LOVES GARFIELD

THE SEMI-OFFICIAL GARFIELD COLLECTORS HANDBOOK

CATHY & ROBERT KOTHE

Loves Garfield

The Semi-Official Garfield Collectors Handbook

"The difference between collectors and hoarders is that collectors have a theme."
- Robert Kothe

Garfield is a registered trademark of Paws, Inc. Other characters are copyrighted by their respective owners. Most photos in this book are from our own collection. Authors are not responsible for factual errors. All information contained in this book has been researched by the authors and is true to the best of their knowledge. Any inaccuracies are purely accidental.

Copyright 2018

ISBN 978-1-949864-03-8

*This book is dedicated to anyone who collects anything -
especially the Garfield collector community.
While some in the world may think we are crazy "Hoarders", in actuality, we
are a community who keep something we love close to us at all times.
And above and beyond that, some of us are especially blessed to come together, get
to know one another, and even develop lifelong friendships.*

CONTENTS

Foreword	vii
1. Why is this Garfield Book Different from Other Garfield Collectibles Books?	1
2. About the Authors (the Who)	7
3. The World Record	19
4. Who are Garfield Collectors? (the Who)	26
5. Don't Let The Term "Collector" Fool You (the Who)	43
6. A Brief History of Garfield (the Who, What and When)	54
7. The Evolution of Garfield (the What)	60
8. Premium and Notable Garfield Collectibles --- (The Who and What)	64
A	67
B	71
C	80
D	100
E	106
F	109
G	119
H	123
I	128
J	131
K	133
L	137
M	140
N	146
O	149
P	154
Q	165
R	167
S	169
T	182
U	185

V	188
W	192
X	201
Y	203
Z	207
9. Not in Our Collection (The What and Who)	209
10. Not Rare (The What)	221
11. Garfield in the Human World (the Who and Where)	226
12. The Garfield Trail (the Where and What)	232
13. The Garfield Cruise (the Who and Where) "It's All About Me at Sea in 2003"	243
14. The Garfield Gathering (the Who, Where, and What)	261
15. 2011, The Year We Hosted the Garfield Gathering (the Who, What, Where, When, Why and How To)	292
16. Life After Hosting the Garfield Gatherings Continued (the Who, What, When, Where, and Why)	307
17. Where to Buy Garfield Items (the Where, What and How To)	324
18. eBAY --- The Granddaddy of Garfield Collectible Websites (the Where, What and How To)	328
19. Craigslist.com (the Where and How To)	342
20. How to Sell A Garfield Collection (the How To)	345
21. Fun Little Stories Not Worthy of a Chapter (the Who, What, and When)	361
22. The Future of Garfield Collectibles and Collecting (the Who, What, When, Where and Why)	379
Acknowledgments	385

FOREWORD

When I received the call from United Feature Syndicate saying they wanted to carry the comic strip, it was one of the happiest days of my career. In my mind, on that day, I was a success. I dared to dream that maybe someday there'd be a book — a collection of Garfield comics. In my wildest dreams, I imagined a TV special. It never occurred to me that people might want to have Garfield on a coffee mug or a T-shirt; in fact, I was wholly unprepared when I was approached by a T-shirt maker, Brandywine, who said they wanted to license Garfield for their product. It was flattering to be sure, but I didn't know if anyone would want to buy a T-shirt with a fat orange cat on it. Turns out they did.

While I tried to stay focused on the comic strip, the truth is, working on the merchandise was a lot of fun. It enabled me to look at the character in different ways and to hear firsthand from people on the "outside" what it was that made them want Garfield for their products. It wasn't his looks — although I've always contended that orange is hard to miss — it was his expressions, the witticisms and sarcastic remarks that we've come to refer to as "Garfisms." "I'll rise but I won't shine." "I'm not overweight, I'm undertall." "Diet is 'die' with a 't'."

Probably the most memorable early product, and the one I'd have to claim as my favorite, was the first book by Ballantine, *Garfield At Large*. It was a compilation of the comic strips, something I had dared to dream about, and boy, I thought Garfield had really arrived when that book came out.

It's been many years ago — maybe 33?— when I first found out there were Garfield collectors, folks who would snatch up every bit of merchandise and memorabilia they could get their hands on. What? Really? I have to confess, I was somewhat flummoxed at this news. First I thought, *well how much stuff could a person have?* After all, Garfield was only seven years old at the time.

And here we are today; 40 years after Garfield's first comic strip appeared in 41 US newspapers on June 19, 1978. Now, it's the most widely syndicated comic strip in the world according to the record keepers, and at this writing, we just released the 65th comic-strip compilation book, and we have many thousands of products in the marketplace around the globe. Who would have thunk?

And speaking of world records, Cathy Kothe, who with the forbearance of her husband, Robert (both co-authors of this book) claimed the record for her Garfield collection — to be the largest in the world. Now, I wouldn't blame Cathy (or Robert) for wanting to make a little money off the sale of this book. How else is she going to keep growing that collection? But it turns out a percentage of the profit will be donated to North Shore Animal League, the largest No-Kill Animal Shelter in the world. I can't think of a more fitting cause — shelter pets need us, and we need them!

When I've asked you why you collect Garfield, you have said that Garfield reminds you of yourself or one of your friends or family.

So essentially, Garfield is a member of your family, and I thank you for that. You'll never know how important you have been to me and to Garfield!

Jim Davis

1

WHY IS THIS GARFIELD BOOK DIFFERENT FROM OTHER GARFIELD COLLECTIBLES BOOKS?

Several books have been written either to attempt to appraise Garfield collectibles or to showcase available items. My wife, Cathy, the holder of the world record for Garfield collectibles, and I call these books, "picture and price books." While some of the books show off impressive Garfield collections, they do not get into the minds of a Garfield collector. This book provides insight on the "who," the "what," the "where," the "when," the "why," as well as the "how-to."

Some books are only a catalog of collectibles. They are just photos and prices. The true irony is that there really is not a set price for any collectible. Any item is simply worth what someone is willing to pay for it at that moment. Prices change, and the book becomes obsolete.

This book is different because it is for collectors, by collectors, and about collectors. It delves into the psyche of a Garfield collector.

Garfield collectors are a bit of a sub-culture. Some of us go to conventions. Some of us went on a Garfield cruise with Jim Davis, the creator of Garfield, and his family. Many Garfield collectors do not get involved with formal events or collector communities. They are happy to stay at home and quietly collect what makes them happy.

The People, the Places, and the Things

In a way, past books on Garfield collectors are only about Garfield as a thing. They are treated as soulless statues and stuffed animals that you put on your shelf. We will have entire sections to help collectors value collectibles. We will also have sections to help people buy and sell collectibles, but what we are most proud of in this book is how we address the people and places of the Garfield collecting world.

The Who (the People)

Who are Garfield collectors? They span generations for many different reasons. This book will give you more insight on how a Garfield collector thinks. Garfield collectors are not the same as Disney collectors or Betty Boop collectors. People collect for many reasons. Paws Inc., the parent company of Garfield, is a completely different type of company than Disney. If you think you know Disney collectors, you do not necessarily know Garfield collectors.

The What (the Things)

This book also will share the what. What are the best Garfield items to collect? What's the deal with major retailers not usually stocking Garfield items even when a major movie is in theaters and the cartoon is on TV?

The Where (the Places)

Where is the best place to buy and sell Garfield items? Where do people go to see more Garfield? Where is Garfield from?

Example of "the Where" ... The Garfield Trail

How many people do you know who would consider a highlight of their life to be a trip to Indiana? You would if you were a Garfield collector. The surrounding area has Garfield statues known as the "Garfield Trail". We will share photos of the Garfield Trail in this book. We will have an entire section on the Garfield Trail and its statues in Chapter 12.

The When

When do Garfield collectors get together in groups? When is the best time to buy or sell Garfield items?

The Why

You will get a better understanding of why Garfield is so admired by some. You will also learn more about how Garfield affected the general population of people who may not have thousands of items in their home but were still touched by Garfield's message or impact.

The How to (People, Places, and Things)

This book also covers more practical matters such as:

- How to sell a Garfield collection
- How to spot the more valuable Garfield collectibles
- How to get the most value while selling Garfield collectibles
- How to buy Garfield items
- How to get in on the fun with Garfield conventions and special events

This book will be more insightful regarding Garfield and his collectors. As we already said, this book is different because it is for collectors, by collectors and about collectors.

The Who (the People)

It would be wrong of us to write this book from an invisible narrator prospective. Cathy and I live one version of the Garfield collector's lifestyle. It is fun to share our little stories and experiences along the way. To top it all off… Cathy holds the world record for Garfield collectibles which, at the very minimum, proves she is committed. Because of the success of our website www.LovesGarfield.com, Cathy is also one of the most visible Garfield collectors in the world.

Collecting Garfield is not some faceless hobby. It is often about spending time with like-minded people who become friends. There is an entire sub-community of people who share their experience of liking Garfield.

Some of these people communicate on the Internet. There are several Facebook groups and forums devoted to Garfield collecting and Garfield collectibles.

The Garfield Gathering is a collectors' convention that now meets every other year. For several years, Cathy and I have taken a very active role in helping to organize the conventions and adding value to them.

There are also book-signings, special events in Muncie, Indiana (where Garfield is produced), appearances at various Comic Cons, movie releases, and other ways to publicly enjoy Garfield.

2
ABOUT THE AUTHORS (THE WHO)

We feel a little funny about writing this section since the book is not a biography about Cathy and me. However, we do have a lot of experience and some fun stories to share. Think of our stories as a way to re-create or understand some of the notable Garfield events, such as the Garfield Cruise or the Garfield Collectors' Conventions. That is the reason we broke tradition and wrote the first chapter to explain why the book is different before we added the "About the Authors" section.

This book is not about us. We are simply the witnesses and tour guides for the book.

The Voice of the Book - Robert

It might feel like this book is written by me and Cathy is absent. The reality is that I wrote the primary narration of the book in my voice. Cathy went over the entire book and checked for accuracy, added a lot of content and tossed in some opinions in my voice. She also deleted a lot of my original writing.

Cathy's presence is often subtle but sometimes it is painfully obvious where she was writing. One example of her input was in the ongoing dispute about how to pronounce Gnorm Gnat. I maintain that the "G" in "Gnorm" and "Gnat" is not silent. In fact, I have Jim Davis on video telling Cathy that the "G" is not silent. It is entirely possible that I might have told him what to tell her but that part is not on video, so she can't prove it.

Cathy here figures "Rob would try to sneak this past me. Rob had been driving me nuts for years calling Jim's first strip Gnorm Gnat and pronouncing both G's." As we were driving out to Paws, Inc. after the 2015 world record was released, we were discussing what questions we would ask Jim. Cathy said, "first and foremost, we are going to resolve this dispute and find out the correct pronunciation of Gnorm Gnat". We got to our hotel room and we were surfing the internet and came across a video of Jim talking about his first strip, Gnorm Gnat, and he DID NOT pronounce the G's, so Cathy said, "OK, that settles that, and we don't need to ask Jim".

As Cathy explains it, "When we got to Paws, and I was talking to the reporter, I didn't realize that Rob was whispering something to Jim. The next thing I know, Jim turns to me and says, 'You know the correct pronunciation is Gnorm Gnat with the G's pronounced.' I just rolled my eyes and said 'Really, he got to you! I thought we finally resolved this last night when we stumbled across the video' and Jim said, 'Oh yeah, the jib jab video, that was fun to do'."

As you'll find out later in this book, Rob likes to find your "hot button" and keep pressing. I do it to him too, so I really can't complain.

This is Robert. It looks like Cathy added something above. My overall point is that Cathy is just as present in this book as I am. For those of you who like to correct people, any inaccuracies on our facts are Cathy's fault since she has final review of the book.

Disclaimer: There are people who know exact dates and more

details than us. We just lived it and collected it. The accuracy is to the best of our ability.

Credibility on the Subject Matter

Another good reason to include the "About the Authors" section in detail is to show our knowledge with the subject. In short, Cathy holds the world record for Garfield collectibles. We are also very involved in the Garfield Collectors community including helping with the Garfield Collectors Convention, called the Garfield Gathering. We will go into more detail later in the book. In Chapter 14, there will also be an entire section on the Garfield Collectors Convention, known as the "Garfield Gathering" or "Garfest."

Finally, I created a website for Cathy, www.LovesGarfield.com. Somehow this website became the most trafficked website on the Internet regarding Garfield collectibles. The website was popular long before Cathy received recognition for holding the world record. We were already the most visible Garfield collectors in the world prior to the record. We will go into more detail about our website www.LovesGarfield.com later.

It all Begins with Cathy - A Brief History

Although I am writing the majority of this book (Cathy's husband, Robert), in order to do this explanation justice, I have to start with Cathy. She is the real collector. I am simply a world-class enabling husband.

Cathy is the original Garfield collector in the marriage. Like most people who grew up in the 1980s, Cathy enjoyed reading Garfield in the comics and had a few Garfield plushes as a child. When friends and family members figured out that Cathy liked

Garfield, she started getting more Garfield items as gifts for special occasions.

It should be noted that the licensing and merchandising did not really take off until the mid-'80s. There were some Garfield plushes on the market, but not to the level of the mid-'80s. In other words, from 1978 to around 1984 there was not a lot of merchandise available.

Cathy in College – Garfield vs. Goofy

When Cathy was in college there was a mild competition between her Garfield collection and her roommate's Disney Mickey Mouse items. For a brief period, Cathy also owned quite a few Disney "Goofy" items, but Garfield won in the end. Perhaps Cathy felt it unfair for her roommate's Mickey Mouse items to have to sleep with one eye open all the time worrying if Garfield the cat was going to pounce on the poor mouse! We still have a few Goofy watches and stuffed animals, but today Garfield is the clear winner. But we may have to put the  Goofy trailer hitch cover on the Range Rover simply because they do not make a Garfield trailer hitch cover. (Ahem! Anyone at Paws, Inc. listening?) ... Trailer hitch cover. Perhaps one that lights up, please.

Enter Robert - Married to the Collection

Cathy here again - I did not start out "collecting" Garfield. In the mid-'80s, I thought he was cute and I liked his sarcasm. One of my favorite sayings or Garfisms, as I like to call them, is "I'm not overweight, I'm under-tall". Even when I started getting more and more Garfield items as gifts, I still didn't consider myself a "collector". I guess when I met

Above is a picture of a Garfield door mat that Cathy's parents gave her as a house-warming present.

Rob in the early '90s and maybe because of his experience with his mother's miniature doll business, he was the first person to call me a "collector". It became more obvious to me in the months before Rob and I were getting married. I was packing up my stuff to move into our apartment. I was packing up a lot of Garfield stuff. I had a couple dozen Garfield plushes. I had my Garfield phone that went to college with me and beach towels, lamps, posters, clothing, watches, an alarm clock. Packing everything up, I thought, "yeah, I am a Garfield collector".

Robert again. Cathy and I were married in November of 1994 and the Garfield collection continued to grow. At first it was slow because in the '90s Garfield was not as popular to traditional retailers and other stores. When eBay became more popular, circa 1999, Cathy's Garfield collection was able to grow by leaps and bounds.

Here is a fun fact; we ended up getting high-speed Internet just so Cathy could browse eBay faster. In 1999, dial-up was practically the only internet access option. We were the first people in our neighborhood to get high speed Internet service just because the pictures of Garfield were loading way too slowly for Cathy's taste.

Today Cathy has over 12,000 Garfield pieces and more arrive every week.

This is a Christmas card photo. Garfield always manages to find his way into our Christmas cards. We always photograph the latest Garfield ornament, clean up the graphic, and use the picture of the ornament on the mailing address label.

www.LovesGarfield.com – Most Visible Garfield Collector

I am a website developer and video producer by trade. This is relevant to our story since I accidentally took Cathy's private collection to the Internet with a pet project called www.LovesGarfield.com. I say "accidentally" because to date, this website dominates the Internet regarding anything about Garfield collections and Garfield collectibles. Apparently, this made us one of the most visible Garfield collectors in the world.

Today we are contacted by people all over the globe. They ask for help appraising items. They ask for help with identifying items. Most often they ask for help in selling collections.

Appraisals and Vendor Consulting

Currently, we have spoken with a number of Garfield licensees and distributors. They were interested in better understanding the "market" and the "mind" of a Garfield collector. They were also interested in where Garfield collectors spend time and might stumble across their merchandise.

It is flattering that sometimes the people at Paws, Inc., the official Garfield company, also gives out our phone number to help new licensees get oriented.

When it comes to websites, I tell my clients all the time not to play games with search engine tricks and cheats. If you want to consistently get found on the internet, content is king. Make a website that is relevant and a resource for whatever someone is looking for. Our website www.LovesGarfield.com is a great example of doing the right thing and getting found.

The success of www.LovesGarfield.com has been a blessing and a bit of a curse. It is a blessing because the site has been a great resource and place for amusement for many people. It is a bit of a curse since it takes just a few keystrokes to find us and many people have contacted us with many Garfield questions ranging from, "Is this cap that used to be on top of a candy jar valuable?" to "Will you purchase our entire collection?"

The truth is that we like getting contacted first, so we get first right of refusal on many great items for sale. We have spoken to many nice people and everyone is grateful to get some help and guidance.

Garfield Related Videos

Because www.LovesGarfield.com gets so many inquiries, we created some videos to help standardize the answers. Our most popular video is, "How to Sell Your Garfield Collection." It is on www.YouTube.com. It is linked to the website and it has had thousands of views. The video is still online, but we will share the information here in this book. The video is not my best acting, but the information is very useful. We get a lot of feedback from viewers on how helpful they find the information.

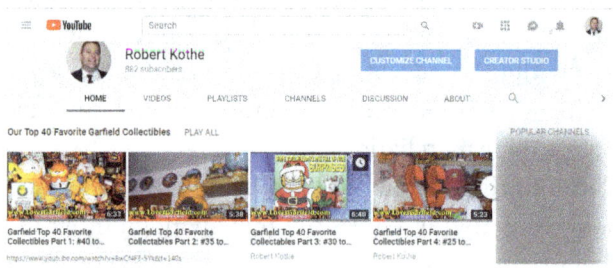

Every now and then we would create another Garfield-related video and put it on YouTube to be stumbled upon. We never had a formal social networking strategy, although I was already active on Facebook and Cathy lives vicariously through my Facebook page.

One day I was reading comments on a business video that I created for a client and somebody said, "More Garfield videos, please." We already had over 700 subscribers on our YouTube channel, but my assortment of videos online ranged between making stupid vacation videos just to taunt people stuck in New York to serious corporate videos that were aired on TV.

At the same time, YouTube changed its monetization policy and anyone with under 1,000 subscribers would no longer get checks for ads on videos. This really was not a big deal since we were only making about $150 per year on ad revenue, which does not exactly pay the bills, but I am always up for a challenge.

All the "How to get subscribers" videos on YouTube were saying the same thing. Pick your brand and lean in to it. We already had the world record for Garfield collectibles and lovesgarfield.com was a number one collectors' website so this was not a hard decision to pick a brand.

What I did not realize was that I created a monster. Cathy was actually enjoying making these videos. In 2018, we released an 8-part video series about our favorite 40 Garfield collectibles in honor of Garfield's 40th birthday that year.

From YouTube changing its monetization policy we were hit cold in the face by Facebook changing its algorithms to the point that only 20 of your friends can see your posts even if you post on a channel with 16 million subscribers, like the official Garfield page. All the experts are now saying to put out videos and it could snowball despite the algorithms.

The good news is that we are enjoying making the videos and the amount of Garfield content that Cathy and I have amassed over the years is enormous. Having full motion video of the Garfield Trail or the Muncie Children's Museum's Garfield exhibit is priceless.

Since a component of my website business is also video production and editing, we can produce content in-house (literally) and inexpensively. Hopefully, Garfield collectors appreciate our efforts and continue to subscribe and watch the videos. Please subscribe to our YouTube channel, www.youtube.com/factxback to stay informed about new video releases. Let us know if there's any specific item you'd like us to highlight.

The Garfield Gathering – Garfield Collectors Convention - Garfest

In 2006, Cathy and I attended our first Garfield Collectors Convention known as the "Garfield Gathering" (or sometimes called "Garfest"). It was in Williamsport, Pennsylvania.

Here are our good friends Tina and Trish. Yes, you do see a man wearing a Garfield plush on his head. That is Roger. Some people wear hats, he wears a Garfield. I would not mess with him because he is a retired police officer and a biker. He is also a really nice guy.

Game Show Host and Auctioneer

In 2009, Cathy wrote, and I hosted, some Garfield relevant games at the Garfield Gathering (Garfield Collectors Convention) and we continued to prepare and host several games in the following years.

In 2012, the contracted auctioneer for the Des Moines, Iowa convention canceled two days before the auction. The event had already started and the organizers were between a rock and a hard place. It did not take long for the event organizers to think of the attendee with the biggest mouth and the gift of gab. I have been the only auctioneer ever since.

In previous years the other auctioneers were contracted and paid. The best part is that I work for free. The bad news is you get what you pay for. As Jim Davis said in the 2015 welcome message to the collectors:

> *"I hear that Robert Kothe will be the auctioneer this year. That's what happens when you don't have a budget for a professional. Be careful or you might end up bidding against yourself."*

I should have been offended by this, but the truth is, I helped write the joke. And yes, somebody did end up bidding against himself.

Auction Openings on YouTube

There are some fun videos of a short monologue I do before the auction every year. Since Cathy and I became regular attendees, we already knew the personalities and quirks of other collectors. Combining that with humorous observations of what happened throughout the days of the convention, I weave in some inside jokes and funny auction rules. Look for them on YouTube. Search Garfield Gathering auction to find them.

The Garfield 25th Birthday Cruise

Cathy and I were fortunate enough to set sail on the Garfield 25th Birthday Cruise with about 400 additional fans. Jim Davis, the creator, was on the cruise with his family and there were Garfield related events, parties, and shore excursions. Read more about the cruise in Chapter 13.

Hosted 2011 Garfield Gathering

Cathy and I hosted the 2011 Garfield Collectors Convention on Long Island, New York. Chapter 15 is an entire section about the year that we hosted. Our goal was to supersize everything from past years, and really make it a convention to remember.

The World Record

Cathy appears in the 2015 world record book for the Largest Collection of Garfield Memorabilia. This can be found in Chapter 3.

Garfield Gathering Co-Moderator and Web Design

The Garfield Gathering also has a Facebook page with several thousand followers. I am one of several moderators for this group along with Nancy and Jen. You will meet them later in the book.

Speaking of Facebook, if you are looking for my wife's Facebook page, good luck. She never set one up. She is vicariously living through my Facebook page. Actually, that is only partially true. She did set up a Facebook page, so she can follow the singer Jewel's dog, Henry. He was all over *Dancing with the Stars* one year and is a real cutie. Friend her, you might be the second.

Finally, I also designed and hosted the Garfield Gathering website to help promote the event. I especially spent a lot of energy making the 2011 pages since Cathy and I hosted that year.

More Later

It is likely some of the above stories will show up again. We will go into more detail about the Garfield Gatherings, the world record, the Garfield Cruise, and other experiences that helped define us. The point is that we are extremely immersed in the Garfield collectors' community.

3

THE WORLD RECORD

In 2013, we discovered that our collection was larger than that of the current world record holder. I guess that Googling "large Garfield collection" led to our website, www.LovesGarfield.com. It is the most visible Garfield collectors' site to date.

The standing record at the time was from two people in California with around 3,000 pieces. We suspected that two people are not supposed to hold a single record, so the world record people were anxious to have someone else take over. So, Cathy and I started going through all the totes in our basement and photographed and kept lists of all the Garfield items. After a couple of weeks and countless hours, we found ourselves completely overwhelmed with information. We still had to organize all of the data and have experts in the field of memorabilia come in and validate the collection. We just kind of gave up and figured we missed the deadline to make it into the 2014 book, anyway.

It was about a year later, out of the blue, that the world record people contacted us again and said that they thought we were interested in beating the old record. We certainly were - and picked up where we had left off and continued photographing and organizing Cathy's Garfield collection. Even though it was a huge undertaking and took way more hours than I would like to admit, it was well worth all the effort in the end.

It turns out that we were able to more than double the previous record, so in April 2014, Cathy's collection was officially validated as the largest collection of Garfield memorabilia in the world.

The interesting thing is that a collection must only contain unique items. In other words, duplicates do not count towards the record. Cathy is now on record for having 6,190 unique items. A footnote could have stated that at the time of publication we had over 12,000 items in Cathy's collection, including duplicates.

I refer to it as Cathy's collection since only one person is credited as an owner. This is appropriate because it is Cathy's collection and I am just the "enabling husband" or perhaps "the Official Cataloger."

As an aside, we are very happy with the number of 6,190. Anything over 6,000 would have been good enough for us at the time. Think about it: if we had 5,900 items everyone would say, "They have ALMOST 6,000 items." Since we have 6,190 on record people now say, "They have OVER 6,000 items." The word "over" is much better than the word "almost." "Almost" seems like a bit of an underachievement.

Recently, there have been way too many people calling us out on the internet saying they want to beat the record so it might just be time to add in the new items we have purchased since 2014 and re-set the record with the new number.

My Wife Can Out-Spend Your Quality Department

To prove that we had enough pieces to beat the old record and to validate the new record, there were several steps that we had to go through. One of the final steps was a database report with photos of each unique item. To make it easy to spot duplicates, I broke the categories down to the ridiculously detailed level.

One example is: Christmas / Christmas Ornaments / Wooden Ornament
or
Plush / With Suction cups / 2 eyes separate

By breaking it down to such detailed categories, the world record data quality department might only be looking at 20 to 30 photos per category at most. This made it easy to spot duplicates. The downside was that there were around 620 categories in the final record.

Before we were officially notified of the record, I got a call from our primary world record contact. She emailed a photo because the quality department believed there was one duplicate in a certain category. They were right. The two photos were of the same item type, so we subtracted one from the count.

Realizing that this could go on forever to catch these duplicates, I mentioned to my contact that Cathy had just received six more shipments of Garfield items in the mail. There were about 14 new items that she did not have before. I asked if I should photograph them and send them in.

I believe at this point my contact realized that my wife can out-spend their quality department. Seeing that this can go on forever she said, "Why don't we agree to lock it down right now." Meaning, let's consider 6,190 items as the official record.

The World Record: WOW Factor Photo

The count was finalized at 6,190 items. If we had any chance of getting Cathy's collection photograph into the book, we needed to take it fast and make sure it was impressive. I looked at the photos that made it into the book and obviously the world record people were looking for a spectacular display.

When Cathy was at work, I staged the living room. To get the most Garfield items in the picture, I blocked doorways with slot machines, pulled things into the middle of the room, and even thumb-tacked a placemat onto a door so there was Garfield as far as the eye could see. Sadly, or Cathy might say, luckily, I did not have to move many items since the living room pretty much looks like the photo. I just had to face everything in the same direction and take some things off the shelves.

I often joke that the only difference between a collector and a hoarder is that collectors have a theme, but if the fire department was around this day they would cite us for not being able to escape in a fire.

Stop the Presses

Cathy was published as a World Records holder on the third page from the back cover. It is called the "Stop Press" section. It is called that because the book had already been typeset, finalized, and ready to print when a notable record came in. It would be too difficult to typeset the entire book again, so they add pages to the back of the book called, "Stop Press." These pages are a catch-all for latecomers that are worthy of publishing. Being so close to the back cover makes it really easy to find her listing.

Just because somebody wins a world record does not mean she is automatically put in a book. Winners are given a certificate to validate the record, but only a small fraction make it into a records book. We are very lucky and happy to be published. It is also possible to re-print the record in future books depending on whether it fits into the goals of the publishers. They may show the information in table form to be able to mention multiple records in a small space on a page with a new record holder.

Jim Davis Book Signing

On October 13, 2014, Cathy and I drove 15 hours to Muncie, Indiana to meet with Jim Davis, the creator of Garfield, and to celebrate the world record. While we were there, a local reporter from the Muncie Star Press wrote an article on the event.

A fun twist was that Jim Davis also has a world record for most widely distributed comic strip with over 2,570 newspapers in syndication. The record was set in 2002 and has not been beaten yet. It was interesting having two Garfield world record holders in the same room. In a way, we made a new record for the most Garfield-related record holders in the same place.

Jim Davis is a very approachable person and is fun to be with. He spoke of how he is still to this day amazed to see the level of devotion people have to a character that he created over 36 years ago.

The newspaper reporter was amazed at how open and friendly Jim was with me and Cathy. Jim explained that most cartoonists are sociable. The reporter also learned that this was not our first time to headquarters. We were there twice before to film Jim for the Garfield Gatherings. We were also on the 25th Birthday cruise with Jim and attended a book signing in our hometown.

Talk about it being a slow news day in Muncie, Indiana. The article about Cathy's world record was on the front page.

Talk about Unfortunate Placement

When the article about Cathy's visit to Muncie, Indiana was published in the local newspaper, it was printed in a rather unfortunate place. The neighboring headline was a story titled, "Molester Draws 40 Year Sentence." The only thing separating that title from Cathy's picture was a little skinny vertical line.

I thought this was so funny that I cropped the photo and the headline and included it in the collections slide show at the 2015 Garfield Collectors Convention. That is the advantage of being responsible for the audio-video at the Garfield Gatherings. I will explain about audio video and the Garfield Gatherings later in the book.

4
WHO ARE GARFIELD COLLECTORS? (THE WHO)

I n chapter 8, we will discuss which Garfield items are more sought after. Here in this section we explain why some people collect Garfield items. We also describe some different types of Garfield collectors.

It is safe to assume that first and foremost people collect Garfield items because they like Garfield. It seems obvious, but this is where it all stems from. There are many reasons why people like Garfield. Here are some reasons that explain our obsession with the fat cat.

Why do People Like Garfield?

Cathy and I have met many Garfield collectors and we have

narrowed down this answer to the following reasons. Every collector has a different story, but these are some of the major categories.

I hate to state the obvious, but Garfield collectors are people who like Garfield and accumulate collectibles. The real question is, why do we collect Garfield? If you ask 100 people you might get 100 different answers.

Garfield Says What People are Already Thinking

Cathy calls these "Garfisms". As it turns out, as you can read in Jim Davis' forward, Jim Davis also calls them "Garfisms". Since he is the creator of Garfield, we have to assume Cathy may have gotten it from him at some point in her life.

"Garfisms" are famous lines from Garfield such as:

- "Big Fat Hairy Deal"
- "I'd like mornings better if they started later"
- "I'm not overweight, I'm under-tall"
- "Good Morning is a Contradiction in terms"
- "Ask me if I care"
- "I'll rise but I won't shine"
- "Never trust a smiling cat"
- And my favorite … "Compute this!"

In a way, Garfield was one of the first "shock jocks." A shock jock is a radio personality who does not censor himself. Garfield is more family-friendly, but he does say what is on his mind. People like that and follow him because of that.

Garfield Represents and Defends Lazy and Overweight People

Another group of people who can relate to Garfield are often people who enjoy the fact that Garfield is a fat cat. He knows it and he is proud of who he is.

As a "person of size myself," it is nice to put a positive spin on a negative topic such as obesity. Once again, Garfield was ahead of his time for having self-esteem regardless of society's norm regarding weight.

High school attendance in the mid-'80s marked the peak of Garfield's popularity. It was a time when aerobics was popular, and some people walked around in skintight spandex clothing. Garfield was a spokescat for people who disagreed with the health fad and said something about it.

I'm not saying that all Garfield collectors are overweight. They are people of all shapes and sizes, but Garfield celebrates the fact that he can eat three trays of lasagna in one sitting or steal Jon's dinner in a blink of an eye and not feel the slightest bit guilty.

These sayings are some of the captions in the comics and on some collectibles. As mentioned above, Garfield says things like:

- "I'm the perfect weight for my shape"
- "If you want to look thinner, hang around people fatter than you"
- "Love me, feed me, never leave me"
- "Diet is "DIE" with a "T""
- "Eat every meal as though it were your last"
- "I am hungry. Therefore I am."

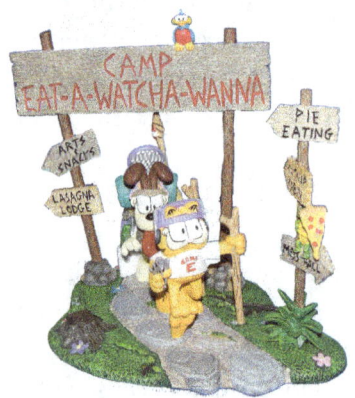

- "I eat too much because I'm depressed, and I'm depressed because I eat too much. It's a vicious circle ... that took years to perfect!"
- "Sorry I only diet between meals"

Proud Lazy People

Along the same line, Garfield is also a spokescat for proud lazy people. In a way he re-frames the conversation to show he is not lazy, he just does not like mornings, waking up, getting out of bed or going to work.

Garfield to the rescue ... Once again it is great to have an influence in life that celebrates the joy of taste buds and the need for rest.

This line of thinking is evidenced by the following Garfield quotes:

- "Take life one nap at a time"
- "Oh no! I overslept! I'm late! For my nap"
- "All I do is eat and sleep. Eat and sleep. Eat and sleep. There must be more to a cat's life than that. But I hope not."
- "If people were meant to pop out of bed, we'd all sleep in toasters"
- "Some people have anxiety attacks; some people have gas attacks...I have nap attacks"
- "Some call it Laziness, I call it Deep Thought"

Represents Everyone and Hates Mondays

Let's be honest, who really does like Mondays? Monday is the day that we go back to school or work. Yes, there are some of you reading this who love school or work or are lucky enough to be retired. But given the choice between school or work or a free weekend, the choice is obvious. There is a little bit of Garfield in everybody. I have also met many people with a lot of Garfield in them.

Garfield is Cute – (Usually)

Who does not love cute? This is my opinion, but one of the first Garfields ever made had a pull-string and talked. The eyes were round, and it was scary to look at. It simply was not cute. If that was the first Ford Model T, it would be highly collectible, but because it was not cute, people would not care that it was one of the first items available for sale.

Sometimes people want an item because it is cute. My wife's favorite plush is him wearing four Garfield slippers on his feet. She doesn't care what year it was made or how many were produced, she just likes it, partly because it was her very first Garfield.

Garfield has an Attitude / Garfield is a Non-Conformist

One reason Garfield is popular is because he has an attitude. He pushes Odie, the dog, off the table. He swats spiders. He plays cards with a mouse when his owner, Jon, wants him to chase the mouse. He says things like:

- "Show me a good mouser and I will show you a cat with bad breath"
- "I Don't do Mornings"
- "I'm only human"
- "Keep your paws off"
- "I'm so Good at Being Bad"
- "Give me Coffee and No One Gets Hurt"
- "I Don't Do Perky"

Garfield is Recognizable and Established

Growing up in the '80s into the '90s when he was most popular, Garfield became a sign of the times. People subscribed to newspapers and read the funnies. Kids watched the Garfield cartoons on Saturday mornings. They saw Garfield star in the Embassy Suites commercial, the Fruit Snacks commercial, the Ravioli commercial, Alpo cat food commercial, or the Plymouth Voyager commercial, among others. People watched TV and saw Jim Davis in the American Express credit card commercial or an episode of "Too Close for Comfort". Garfield has been referenced in many shows, like one of Cathy's favorites - "Alf" - and even just a couple years ago in an episode of "The Big Bang Theory". Garfield is the biggest reason that Cathy and I started watching the television show, "The Goldbergs". We've always keeping an eye out for the Garfield telephone, or corkboard or ball.

One thing is for sure: if you mixed a picture of Garfield into a bunch of photos of world leaders, I guarantee that Garfield would be recognized more than Barack Obama. I pity the leader of the Netherlands in this game.

Garfield Reminds People of the Good Old Days

In a way, Garfield has become an anchor to our past. Some call it the good old days. Others just think it is the good old days, not remembering the challenges of the past.

Sometimes collectibles bring people back to happier times when life was carefree. My mother collects miniature dolls and is in the miniature business and often describes herself as a frustrated decorator. She decorates tiny houses instead of real houses.

Garfield was first published in 1978. Many of us were kids or teenagers and it is an anchor point to our childhood. Even if you do not have over 12,000 items in your house, like my wife, there are many people who admit to going straight to the funny pages and reading Garfield. They have a good laugh and go on with their day. My parents subscribed to New York Newsday when I grew up and I only read the funnies and enjoyed Garfield. I am not the collector - my wife is - I'm just the world class enabling husband.

Garfield has Human-Like Qualities

Although Garfield is a cat, it is easy to mistake him for a person. Some people can relate to him as a person rather than as a cat. Much of his commentary is anti-exercise, anti-health food, and anti-work.

- "You can bet it wasn't an exercise freak who invented power steering."
- "I need less week and more weekend."
- "This is it. I've reached the pinnacle of laziness and gluttony . . . How depressing. There's no place to go after you've reached the top."

Jim Davis mentioned in the forward that Garfield reminds people of themselves or family members so, in a way, Garfield is family.

Garfield is Edgy, Yet Safe

Garfield has a clever attitude and will often come off as a non-conformist. At the same time, he stays within set boundaries to be considered safe. Jim Davis, the creator, talks about how he never wants a parent to be shocked by what a child might read in a Garfield comic or Garfield book. The parents should always know that Garfield is a safe space that will never go into religion, politics, controversy, nationalism or be vulgar.

When I say that it will not go into nationalism, keep in mind that Garfield is published in many different countries and many different languages. By acknowledging national holidays, it could be offending other readers from other countries.

The only time Garfield continues to inflame the wishes of a group critical to his action is when Garfield insists on squashing spiders. The company has received many complaints about "insect rights." Once the letters start to die down, Garfield squashes another spider. Keep in mind that comic spiders do not die. They are like a cartoon character that just falls from a cliff and still appears to be in the next episode. In a way, no spiders are ever harmed by Garfield since they bounce back.

People Collect what Makes them Happy – Sub-Sets

Believe it or not, many Garfield collectors do not indiscriminately purchase anything just because it has Garfield on it. Many collectors have themes.

My wife likes things that remind her of boating, beaches, Florida, or the tropics. We have dozens of beach towels for some day when we buy a house in Florida where it is warmer than New York. My wife and I are boaters. We have Garfield life jackets, although they are way too small for us. We like the summer time and a significant portion of her collection reflects that fact. We have Garfield pool toys and we do not have a pool that we can swim in. We do have an inflatable Garfield kiddie pool.

Another collector and good friend, Gary, is a fireman and a volunteer emergency medical technician (EMT). He will outbid anyone at the conventions for Garfield items depicting firemen or ambulances. At one convention he was willing to bid up a Garfield pedal car shaped like a fire truck.

Nancy, the convention organizer and host of the 2004 and 2019 Garfield conventions and one of the founders of the Garfield Gathering, simply loves Garfield Western items. It is no surprise that Nancy also wears a cowboy hat when emceeing the conventions. It is an unwritten rule not to bid against Nancy at the auction for Western items. She works so hard putting on the event that is only fair not to give her any resistance at the auction. Her husband Manny also likes Garfield baking items because he loves to bake.

Tony, another long-time collector and host of the 2000 Garfield convention, tended towards Garfield clocks and mugs. Tony has since tragically passed away, but he is in the spirit of hundreds of collectors.

Another collector and host of the 2008 Garfield convention, Pat, collects every Garfield Christmas item he can get his hands on. Pat is also a devout Yankees fan, so he accumulates Garfield baseball items too.

Several collectors, like Bill, are avid golfers and will purchase anything that relates to golf and Garfield. Golf items are practical because you can put Garfield club covers on your golf clubs. You can use a Garfield golf towel on your golf bag and even play with Garfield golf balls.

Below are just a few golf items from Cathy's collection. The rest are on her golf clubs.

Golf is also an artistic category because there are many collectors' cels, paintings, prints, and statues of Garfield playing golf.

In a way, a Garfield collection is sometimes a reflection of who somebody is or wants to be. It is no coincidence that Enesco, one of the Garfield licensees, made hundreds of different Garfield mugs: World's Best Nurse, Best Doctor, Best Teacher, Fireman, Retiree, etc. The list goes on and on. At the time, Enesco ceramics were an inexpensive gift you could purchase in a local card store. They were affordable and reflected a wide array of occupations. Today, since ceramic is so fragile, many Enesco pieces are considered highly collectible and sometimes rare.

We are going to repeat ourselves in the "How to sell your Garfield collection" section of this book, but this current point deserves emphasis. Because Garfield collectors are unique and often purchase within personal themes, many items online sell for way above market value just because they fit someone's theme and were really wanted. That is why Cathy and I snicker at Garfield collectors' books that suggest that the average plush might be worth $10 to $20. They are not taking into account that when a collector wants something he will pay top dollar for it.

Cat People

Jim Davis, the creator of Garfield, started out his animation career drawing a character named Gnorm Gnat. As it sounds, Gnorm was a gnat. For those of you who do not know, a gnat is a tiny fly-like insect that bites people around sundown. Footnote from Cathy, the g's in Gnorm Gnat are SILENT, regardless of what other people (Rob) might tell you!

Jim Davis created a bunch of characters besides the gnat that were all insects. He was having a hard time selling his comic strip. The story goes that somebody told him that nobody cares about bugs.

Jim Davis has said publicly many times that at the time that he wanted to be a cartoonist, there were many famous dogs filling the comic strip section but there were not any cats that stood out. Snoopy and Marmaduke (to name a few) were popular, but no cats.

Jim Davis also knew a lot about cats. He grew up on a farm and there were many cats on the farm to watch and observe their behavior and personalities.

I give this brief background because in a way, Garfield is the "spokes-cat" for the feline species. It is no coincidence that many Garfield fans and Garfield collectors have cats.

Cat Fancy magazine used Garfield as its figurehead. People who read *Cat Fancy* magazine obviously like cats. My sister subscribed to *Cat Fancy* magazine and would cut out the monthly Garfield articles and give them to Cathy.

As Garfield says, "Cats Rule, Dogs Drool!" Cathy and I have a dirty little secret.

Our Dirty Little Secret

Here is our dirty little secret. Cathy and I are, gasp, dog people. We have been married for over 20 years and a cat has never set foot in our house. We have dogs. We got our first dog, Sweetie, in 1999. She was quite a handful, so in 2001 we got her a friend, Oreo. They have both since passed and we now have a Pomeranian, Zeta. We also foster dogs for North Shore Animal League America, the world's largest no-kill animal shelter in the world. Zeta was our first foster and we just had to keep her.

In 2016, Cathy and I were honored to be awarded the "Fosters of the Year" for 2015 at North Shore Animal League America. At that time, we fostered over 22 dogs in a year and a half. As of the publishing of this book, we have fostered over 40 dogs.

Growing up, my family has always had a cat in the house. We had outside cats and inside cats. I enjoyed having a pet in the home but there was something in my soul that yearned for a dog. Eventually, we got a Pug; they are almost dogs. You want to talk about strange dogs, Pugs fit the description. It is no wonder they cast one as an alien in the "Men in Black" movies. The dog was my pet and the cat was my sister's pet.

This precious little ball of fur is our current dog, Zeta. She was our first foster dog who we absolutely fell in love with and adopted. Today she is an ambassador to our other foster dogs, especially those from puppy mills. She was from a puppy mill and she has a way with frightened new arrivals that we foster.

Cathy and I do not dislike cats at all. We just cannot relate to cats. We are going to get some angry letters when I say this but when people describe the perfect cat they say it comes when you call it, it is friendly, and it knows some tricks. You just described just about every dog in the world. The perfect cat is one in a thousand and the rest of them are standoffish, only let you pet them when they feel like it, and only care about you if it is feeding time. I better stop before there are boycotts and organized book burnings for our views. You do have to enjoy the irony that the largest Garfield collectors in the world are dog people.

Shown above is our first dog, Sweetie, as a puppy, sporting her home-made Garfield costume. We took her trick-or-treating only to the dog people on our block to introduce them to our new puppy. She was adopted from North Shore Animal League America. Every other dog we adopted was from them as well.

Cathy never had a cat growing up. Her grandparents always had cats. Her favorite was their Siamese cat name Tuffer. She and her brothers would always fight with each other on whose turn it was to play with the cat. She tells me that poor cat would never get to use the litter box in peace if they were in town!

Spoiler Alert regarding the movie, "The War of the Roses". If you do not want to have the movie ending ruined go right to the next section now.

In the 1989 movie, "The War of the Roses", Kathleen Turner and Michael Douglas, the main characters, are going through a progressively violent divorce. Danny DeVito plays the character of an attorney and the movie narrator. At the end of the movie, his conclusion is that cat people should never marry dog people.

The reason I brought up "The War of the Roses" is that Cathy and I are both dog people. We are happily married. We love cat people, but we are not cat people and that is perfectly fine with everyone. As I already said, there is some irony in the world record Garfield collector being a dog person.

Some Foster Dogs and Zeta in our living room

Garfield is Practically the Spokescat for the Cat Family

Jim thought about wanting to be a cartoonist and began to ask himself, "What do people care about?" At the time, there were several successful dogs such as Snoopy and Marmaduke in the comic strips, but no cats. The idea for Garfield was born.

Ironically, Jim Davis grew up on a farm but was too asthmatic

to help on the farm. He spent a lot of time drawing in his room. The farm had dozens of cats on the property, so he was already a cat person and was able to be more familiar with cat behavior.

Another fun fact is that the original Garfield design did not have stripes. One newspaper editor said he loved the idea, the gags were great, but the cat needed stripes. Jim agreed, but looking back now, he and his staff must have painstakingly drawn millions of stripes that could have been a plain cat. Hours of their lives were lost to adding in the stripes. Would Garfield be as successful without his black stripes? We'll never know.

Getting back on topic ... I was saying that people like Garfield because he is practically the spokescat for cats. Cat people all over the world think that Garfield sometimes reminds them of their own cats. Garfield runs the house, is demanding and disobedient, and a bit of a brat.

Magazines such as *Cat Fancy* had a long-standing relationship with Garfield and the strip was published in many issues. Pet food, pet toy companies and kitty litter companies also licensed Garfield to represent their brand. It's no wonder that cat people think Garfield is the spokescat for cats all over the world.

5

DON'T LET THE TERM "COLLECTOR" FOOL YOU (THE WHO)

It is dangerous to lump people into the same category. Often, collectors are considered people who buy something as an investment and plan on selling it when the item becomes rare and sought after. Art collectors are a good example of this. To further muddy the water, some Garfield items are fine art such as lithographs, sericels, acrylic paintings, and limited-edition prints. One might assume that they were purchased as an investment. For some Garfield collectors, this can be miles away from the truth.

Garfield collectors do not necessarily keep items in mint condition, or even keep the box. My wife and I personally have many items that we use every day for what they were intended to be: a telephone plugged into the phone jack, an alarm clock to wake us up, and mud flaps screwed to the back of our car, floor mats and seat covers inside our cars. We drink out of Garfield glasses and eat out of Garfield

bowls. If we had a cat, we would use the Garfield kitty litter scoop for what it was intended, and that is not a good life for any item.

Clearly, being screwed to the back of a car and designed to stop mud will likely ruin the resale value of a Garfield mud flap. Just because we are called collectors does not mean it is to buy, hold and invest.

The reality is that many Garfield items can be used for a purpose. They were not designed to be put behind glass and looked at. They are practical and cute.

Pictured are cupcakes made using the Garfield muffin tin by a collector and good friend, Trish. If you know how to bake why would you keep muffin tins and cookie forms behind velvet ropes? Trish knows how to bake.

Preserve vs. Using

Most Garfield collectors that we know both preserve collectible items as well as use practical ones. In a way, our homes are like living museums. We drink out of the Garfield coffee mugs that are part of the exhibit and are careful not to break them.

One for Showing and One for Blowing

We personally like to purchase multiple copies of many items. We may buy all the Garfield greetings cards that a store has. We might keep one for preservation and mail the rest out on people's birthdays.

You can't take it with you, so you might as well enjoy what you have and use what you can. In many cases such as with drinking glasses, you can use them for years and with yet another washing they are as good as new. I would suggest hand washing with a mild soap detergent to limit the amount of fading. Simply put them on a shelf and now they're collectibles.

Cathy here again. As I was doing a lot of the research for this book, specifically checking eBay for current prices, I came across so many listings that I would consider to be way over-priced. The descriptions would read something like, "always boxed" or "never displayed". So, the person expected to get more than he originally paid for the item. I know that Rob has already said that the most an item might be worth is what you originally paid for the item. That may be very true, and I would like to say that you should display your items and enjoy them. You can protect them as best you can from damage, keep artwork away from sunlight, keep delicate items in an enclosed cabinet.

The only reason why I have so many items packed away is simply because our house is way too small to display everything. I would love to put everything out, but until we win the lottery, there is just no room.

Perceived Value vs. Future Value

Most collectors that we know have met Jim Davis, the creator of Garfield. He is a really nice guy and very kind to collectors. We would rather he live forever and never retire than to think about a world where his brain is not active.

One of my clients sells sports memorabilia. When the news announces the death of a former sports figure, the industry immediately doubles or triples the price of any of that athlete's memorabilia. Frankly, the whole thing is morbid to me.

Most Garfield collectors I know do not purchase something as an investment. They purchase an item because it makes them smile to be in possession of it.

The "Stuck on You" Craze – 1 Turns into 2 – A Collection is Born

In the late '80s and early '90s, a Garfield "Stuck on You" was produced. It was a stuffed Garfield with suction cups on his feet. It was all the rage. They were everywhere. You would especially see them on the inside of cars. My sister had one on her car. She was 19 at the time and my wife, Cathy, had one in her car. This was long before Cathy had a world class collection. In a way, it seeded the collection.

In Chapter 23, I'll go into more detail, but Cathy was a victim of the '80s craze where people would steal the Garfield "stuck on you" out of people's cars. This was a craze that I am sure Paws, Inc. was not behind and was not particularly proud of. Cathy also had a Garfield ice scraper in that car that was also stolen at a different time and a different location.

A bunch of Stuck on You Garfield Plush

Sometimes a collector simply starts out by owning one or two Garfield items. Over time, whether it's getting gifts or making additional purchases, before you know it you have a whole bunch of Garfield items. A collection is born.

One of my clients, who lectures about and sells sports collectibles, says if you have more than one of something, you could be a collector. He says everybody collects something.

When we go to the Garfield Gathering, the Garfield Collectors Convention, we meet people who are proud of their Garfield room, or their Garfield shelf, or cabinet filled with Garfields. Surprisingly, people who go out of their way to go on vacation with other Garfield people do not all have ridiculously over-the-top collections like my wife.

I know my wife holds the world record for Garfield collectibles, so by default her collection is larger than life. The truth is that being a collector is not about the final item count; it is about how having Garfield in your life makes you feel.

"By-the-Book Collectors"

It should be obvious that collecting Garfield items can also be treated as a discipline. Just like some people collect paintings and others collect baseball cards, some Garfield collectors do it for the possible increase in value as well as to have more sought-after collectible pieces.

Enesco ceramics are very popular among the "By-the-Book" Collectors

I call them "by-the-book" collectors because there are a few published books that try to appraise Garfield collectibles. Unlike stamp collecting, where books are more common and more accurate, there really is not an open "Trading Market" that can pinpoint the value. The closest "trading market" would be eBay, since it has millions of users and bidding can establish market values.

Unlike a commodities market with supply and demand, eBay has a lot of buyers who purchase based on wants, for the simple fact that it makes them happy. Actual selling prices are all over the map from high to low and in between.

Copy-Cat Collectors

Hopefully this title does not offend anyone, but we consider a copy-cat collector someone who purchases something because he previously saw it sell for a lot of money.

In a way, this is how markets are made in the first place. As the price of something rises, more and more people want it despite the higher price. The collectors may not want an "Oreo cookie jar" because they love cookies and always dreamed of having one. They may purchase one because they are reported to be rare and sought after.

This strategy could be dangerous. Do not let public opinion dictate the personality of your Garfield collection. In a way, this is peer pressure or "trying to keep up with the Joneses." Garfield can provide something for anyone, so let your collection reflect your personality.

The Irony of Enesco

Today, Enesco is looked at as the producer of fine, hand-crafted ceramics. Their products are often treated as if they are the finest Garfield collectibles available on the market. The irony is that Enesco was made to be affordable - cute items you can get at a card store when you needed a quick gift for a friend.

Don't Let The Term "Collector" Fool You (the Who) | 49

Enesco's products include items like:

- "World's Greatest ... Teacher, Mom, Fireman, Doctor," etc. mugs
- Golf, soccer, football, and skiing trophies
- Sarcastic statues about food, weight, and lack of exercise
- Little boxes to hold keys or jewelry
- "Happy ... Birthday, Anniversary, Graduation", etc. statues

Let's look at the patterns. These are everyday gifts for everyday people with everyday hobbies, professions, or roles.

In the above photo there are mostly Enesco graduation items.

Why did Enesco Become so Valuable?

Since this section is called copy-cat collectors, this is a very big part of it. There is a bit of a feeding frenzy on eBay and other auction sites. The more it sells for, the more it is perceived as a classic.

Enesco is no longer a licensee, so their items are not produced anymore. At some point, any company might not renew its license. Just because an item is not made any longer, does not automatically make it a collectible. There may not be a huge after-market for old bags of kitty litter with Garfield's face on them. But because of Enesco items' cuteness and other reasons I'll go into next, they have been known to not only keep their value, but some have been sold for way more than their original retail price.

One of the problems is that many Enesco items are made of ceramics and porcelain. Ceramics and porcelain can break. Over time, as the world's greatest teachers accidentally drop their mugs off their desks, these broken pieces will be thrown into the garbage. The more this happens, the fewer items there are to re-sell. Many times, when Cathy ordered Enesco items online, the seller wrapped them so poorly that they arrived broken. Sure, we had insurance on the purchase, but now there are fewer fragile ceramic Garfield collectibles in the world.

Finally, since the list above implies that Enesco was targeting all-things-for-all-people, perhaps the teachers of today will want to sport a "World's Best Teacher" Garfield mug on their desks. After all, they are still proud of what they do!

Wishy-Washy and Timeless – The blessing and the curse

Garfield collectors live in a wishy-washy world. Except for the evolution of the collectibles and the physical design of Garfield over the years, he is a character that makes time stand still. Humans are the only ones who are counting the years since his creation. Garfield lives in a comic world where nobody ages and you can fall off a table 1,000 times and never get hurt. This could be yet another reason why people like Garfield.

I realize that this reality is a blessing and a curse. It is a blessing since Garfield is not a reminder that we age, or we can get hurt.

It is a curse because as collectors there are very few bread-crumbs that one can follow regarding how old a collectible is or what company produced it.

Wishy-Washy Things Garfield Collectors must live with:

- Everything is marketed as Garfield
- Most of the manufacturers do not really matter
- The copyright dates are vague, and it is likely many say "1978"
- Garfield has looked the same for over 40 years with minimal design changes
- When somebody buys something, he throws away the packaging and removes the tags
- Many items do not come with tags or packaging
- Even the parent company, Paws, Inc., does not have clearly organized records of what has been licensed over the years.

The last bullet point is only known if you are fortunate enough to get a tour of the facility in Indiana. It seems that they have consulted with a professional cataloger who admits that they would not know where to start when it comes to organizing the company archives.

It is for these reasons that I am going to apologize early and often for a lack of accurate dates, manufacturers and concrete details about most of the collectibles featured in this book.

Cathy is simply the world record holder and I am an enabling husband who likes to have fun with fellow collectors. We are not psychic. We do not have amazing memories for facts and she did actually purchase over 12,000 Garfield items not knowing the manufacturer, the date of creation, how long it was licensed, how many were made and what markets they were released in.

Like many of you, she purchased items that she wanted, and they make her smile.

Perhaps someday a cataloger will have the resources and energy to make a total accounting of every Garfield item ever made. I am not sure if we would ever need to reference that book for anything other than morbid curiosity.

Garfield is not a commodity that is traded on the commodity market. Garfield is a character who has waddled his way into many people's hearts for many of the reasons stated earlier. There are even more reasons that we did not list but the fact is that Garfield makes many people smile and therefore some of us surround ourselves with him in our homes.

6

A BRIEF HISTORY OF GARFIELD (THE WHO, WHAT AND WHEN)

On June 19, 1978, Jim Davis released his first comic strip with Garfield the cat and his owner Jon. It was well-written, funny, and over time it was syndicated to many newspapers. They hold the world record for "most syndicated comic strip" with over 2,500 newspapers printing the strip.

As the character grew in popularity, merchandise came out such as mugs, stuffed animals (called plushes), clothing, automobile accessories, and much, much, much more.

Once enough comic strips came out, an entire book publishing empire was born. By repackaging the daily comics into numbered volumes, millions of books were sold. The story goes that the Garfield books were so popular that they had to create a special category on the New York Times Best Seller list just so regular authors could get back on the list.

A Brief History of Garfield (the Who, What and When) | 55

Get it? History of Garfield

All the while, the entire business of Paws, Inc., the parent company of Garfield, was run out of a headquarters tucked away in Muncie, Indiana. Muncie was not usually associated with big business. Ball State University had always been the biggest reason why Muncie, Indiana had become a destination.

Although the Paws headquarters is surrounded by corn fields, its building is state of the art with backup generators, high-tech security, and impressive architecture. This multi-million-dollar compound housed the entire organization, from the creative side to the licensing side. The building can generate its own electricity in an emergency and feature a full cafeteria, exercise room, and glass atrium. A true Garfield collector would not have been concerned with an exercise room. Garfield would have considered that a waste of space. At the height of its popularity, Paws even boasted a private Jumbo jet.

Its showroom upstairs is filled with thousands of Garfield items, both old and new. Since many collectors do not get the chance to visit the headquarters, we wish to share some highlights of the tour.

The building is a working studio for comic strips, animations, cartoons, movies, software, cell phone apps, sculptures, and much more. Some of us even consider Muncie to be the mother ship for Garfield and an extremely special place.

United Feature Syndicate and Paws

From 1978, United Feature Syndicate was the sole licensee that owned the merchandising rights. Most earlier pieces say "copyright United Feature Syndicate."

In 1981, Jim Davis founded Paws, Inc. to control the licensing and future of Garfield merchandise.

In 1978 there was not a lot of Garfield merchandise on the market. As you can see from Jim Davis' forward, he was elated just to be picked up as a strip and had his doubts that anyone would want a Garfield Statue.

Even with the lack of merchandising, some of the earliest memorabilia would come from communications and early workings of the processes that went into making Garfield. Many of their drafts and pencil sketches were thrown out but occasionally something surfaces that is from the early days.

Above are two packets of a Garfield Licensing instruction booklet. It helps non-Paws, Inc. artists produce accurate Garfield and friends drawings to be incorporated into future products. I carefully opened and read these booklets and they are amazing. They show poses, facial expressions, they show scale, perspective, color codes, and anything else a new artist needs to know about drawing Garfield.

If I were a company with an idea for a Garfield Christmas tree topper, the only Garfield Christmas item never made (Hint, Hint) I might submit a prototype of a mischievous Garfield at the top of the Christmas tree swatting at the ornaments.

As we stated earlier, United Features Syndicate was the first company to manage the merchandising, but it did not start immediately.

Speaking of Christmas tree toppers, here is an Angel plush that we must use for the top of our Christmas tree.

Full Media Company

Although Garfield has its roots in publishing, it has expanded to feature films, cartoons, video games, amusement parks, and perhaps a Broadway play soon.

Several wide-released movies were in the theaters. "Garfield the Movie" (2004) and "Garfield: A Tale of Two Kitties" (2006) could be seen on the big-screen. The voice of Garfield was portrayed by the legendary Bill Murray.

Licensing

Garfield merchandise is marketed by companies that license the rights from Paws, Inc. Companies all over the world, and in many different languages, are producing and selling merchandise.

In addition to products, the Garfield character is licensed to hotels, amusement parks, stage shows, TV commercials, and even a credit card.

In the '80s at the height of all things Garfield, he even let his creator, Jim Davis, get in on some of the action. They appeared together in TV commercials for the American Express Card.

Hands-Off and Hands-On

Paws, Inc., the parent company of Garfield, is a model of business efficiency. First, they do what they do well, and they do a lot of it all in-house. The creativity, the art, and the necessary steps for the daily comic strip are all done with internal employees.

The licensing appears to be a bit reactive, not proactive. Manufacturers and companies approach Paws, Inc. with their ideas. They may already have a design or a prototype in mind. Paws, Inc. can provide some resources to complete the project, such as art or sculpture, but overall it is the responsibility of the manufacturer to produce and market the final product. The royalties are worked out between Paws, Inc. and the licensee.

I call this a model of efficiency because Garfield is often compared to Disney. According to Google, Disney, employs around

74,000 workers and owns dozens of multi-billion-dollar properties and interests in a plethora of media companies.

Despite having under 40 employees, Paws commands worldwide recognition. They are good at what they do and if someone comes along with an idea for a movie, a product, or a fast-food branding campaign, they are open to listen. All the while, they do not have to make payroll on theme parks or retail stores.

Jim Davis has said many times that his original goal was to be printed for ten years to become syndicated. He never imagined it would syndicate so fast to more than 2,500 papers. He never thought Garfield would become so popular. He never dreamed that Garfield would be around 40 years later!

7
THE EVOLUTION OF GARFIELD (THE WHAT)

Like everything in life, the only constant is change. Even Garfield has evolved and morphed over time.

Look at the eyes

The first Garfield had two separate eyes that were round. As time went on, the eyes got bigger, more oval, and became connected together.

The story goes that as newsprint became more expensive, to save money, newspapers made the comics smaller. This was a problem for cartoonists like Jim Davis because there is only so small that you can make it for people to know what was going on and to get the gag.

One solution was to make the expressive parts of the character larger - such as the face and the eyes. As the eyes got bigger, so did the merchandising.

You will read throughout the book that I reference the importance of looking at the eyes to estimate the age of a Garfield collectible. Below is a graphic that demonstrates how the eyes alone have drastically changed over the years.

© 1978 Paws, Inc.

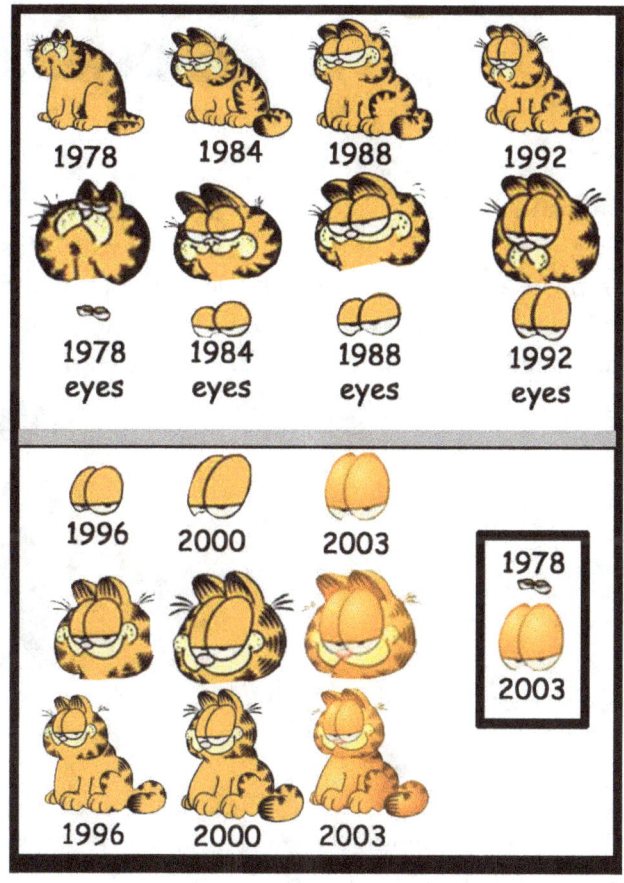

Garfield in 3D

Some cartoons used the technology available to them and transformed Garfield into 3D. The comic strip is two dimensional, so the texturing and coloration was different for the 3D version.

Movie Garfield

In 2004, the first Garfield movie was released. Instead of making Garfield a comic strip, they made him lifelike and believable. Now he looked more like a real cat. The movie merchandising was also upgraded to match the look of the Movie Garfield.

The Color

Over the years, the color of Garfield has ranged from an orange to an orange-yellow. Garfield is not pumpkin-orange. When

Garfield is too orange this is often the work of an illegal, unlicensed copy.

Ceramics Color:

In the world of ceramics such as Enesco, Garfield is browner rather than orange. There are only a few glazes available in the ceramics industry. The best glaze for Garfield is browner because it is more realistic than the orange colors. Even in the '80s when pouring ceramics was popular, people often made the mistake of making Garfield look like a pumpkin.

8

PREMIUM AND NOTABLE GARFIELD COLLECTIBLES --- (THE WHO AND WHAT)

I already mentioned that this is not going to be yet another book with a few hundred pictures and a wishy-washy appraisal of the items featured. This book will, however, feature more of the sought after, rare, and fun collectibles. Most of them are from Cathy's personal collection. A few photos were provided from fellow collectors.

If Cathy and I had to publish a book with over 6,190 unique items, the number of items listed in the book of world records, this book would cost $300 dollars and be thicker than a set of encyclopedias. Would you be amused by pictures of all 22 Garfield Pez dispensers that were made? Most people would not.

Scratch that last statement. If you are a Garfield collector, you would love a book with 6,190 photos in it. I forgot who I was talking to!

The following are some of the good stuff and the fun stuff. Sometimes we will mention prices. Sometimes we will not mention

Premium and Notable Garfield Collectibles --- (The Who and What) | 65

prices. Every item is only worth what someone else is willing to pay for it. We may also be unsure about the manufacturer and the years the items came out. The truth is, much of the time we don't know. Almost everything says, "Copyright 1978," even if it was made yesterday. Unless the actual year the item was produced is printed on it, it is often hard to find out the exact production year.

Garfield Stuff Catalog

Before there was the Internet, there was direct mail. It was the heyday of the United States Postal Service. Elvis sang songs about letters, and mail bags were stuffed with catalogs. The most popular catalog for Garfield Collectors was called "Garfield Stuff" and it came out at least four times a year depending on the availability of merchandise and upcoming events, like Christmas and Back to School.

We will be using the "Garfield Stuff" catalog as a basis for the original price for some Garfield collectibles. This is not an appraisal; it is just a way to gauge the starting price of items. In our opinion, some items in the catalog were already overpriced, so they might have finally been sold out in the clearance area that occasionally showed up in the middle of the catalog. Cathy would always place a large order from the clearance section. The catalog debuted in 1997 and ran approximately until 2005.

Alphabetical Order

There is no right or wrong answer. I already mentioned that many Garfield collectors purchase what makes them smile. It would be judgmental of us to rank the collectibles in order of value since the real value comes from whatever someone is willing to pay for it in the current moment.

To avoid bias, we will be listing the items in "convenient alphabetical order". What is "convenient alphabetical order"? Since each piece is not officially named and cataloged like a library book using the Dewey Decimal system, we will use the best name we can come up with. We will also use multiple names in different places to cross-reference the item. Finally, we will conveniently make up names that make sure we fill in every letter of our alphabet. The Q's and Z's were especially tricky.

Check out our video series of Cathy's and my favorite top 40 Garfield collectibles. In this countdown we do play favorites.

A

Amusement Park Signage

These are good to collect, since in the history of Garfield there were only a handful of amusement parks that ever had a license. Amusement park signs are not sold in retail stores. They are often destroyed before they can be made available to the public.

We have a few Amusement park signs. Pictured here is a sign we got at the Garfield Gathering. It was probably acquired directly from Paws, Inc. as a production proof or a sample.

This one is extraordinarily special to us because it is about a ride, "Garfield's Nightmare." We had previously purchased the Jim Davis signed pencil sketch of a proof of the same ride. It can be seen in the section called "Pencil Sketches."

Amusement Rides (Coin Operated)

We know of two variations of coin-operated amusement kiddie rides. These were made for the entertainment industry to be kiddie rides in malls and public places. They are a way for small children and full-grown, obsessed collectors to be amused for approximately three minutes.

Garfield in a Car Kiddie Ride

A smaller Garfield is sitting in a car. The child (or collector) will sit next to Garfield and enjoy the ride. The collector will later post the picture on Social Media and the child will simply move on with his or her life.

We are using our Garfield in a car kiddie ride as a desk. The fact is, when you have over 12,000 Garfields in one house, you must get creative with space. We purchased two from an amusement ride vendor. We left one alone and I fabricated a desktop that fits over the ride to use as my computer desk. The desk comes off and does not damage the piece.

If anyone takes our desk idea, remember to never plug in the ride or your desk will immediately become an earthquake simulation table for your computers.

Garfield Kiddie Ride with Long Tail

This one is very visual. Nothing but a giant fiberglass Garfield with a larger than life tail. It looks great, but it is dull to ride. There are YouTube videos with toddlers riding this. Even they have a look on their face like, "that's it?"

It goes back and forth slowly while the song "Here Comes Garfield" plays.

Ours barely fit in the door. We won it on eBay and paid extra to have it crated and shipped. We had to pay for a lift truck since our house does not have a loading dock. Five neighbors helped us get it in the door. I think we had to crack the plaster to make a turn into the living room.

Fun Story from Paws, Inc.

When we were with our contact on the tour of Paws, Inc., we also saw this amusement ride in their atrium. They must leave it unplugged because, when it is plugged in, every five to ten minutes a recording of a British child tries to entice children to ride it.

The problem was that the high-tech security system for Paws, Inc. headquarters also has audio. There was a call from a security guard that a child might be trapped in the building. It was only the amusement ride recording. Rescue workers were sent to their office to save the child who did not actually exist.

B

anks
There is a wide variety of banks ranging from ceramic piggy style banks up to Enesco ceramic banks.

Pictured is a ceramic piggy style bank in the spirit of Garfield. Spencer's sold them in the mid-'90s. They were also available in the "Garfield Stuff" catalog with a price of $21.95.

Bedtime for Garfield

"Bedtime for Garfield" was made by Danbury Mint in the mid-'90s. Each one was hand signed by Jim Davis on the bottom ribbon by the slippers.

It is 18 inches tall and a foot wide. It is posable. When it was new, it sold for $147.50. Unfortunately, it usually trends between $50 to $100 on eBay.

This item is only complete if it has the best friend 18kt gold electroplated necklaces and the red leather-covered book with story by Jim Davis.

Cathy's is displayed in a custom acrylic case that was manufactured to fit the exact footprint of our curio cabinet. It was made by Cathy's parents' next door neighbor and friend, who owns a company, FirstTech Corp., in New Jersey.

We would classify this item as a rare yet common collector's piece. In other words, sooner or later every serious collector will eventually own one, so they are very common for serious collectors. This also holds true for the Danbury mint plates and the Christmas village.

Bedtime for Odie

"Bedtime for Odie" is also made by Danbury Mint; this was the follow up to "Bedtime for Garfield". They probably did not make as many of the Odie version of this series since often Garfield collectors are just that ... Garfield collectors. Odie and the other fringe characters are not as popular as Garfield himself.

The one shown is actually incomplete. It is missing the pink teddy bear that Odie should be holding and the wooden base. Sometimes you can get items at really good prices if you are okay with missing pieces. Cathy didn't accumulate over 12,000 pieces by paying full retail.

On the contrary, there are quite a few pure Odie, Pooky, Arlene, Nermal and, dare I say, Jon collectors. These people can relate better to the characters for their own personal reasons. These fringe characters are often not available, or simply an accessory to the Garfield that comes with it. You might get a Pooky that is being held by Garfield. There might be a statue of Garfield kissing Arlene.

Odie is often available on a stand-alone basis since the character speaks directly to dog people and it is not a risk making dog toys, dog bowls, Odie collars, and other canine accessories.

I am not sure if this is the time or place to mention this, but Odie was created as a contrast for Garfield. He is the opposite of Garfield on purpose. Garfield is smart. Odie is stupid. Garfield is aggressive. Odie is a victim. Garfield is calculating. Odie is reactive and never sees things coming. How many times can a dog be kicked off a table without anticipating the next one? Even Charlie Brown knows that Lucy will likely pull the football away from him when he tries to kick it. He just believes her when she says she will not. Odie will never get it. He is just a dim-witted, slobbering, happy-go-lucky dog.

As dog people ourselves, this is one of the main reasons we have dogs. It's the unconditional love and the reassurance that our pet is not plotting the next injury that will happen to us. Cat people often must live in fear of retaliation.

Beer Stein

This is a total gray area when it comes to walking right up to the "line" and standing with your tippy toes right on that "line". Garfield staffers always try to avoid items that relate to drinking, smoking, and other vices. Danbury Mint must have caught them at a weak moment since this is vaguely alcohol-related. An interesting fact is the advertisement from Danbury Mint only calls it a "stein" not a "beer stein".

Thank goodness for that weak moment, because it is a beautiful piece and the brand is not in jeopardy letting one mug go that is so large that your blood alcohol level will fail a breathalyzer test from one glass. The purists can easily argue it is a Garfield size coffee mug. The original price was $59.00 plus $7.50 shipping.

Birdfeeder (and Windchimes)

This item barely deserves to make the list for the very reason that it is on the list. We learned the hard way that although it was intended to feed birds, the metal that they used for the chain and the eye bolt rust out and stain the

piece. All the pores in the design attract dirt. Once it is used for its intended purpose it becomes ruined and loses all value.

In a way we are rewarding a manufacturer for completely missing the target to have an item function properly for its intended purpose. Once again, for that very reason that we ruined the first one using it as a bird feeder, we quickly learned to keep the new one inside and in its box.

So, congratulations to whomever made this item for earning the "Participation Medal" of Garfield collectibles and making it in this book. It is a well-sculpted piece that cannot be used for its intended function unless you have an indoor bird cage.

This is just a prediction, but I would imagine these items could become harder to find because if they were used, they were thrown out. Imagine a Garfield drinking glass that is not machine washable and disintegrates if it gets wet? That's what the birdfeeder people made.

Just a footnote. The same company also made the Garfield windchimes, so leave them inside also. In the Spring 1998 "Garfield Stuff" catalog the birdfeeder was priced at $14.95 and the windchimes were $6.95.

Books (only some books)

Paws, Inc. does publishing very well. Our research shows they have sold over 200 million books over the last 40 years and counting. You will soon read that we classify most of the books as "not rare" in chapter 10. Some books are definitely more valuable.

Here is a picture of the 20th birthday book published in 1998 by Easton Press, a division of Danbury Mint. It is leather bound with 22kt gold accents. This was the easiest item to date since it is a 20-year book and Garfield started in 1978.

Boomerang

This item may not be on par with Enesco figurines or slot machines, but it holds a special place in my heart because I made Cathy bid on it for me during the 2009 Garfield Gathering,

The mere fact that it was in a Garfield Gathering auction alone makes it a stand-out piece, but something was telling me I wanted this item. The packaging was in Italian so at least it is manufactured for foreign markets. We have never seen one since we won it at auction. There is no telling if they were ever produced; often times auction items are samples or prototypes.

Bowling balls

One bowling ball has Garfield etched into the ball. Other bowling balls have the color images on the surface of the balls. What make this fun is the fact that our bowling balls are drilled and used for bowling.

They also made a yellow Odie bowling ball.

Boxing (and MMA for Chad)

In keeping with the sports theme, if there is a group of people that participate in something, then there is a collectible for them to get their hands on. This is no exception when it comes to boxing. To modernize the items, I am also including Mixed Martial Arts (MMA). I subtitled it, "for Chad". Chad is the husband of a high-end collector, Jo "Boom Boom" Herrman. She co-hosted the 2015 convention with Cheryl and is a good friend of ours.

When describing why people collect certain items, we previously said they purchase items showcasing the hobbies and sports that they are interested in. Chad used to fight in Mixed Martial Arts, and these days he owns a company that makes fighting rings and cages.

This story is important because I am not only making a personal friend say, "Hey, they are talking about me." It also is important to note that when a plush Garfield wearing a karate uniform came up in the auction, Jo did not let up on the bidding. Failure was not an option, and only Sylvester Stallone himself, as

a millionaire, could have outbid her that day.

This is a major reason why this entire directory barely has prices. For every Jo "Boom Boom" Herrman at the Garfield Gathering, there are hundreds more on-line bidding for items showcasing what sports and hobbies they enjoy. Putting an arbitrary price of $10 for a plush would not do it justice when

others might be willing to pay hundreds. *Note to Chad …. She only spent a few dollars. Yeah, that's the ticket.*

Burton and Burton

A major licensee in the past is Burton and Burton. The look and feel are a bit different from Enesco even though they both make Garfield ceramics. Just by looking at the eyes, you would know that they came after Enesco. The eyes are bigger and more expressive.

Since we are discussing ceramic timelines, Westland was another manufacturer who came after Burton and Burton and also made Garfield ceramics.

Shown is a Burton and Burton Flower pot. Jim Davis always jokes that he curses the day that he decided to make Garfield a striped cat because of all the extra work it has created for them. I am sure the people who painted this item will also agree.

Above is a Burton and Burton coffee server and mugs. Some would argue that it is a tea set but we all know that Garfield is fueled by coffee.

Butler Table

This almost four-foot-tall cast resin item is antiqued and has a retro feel to it. Garfield is dressed as a butler and is holding an oval tray.

This manufacturer made a few pieces within the same series and they have a very special look and feel to them.

This photo is credited to Nancy and Manny Vega. We have one, but ours is missing the tray.

C

Canisters
Danbury Mint produced a set of four canisters in the mid-'90s They were Jim Davis' vision of an imaginary "Main Street". The set sold for $168. The largest, Garfield's Bakery, holds 72oz. The next size down is Odie's Grocery which holds 56oz. Next is Arlene's Café that holds 32oz. Finally, there is Pooky's flowers that holds 20oz.

The lids are rubberized for a snug fit to help keep contents fresh.

Carousel

This item was made by Danbury Mint in the early to mid-'90s. It almost always fetches over $100 when it comes up for sale. The original price was $115.

The piece is built on a rotating base. The horses are mounted on 23kt gold-plated poles. This piece does not play music. It also spins round and round if turned by hand. Each one originally came with a certificate of authenticity from Danbury Mint. If you don't have one, do not fear. We cannot say there was ever any bootlegging of these items. The certificates were a clever way for the marketing department to make it feel rarer and more collectible.

This piece is yet another common yet rare item that every serious collector will get his hands on eventually.

"Celebration of Art" T-shirt

The first time we ever saw this shirt was when Jim Davis wore it on the 25th birthday cruise as shown in this photo.

Later, during the 2017 Garfield Gathering we managed to purchase the same design shirt from the Garfield sales room. It holds a special place in our heart and our collection since it reminds us of the cruise and how Jim Davis managed to wear something that the most devoted 400 collectors on the cruise did not own. We saw a lot of nice Garfield shirts on the cruise but only one of these.

The design is genius. Odie strategically covers up any risqué body parts with his face and his ears. Our research shows that the oil painting in the background is called the "Grande Odalisque" painted in 1814 by Jean Auguste Dominique Ingres.

We can't be certain, but considering we purchased the shirt from Paws Inc. directly, Cathy likes to think it is possible that this could be the actual shirt worn by Jim on the cruise. Hey, you never know.

Cels (Collector's Cel)

American Royal Arts held the license to sell animated production cels that were part of some cartoons. They had a catalog of cels that were available for purchase. We were lucky enough to have an American Royal Arts retail outlet not far from our house. On a Saturday in March of 1995, Jim Davis was in town 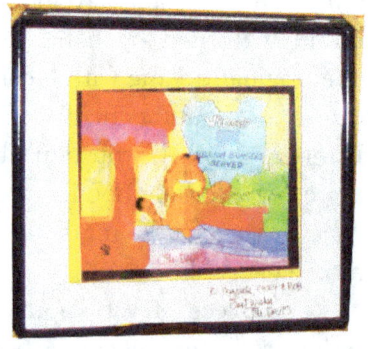 for a special signing event. Jim would personalize any cel, and American Royal Arts matted and framed it.

We were not able to attend and meet Jim Davis. I was away on business and Cathy was a bridesmaid in her friend's wedding on that day. We were able to leave instructions for the personalization. It would be another 8 years before we would get to meet Jim Davis in person. At the time of release, the prices started around $350 and went up from there. You can still find some cels being sold on cruise ships at their art auctions. You can also purchase cels and other collectible items directly from Paws, Inc.

From a Collection A Nod to Gary Skinner

Gary Skinner is one of the first serious collectors, who also organized one of the first collectors' get-togethers known. Because he lives in the Indiana area, he has access to Paws, Inc. and has quickly become a friend of the company.

The reason he is mentioned here is that he was the person to convince Paws, Inc, that they were throwing away money. In the early days, an original pencil sketch went into the garbage after it was not needed any longer. Probably cels were also tossed when the animated cartoon was complete.

Gary says that, at first, when he visited headquarters, the staff would joke, "Gary's here, protect your garbage pails." He later became a valuable liaison between the collectors' community and Paws, Inc.

Gary is a regular representa-

This one we acquired as part of a collection that we purchased on Long Island. The previous owner had excellent taste in collectibles.

tive sent from Paws, Inc. to sell their personal Garfield items. Since he is also an avid collector, he can relate to the market. I will say it here: if Gary cared about the world record, he could probably have taken it from Cathy at any time or gotten it long before Cathy came along.

Gary also owned a store for many years that only sold Garfield items. He supplied many gift shops with special items and purchased entire collections to retail.

CD Holder / Antiqued Clock

This item was made by the same manufacturer as the butler table. They manufactured several additional items: Garfield laying on top of a CD holder, Garfield standing by a clock, Garfield standing by a candle holder, Garfield grasping a paper towel holder, Garfield holding a key fob. The CD holder is a cast resin material with an antique looking finish. It stands almost four feet tall and holds around 80 compact disc cases. It was sold in the "Garfield Stuff" catalog for $250.

The deliberately antiqued fit and finish makes this series of collectibles an instant classic. They are big and bold and beautiful.

This line of items, like many Garfield collectibles, had both form and function. They had a useful purpose and were beautiful to look at.

Here is a photo of the complete piece. It was photographed at the Paws, Inc. showroom on a visit to Muncie Indiana.

Years later, all of these items are harder to come by, and therefore a great item for any collection. When new, they each cost well over $100, and I've seen them sell on eBay for much more in recent years. Cathy has been able to get her hands on them fairly cheaply since she is willing to buy them damaged. Our butler is missing the tray so we call him "low five Garfield". Our clock figure is missing the clock so we call him "the Thinker".

Christmas

You name it, and they made it, except for a Christmas tree topper. Almost every imaginable Christmas-related item has been created in Garfield's image. You can fill multiple Christmas trees with all of the ornaments produced over the years.

There are all sorts of Garfield Christmas decorations. One of the largest Garfield plushes you will ever see is also a Christmas item. It is coming up under "Macy's Giant Plush".

Christmas Animations

Several large animated plush decorations were made. The fuzzy holiday decorations play music and the arms move. They are almost two feet tall and are really fun pieces.

These decorations can easily be used inside a high-end Christmas exhibit shown by people who decorate their entire property into an amazing winter

wonderland. Just picture the Garfield room surrounded by velvet ropes with each one playing and moving.

Shown here is Garfield ringing a bell and Garfield skiing. The arms move up and down and the music would cycle through 18 Christmas songs. Around six different designs were made, and these are always a great item to put on the piano to signal that Christmas is coming. Just remember to take the batteries out when you store them or you could ruin them with battery acid. They also came with an AC adapter to plug into a wall outlet. They were sold at Spencer's and other Christmas stores, like Harrow's and specialty outlets. They retailed in the range of $50. They do come up for sale quite often, but make sure they still work if you're going to pay top dollar.

Christmas Danbury Mint Band

In the mid-'90s, as a great accompaniment to the Garfield Christmas Village, Garfield small Christmas train, Garfield large Christmas train and Garfield Christmas plates, Danbury Mint also offered the six-piece set, Garfield's Christmas Band, shown below. It's a really great piece because it includes the entire gang from the comic strip; even Garfield's friends, the mice, get to hold up the Garfield's Christmas Band sign. The original retail price was $115.

Christmas Lights

In the mid-'90s, a string of 10 Christmas lights was produced by Kurt S. Adler and has not been made since. They retailed for $19.99. At the Garfield Gathering in 2017, a string of lights sold for over $100 at auction. This isn't necessarily an appraisal since the purchaser goes by the nickname of "Crazy Gary" and he will pay anything to win the items that he wants. Fortunately for those of us who are online, Gary does not know that eBay and the Internet exist. We are certainly not going to tell him even though we are good friends.

They also made a bunch of Christmas ornaments in the '90s into the 2000s.

Christmas Ornaments

Over the years, there were hundreds of Christmas ornaments produced. The ornaments alone can be the subject of a very thick book. Some are rare, some are ordinary, and some are extraordinary. Cathy and I have most of the ornaments, but we are not really as obsessed with the Christmas items as other collectors are. We don't usually put up a Christmas tree because we spend Christmas and New Year's with Cathy's parents in Florida. I've spent the last 6 or so Christmases decorating her father's pontoon boat to look like a Christmas train, smoke and all. Check it out on www.youtube.com.

Bradford Exchange

I call them the "Fragile Round Ornaments". These are a series of eight ornaments made in 1999. You would order the set

and they would ship two at a time until you owned all eight.

Possible Dreams Ornaments

These, too, are round and fragile. They come in gold, green, and red. Gold is the rarest, and the red one seems to appear most often. They each have a different Garfield placed on top of the Christmas ball. There were also some weighted stocking hangers. Be careful when using them and stuffing the stocking that you don't weigh down the stocking too much so the holder falls off the cabinet, mantle or wherever you hang your stockings. Cathy found that out the hard way. These items are well made and very sought after.

Hallmark Ornaments

It would be unfair to say the Hallmark ornaments are incredibly rare. They were made of some type of plastic resin and they were made quite well. Because of their fine quality, the survival rate is pretty high. You can throw them all in a plastic tote without wrapping them individually and they should last a long time. We know because one of the collections we purchased had probably 100 ornaments in a tote and most of them were not broken. Hallmark is a good name and these should be the cornerstone of any Christmas tree. Hallmark stopped producing Garfield ornaments in 1995. You can still get them for under $20 online.

Carlton Cards Ornaments by American Greetings

In the late '90s, Carlton Cards took over the production of Garfield

Christmas ornaments. As of the writing of this book, they still produce an ornament every year. Look for them in your local American Greetings card store. They retail for around $16.95, and sometimes they have a "buy 2, get one free" promotion. Get some of your Garfield collector buddies together and split the purchase. Or, keep one for displaying, one for a gift and one mint in box. I'm not saying they will be worth a fortune since they are mass produced, but it's always nice to have a back-up in case one breaks. I hear cats can wreak havoc on Christmas trees.

Lighted Ornament

This ornament would plug into a string of Christmas lights and red bulbs would chase in circles. No matter what you had on your Christmas tree, this ornament would demand attention from anywhere in the room.

There was a time when you could buy them in stores, but today you rarely see them for sale on eBay. The truth is that once you have one, you never want to let it go. In fact, many people frown about having duplicate ornaments on their Christmas tree, but this item is so much fun that you need one every few feet. They sold for $9.99 in the mid '90s.

Enesco Ornaments and Enesco Christmas Items

In the early to mid-'80s almost everything Garfield was produced by Enesco. They made Christmas ornaments, bells, statues, mugs, figurines and salt and pepper shakers, among many other items. Some were dated like the Christmas bells, so, of course you would have get one every year until they ended the series.

Over the years, the ceramic ornaments became cracked, broken or thrown out. Enesco stopped making them in the late '80s. Since Enesco was one of the first ornament suppliers, they are now the oldest ornaments made with Garfield's image on them. Over time they have become more sought after. Some items are more common than others and the prices are all over the place. It comes down to either what you are willing to pay for an item or what you are willing to sell the item for.

In the set below, look at the eyes. The eyes are small and separate. This indicates an earlier version of Garfield. As newsprint got more expensive, the funnies were drawn smaller. Jim Davis, the creator of Garfield, had to exaggerate the faces so the comic strips would be understood. This is why the eyes are bigger today.

The Enesco ornaments above are older given the size and shape of the eyes.

Enesco Christmas Bells

The best thing about the bells is that they have the year molded right into them so there is no second guessing as to the age of the item. Shown here is 1984 to 1990. Interestingly enough, there was no bell manufactured in 1983.

Dakin Ornaments

In the early '80s, several ornaments were also made out of wood. They are sturdier than ceramic and glass. The clunky nostalgic look makes them more sought after today. It is like the nostalgia that black and white photography brings even if color film is available. Wooden ornaments appear a bit retro as if Santa's elves made them. They make me think of what Christmas ornaments looked like in the 1950s.

Kurt S. Adler Ornaments - Polonaise Glass Ornaments

They made a half dozen or so different types of glass polonaise ornaments. Some of them are rarer than others. There were some stand alone Odie ornaments that were really nice and very fragile. They originally retailed for around $40. I've seen some sell for double that in recent years.

Talk about fragile, these glass ornaments have a European, retro, high-end look and feel - the kind you would find on a millionaire's Christmas tree.

Christmas "Tips"

This fun set of Enesco statues feature Garfield's tips regarding the Christmas holiday.

From left to right – Christmas Tip

1. "Leave something for Santa"
2. "Tis better to get than to give"
3. "Tell 'em your size"
4. "Remember to take your foot out first"

Christmas Train(s)

There is a big Christmas train and a small Christmas train. Both trains have five pieces. The large train originally sold for $199.50.

Shown above is the small Christmas train. It was a follow-up to the large Christmas train. Both were produced by Danbury Mint.

Still in its protective styrofoam box is the large train set. Unlike other Danbury Mint items, you received the entire set all at once.

Christmas Village

Danbury Mint also made a Garfield Christmas village in 1994. Some people will tell you that Danbury made six houses and other people will tell you they made a series of ten of them. They initially promoted it as a 6-piece collection. After you purchased all six, Danbury Mint offered an optional four more. Since many people did not purchase the extra four, today the extra four houses are very sought after.

Each house originally sold for $84, plus shipping.

Clocks

Clocks are a category that can also be a subject of a book by itself. There are dozens of Garfield clocks made by many manufacturers. Sunbeam probably manufactured most of them in the '80s and '90s. Don't let size fool you, though. Just because a clock is small, it doesn't necessarily mean that it will be inexpensive. We've seen some small clocks sell for large dollars.

Clock with lights and panels

Danbury Mint came out with a clock for all seasons in the late '90s. This clock body acts as a light-box and there are four inserts that can be changed to represent each season. It originally sold for $150 directly from Danbury Mint. It's a rare-ish piece that you don't see for sale very often. It either takes batteries or can be plugged in with the AC adapter that is included.

Colecticritters

I write this section with some conflict in my soul. My concern is that Cathy and I are becoming agents to slick marketers who create a narrative that suits their wallets. Let's be honest: all licensees and manufacturers want to sell as many items as they can. I have a bit of a queasy feeling when the hype is amped up and is targeted to the buyer. Cathy and I are guilty as charged because it should be no secret that we are hoping the book also sells well. We would be crossing a line if we promoted the book as if "it is a limited run, so act now."

I look back on the Beanie Baby craze and see that some victims believed the hype. They believed that a stuffed animal mass produced last month is worth cashing in their retirement plans to purchase. Fuel was added to the fire when home shopping channels got in on the act and marked the prices of the items up from the beginning. The hosts of the channels acted as if they were investments. This could almost be called deception or fraud.

With that said, Collecticritters made two types of Garfield bears. The white one was a limited edition of 10,000 pieces. The cream colored one was a limited edition of 2,000.

To be blunt, Cathy paid $10 for one and under $10 for the other. We don't want to create a bidding war out there. If you think they are cute, buy them - but not as an investment. Buy them if you want them and they make you smile. If you are looking for an investment, might we suggest a nice safe bond or stock that was well-researched.

Credit Card in Frame

MBNA America Bank created a credit card with Garfield on it. As a perk for using the card, (I think you had to put $1,000 on the card in the first 90 days), they sent you a plaque. If you stayed in good standing and spent a certain amount every year, they would send another credit card blank to put on the next year's space.

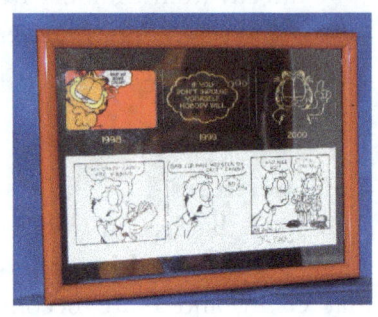

It held three credit cards and had a Garfield comic strip at the bottom. It was signed by Jim Davis. You would also earn points to get discount coupons to use on your purchases from the "Garfield Stuff" catalog.

Crystal Garfield

In our opinion, one of the rarest Garfield collectibles ever made was the Garfield Crystal. We have seen only one in existence. Fortunately, we saw it when we were purchasing someone's collection. Besides our own, we have never seen one in person or for sale since.

Cathy was also once contacted by someone about a Pooky crystal. She sent a picture and we have never seen one of them beyond that photo. There were about a half dozen different crystals produced probably in the mid-'80s.

If you have a crystal, treasure it and protect it.

Cookie jars

There have been several Garfield cookie jars made by several companies: Enesco, Burton and Burton and Westland, to name a few. They have been manufactured since the '80s and continue well into the '10s .

Because the cookie jars are made of ceramics, they are prone to break. The more they break, the less there are in the world. This is especially true when you try to ship them via popular freight carriers.

Cookies jars can fetch a nice price because they are highly collectible by a wide range of people. Many people collect a wide assortment of cookie jars, not just of one character, so take very good care of your cookie jars.

The ones that come to mind follow:

White Cookie Jar

The White Cookie Jar has a matching creamer, sugar bowl, and other similar items. They were only glazed, but not painted any colors.

Oreo Cookie Jar

Probably one of the more sought-after cookie jars. This is Garfield laying on (protecting) a stack of Oreo cookies. Made in the mid-'80s, these pieces are highly sought after and very collectible. Because they are ceramic, the survival rate decreases every year. It is even rumored that Paws, Inc. even broke a few themselves.

D

Danbury Mint
Throughout the '90s and into the 2000s The Danbury Mint, a company located in Norwalk, Connecticut, had offered hundreds of high quality Garfield collectibles. They range from collector plates and mugs, small figurines and model cars to large figurines and many more. Chances are you own many of their items. Some items are rarer than others because the production run was short. Check the internet selling sites and you will see most of the items that were available. The Danbury Mint does not offer Garfield items for sale any longer. Most of the items they sold were part of a series:

- "Dear Diary" set of eight plates
- "A Day with Garfield" set of twelve plates
- Garfield Music Box Collection set of four musical jewelry boxes
- Set of twelve "Classic Garfield" figurines

All the items came with a certificate of authenticity and they would be numbered with the same serial number to show that the entire series was sold to the same person. You could opt out at any time since they would send one or two items each month. That is why you'll see a lot of incomplete sets for sale, which is fine, if you are looking to replace ones that got broken or damaged. If you are looking for a complete set, be sure to do your own research. I can guarantee you that the set of calendar plates has twelve plates in the series.

There's A LOT of details on some the statues and figurines; be sure to ask for multiple pictures from every angle when purchasing them online. Also, make sure you ask the person to take very special care when packaging them for shipping. Cathy bought two of the large statues from someone years ago and they only wrapped tissue paper around them. By the time, we received the package, we had quite a puzzle on our hands trying to even figure out which pieces belonged to which statue.

The music boxes shown below were sold in the "Garfield Stuff" catalog for $59.95.

The original prices on the statues shown below range from $59.95 to $74.95.

Dip and Chips Plate

Nothing says, "I love Garfield" at a cocktail party like a dip and chip platter. It was distributed by Spencer's Gifts.

I must admit, this piece is adorable and yet so functional. The dip goes in the bird-

bath with Garfield and the chips go along the outside with the birds.

As rare as this piece is, I guarantee you that Garfield collectors have used and continue to use this to serve food.

Doc Davis

Doc Davis is Jim Davis' brother and the inspiration for the character "Doc Boy". No, we do not have Doc Davis locked away in our basement, however Doc Davis is an important part of the Garfield story.

Anyone who regularly follows the Garfield comic strip probably already knows that the strip is, to some extent, an autobiographical look into the Davis' past life of growing up on a farm in Indiana. So many of the strips that feature Doc Boy are taken directly from their experiences growing up.

Doc Davis retired in 2006, but prior to that he was instrumental as the liaison between Paws, Inc. and the collectors. He attended many conventions and was extremely generous to the collectors. More on that later in the book.

There are several items that we purchased personally from Doc at the Garfield Gathering. Some items were from his own personal collection that he sold off to the collectors.

Coming up under "P" is the "Pencil Sketch" original artwork we purchased from Doc Davis. There is a nice photo in the section about the 2006 Garfield Gathering of Cathy and Doc holding an acrylic painting that we purchased from him. As part of the purchase, he "threw in" a framed, uncut sheet of the 1995 Garfield krome trading cards. This can be found coming up under "K".

Doc Davis Polo Shirts

These polo shirts were owned and worn by Doc Davis. After he retired, he consolidated his collection and went to the 2008 Garfield Gathering in Tennessee and sold some personal items. They are beautiful shirts on their own but knowing that they were once owned by Doc Davis makes them even more special. We purchased the only two he had for sale. Cathy remembered him wearing one on the Garfield cruise. That picture below is Doc behind his camera on the 25th birthday cruise.

In one of the "Garfield Stuff" catalogs, Jim Davis is shown wearing this same golf shirt. It originally sold for $49.95 as a "Garfield Stuff" catalog exclusive.

Doc Davis Acrylic Painting

This is not named after Doc Davis, but we did purchase it from him at the 2006 Garfield Gathering. 2006 was the first year that Cathy and I attended so it was a big deal to have Garfield royalty at the event. We learned

that the family is very friendly and very approachable.

Doorbell

This electrical beauty is a plush, indoor personal room doorbell that has a button on one side and a chime on the other side of the wire. On the outside of the door you squeeze the little  "Pooky" button and the Garfield face chimes on the inside of the doorbell.

I am sure it was designed with a twelve-year-old child's bedroom in mind but it totally comes in handy on our bathroom door. They were sold at Fashion Bug stores in the early 2000s. There were two different versions. They were also featured in the "Garfield Stuff" catalog with a retail price of $12.95.

E

Enesco As already mentioned multiple times in this book (only because they are an essential part of any Garfield collection), years ago, when Garfield was gaining popularity in the '80s and '90s, just about every card and gift store had cute mugs and statues made of ceramic. They were inexpensive, impulse gifts for graduates, teachers, skiers, and just about any other sportsperson or activist you could think of. At the time, they were not treated as rare and valuable collectibles.

Once again, since they were made of ceramic, there has been a lot of broken ones over the years. Today, many Enesco ceramics are treated as rare and sought-after limited pieces. It helps that they have not been produced in years. Some are rarer than others and can go for a pretty penny at auction.

Embassy Suites Hotel

Back in the late '80s, Garfield was the spokescat for the Embassy Suites Hotels. Their logo was "You Don't Have to be a Fat Cat to Enjoy the Suite Life". They featured Garfield in their commercials and print ads. They used Garfield's picture on their "do not disturb" signs in the hotels. They also made promotional pins and mugs with Embassy Suites Hotels' information on one side and Garfield on the other.

Easter

If there is a universally recognized holiday, there are many Garfield items to help celebrate. Easter is no exception. Not the religious dimension of the holiday, rather the fuzzy Easter bunny and dyed eggs version. Russell Stover was right there with an annual license to spread chocolate and plushes and figurines to all the good girls, boys and Garfield collectors.

Enesco also had its share of ceramic holiday items. Some are seen in this holiday Enesco group photo. In the front left you can see Garfield and Odie sporting white bunny outfits. For those of you dying to call out our mistakes, yes, the birthday cake in the back left is not an Enesco. This is our general celebration group photo.

Easter Candy

In this picture are mostly Russell Stover Easter candy boxes. They were packaged with a Garfield figurine and were marketed around Easter. They also made fully-stocked Easter baskets and a larger Garfield plush came with those. They had different variations every year throughout the '90s into the '00s.

F

Fabric
If there were such a thing as an "Endangered Species List" of Garfield items, sewing fabric is practically extinct. Fabric from a roll or bolt used to be available for crafty people to make their own Garfield clothing, bags, pillows, and other household goods.

We already established that some Garfield collectors use items for what they are intended to do. That is fine when it comes to a mug or drinking glass; you just rinse it off, put it away and use it over and over. Fabric, on the other hand, gets cut up into little pieces and re-purposed into a new type of item. As more and more items are made, the available stock dwindles. Soon, what you see in the next photo will be the only evidence of the Garfield fabric. Hopefully it lives on as completed pillows, shirts or other items.

A tribute to Jubilant Joy and Jessie

There is no better place to immortalize two beloved Garfield Gathering insiders, who we called "Jubilant Joy" and her husband Jessie. As her name implied Jubilant Joy was always upbeat and always made the room light up when she was in it.

Why did we put the tribute directly under "Fabric"? Great question. Jubilant Joy used to sew the most amazing top to bottom, matching outfits for her and Jessie. While the rest of us wore off-the rack T-shirts, they leaned in and really owned it.

Jubilant Joy and Jessie were always involved with volunteering to help make the organizers' and hosts' lives easier by setting up the rooms before a meal, organizing the auction items, selling raffle tickets and anything else you needed them to do. Jubilant Joy would be in the Paws room helping Gary Skinner with pricing and organizing items.

The year that Cathy and I hosted the Garfield Gathering, Jubilant Joy gladly put on the warm, heavy Garfield costume and graced the room with her presence. That was not even the first time she performed in the Garfield costume to amuse the group.

Sadly, she passed away in 2016 and she has been profoundly missed. Hopefully, this book will help keep her memory alive in the hearts of collectors.

Fast Food Toys and Signage

Sure, millions of people can purchase kids' meals and receive the fast food toys, but it is a good idea to try to get your hands on the signs and any promotional tools used to promote the toys. The signs are usually destroyed after the promotion is over. Years later, they are more collectible than the toys that they promoted.

Fast food toys and signage are collectible by a wide range of people. There are many people that collect the toys regardless of the character portrayed.

Don't expect to make your fortune from these, unless you have samples that never actually went into production or foreign market toys or very limited runs.

Fast Food Signage Fun Story

In June of 2017, at the Garfield Gathering in Asheville, North Carolina, there was a funny story that addressed fast food signage.

Just to set the stage, Cathy and I had been helping Nancy and Manny, the organizers, get ready for the convention. We went to their home in Pennsylvania a few times to help pick out the auction items and get them packed up for the trip.

One of the items in the auction was to be a foreign market Wendy's fast food sign with Wendy's toys. Nancy had the sign from Paws, Inc. and Cathy promised Nancy that she would look through her collection and find an extra set of Wendy's toys.

When we got home, it took us over two full weekends to find the toys. We had to open over 150 totes to look for them.

Just a little more background and I can get on with the story. You may not have found out yet that I have also been the auctioneer for the Garfield Gathering since 2012. (That is another story for another time).

On Saturday, the night of the auction, the Wendy's toys and poster came up. I started the bidding at $10. For a moment, the room had no action. I kept repeating "Ten dollars, where is my ten-dollar bid?" Still no bids. So, I said, "Cathy (my wife) will even bid the ten dollars." She looked at me like I had three heads. I told her to raise her paddle and reluctantly she bid.

She and Nancy could not stop laughing because the toys came from our house in the first place and we had given them up at no charge and now we were buying them back. Truth be told, I was just trying to loosen up the room so other people would join in. I figured I would break the ice and someone else would win it.

There were no more bids in the room and it was dropped on us for $10. It actually was a really good deal because the toys were worth pennies, but the signs that we did not already have were the real value to the win.

More importantly, I have not seen Cathy laugh so hard since we watched an extremely overweight person try to get out of a canoe in upstate New York. Don't judge. It was really funny.

Signage Screen Shot

Since I am jumping around with items and stories, here is as good a place as any to talk about the video screen shot that we used to represent fast food packaging.

The screen shot came from a video series that Cathy and I made for Garfield's 40th birthday. We already mentioned in the "about the authors" chapter that Cathy and I have done many Garfield collectible-related videos. Our most ambitious project was an eight-part series that featured our favorite 40 collectibles.

We were almost done writing this book and wanted a way to bring to life our collection and acknowledge the 40th birthday. We encourage you to seek out the videos on YouTube, Facebook, or www.LovesGarfield.com.

Fish Bowl

As part of a collection we acquired, this Garfield fish bowl was included. According to the box, the tank rotates to see all three of Garfield's expressions and to "drive your fish crazy." The bottom of the box says the "Graphic coordination by Tasteful Ideas" in Mission, Kansas.

Fish Tank

A two-gallon fish tank with pump and light is a popular collectible. They range in price from $50 to over $100 depending on whether it has the box and if it is unused. This is a fun item since many Garfield collectors use items for what they are intended. When I was a manager at a retail store in my 20s, I had ours in my office with goldfish in it. We think this is a great representation of the sense of humor the people at Paws, Inc. must have. It's a real cute piece and fun to look at.

Folding Chairs

Here's another item that Fashion Bug marketed as part of its entire line of Garfield items in the 2000s. They are canvas folding chairs that fit in a Garfield sleeve style bag.

2006 Garfield Gathering – No room in the car

Shown here are our chairs that we brought to the 2006 Garfield Gathering. It was the first year that we attended. The hotel rooms were so inexpensive that we booked a hot tub suite. Not knowing that we would purchase tons of items at the event, we made the mistake of bringing Garfield decorations to spruce up our hotel room and show off some of our collection to fellow collectors.

The problem was that we needed to drive home with what we brought with us as well as all of the stuff we purchased at the event. To make matters worse, we drove in our small Saturn sedan because it had the lowest mileage on it and got better gas mileage. Somehow, we got everything home, but I could not see out the back window.

We have since learned to bring the largest car that we own, and bring it as empty as we can. To the next convention we are bringing the Range Rover and maybe even tow an enclosed trailer, since it won't be a long drive, for a change.

Don't even get me started on the years we had to fly to the conventions. I'm lucky Cathy let me pack clothing to wear! Here's a random tip for people who have to travel by airplane. Pack a suitcase inside another suitcase on your way to your destination. That way, if you buy too many souvenirs or clothing or whatever, you can have an extra suitcase ready to go. A lot of people figure they will ship items home, but even if you have to pay for the suitcase, many times it's still cheaper than shipping. Most airlines allow 50 pounds per suitcase.

Foreign Figurines

Cathy was lucky to find these statues made for foreign markets. For the hundreds of hours that she has logged on eBay, she has only seen them once. Luckily it was the one time that she won the bid. They were shipped to her from the Netherlands.

Foreign Mugs

The mugs shown below were also available for the foreign market. Cathy purchased them on eBay sometime around 2016.

Fountain

This musical garden fountain was sold in the "Garfield Stuff" catalog at a price of $39.95. It's a three-tier fountain that plays a medley of four songs. It's battery-operated and features the whole gang in various spots playing in the water.

Fuzzy Garfield – Garfield Blown Dry

As the proud owners of a rescued Pomeranian, we can see that this style of plush is so wrong that it is right. There were several

Dakin plushes that came out in the mid-to-late '80s that imagined Garfield with long hair. This included a hand puppet and a marionette puppet. The copyright still reads, "Copyright United Feature Syndicate" so we know it was in the early days of licensing.

The one pictured here is not the hand puppet despite how hard Cathy just tried to stick her hand in it. Different is often strange, but when many of the traditional Garfields all look similar, than sometimes different is good.

This line of Dakin plushes sells well online, making it popular and desirable, especially if it still has the hang tags.

G

Garfred Rogers 25th Birthday Statue
(See "Statues" in this chapter and also learn more regarding the 25th Birthday fundraiser statues in Chapter 14)

Gift wrapping / Gift Boxes and Gift Bags

Although these items were cheap and consumable, that is the actual problem. People had the audacity to use these items for their intended purposes. Giftwrap was used to wrap packages and would be torn off and thrown away. Knowing that Cathy was a huge Garfield fan, her mother would pre-wrap gift boxes with Garfield gift wrap and Cathy would just have to lift off the lid

and not damage the wrapping paper.

In hindsight, consumable and disposable items become more sought-after since they are available in diminished quantities. It's why some baseball cards are so valuable today because as soon as kids left home, their mothers threw away their collections. A gift box is usually the vessel to the gift, not the collectible itself. Of course, there were several different sizes of Garfield gift boxes available in the '80s. I've seen these items sell for way more than their original purchase prices on the internet selling sites.

Giant Christmas Plush

(see Macy's Giant Christmas Plush)

Golf Items

When I was profiling Garfield collectors, I mentioned that people often collect what they can relate to and they enjoy. It is no surprise that golf is a pastime that people often live their lives around.

In the "W"s you will learn more about the "World of Golf" statue. Shown here are some of our golf items.

There have been many golf items produced throughout Garfield's existence - at least half a dozen different plushes, golf club covers, gloves, statues, trophies, towels, balls, divot repairers, ball markers, caps, and any other golf accessory you can think of.

It should be noted that Jim Davis is an avid golfer and it is entirely possible that the line of golf items were produced purely for his own enjoyment.

A couple of years ago when Cathy and I were visiting her parents in Florida, Cathy came across an ad on Craigslist selling Jim Davis' golf bag. It seemed legit, but we didn't have enough time to get to the location as we were leaving early the very next day. Cathy tried to convince me to change our plane tickets, but we had to get home. It just goes to show you that you should always be checking the internet wherever you are because you just never know when and where you might find something. Several years later, Cathy was able to snag a Garfield meets Rockwell lithograph while visiting her parents.

Globe

A cute globe of the world is a nice shelf piece. The globe is just over a foot tall. Considering it was made in the '90s it would probably be a bad idea to use this globe as a reference for a book report. At least the continents are still in the right place.

Garfield's tail is cleverly holding up the world. Considering Garfield is syndicated in hundreds of countries and translated into dozens of languages, this is either a metaphor or just plain boasting. It was listed in the "Garfield Stuff" catalog for $29.95.

Gumball Machines (Bubble Gum Machines)

Fun, useful, and dispenses edible items makes up the trifecta of Garfield Collectibles. Garfield gumball machines range between novelty keychains all the way up to ones with metal bases and full-size gumballs.

In the photo are two larger gumball machines. The larger ones will dispense gumballs when a coin is inserted. They are residential quality. There is no way they will withstand the abuse they would receive in a store. For a bedroom, they can make fun piggy banks and the money can be retrieved easily.

The photo also shows an entire case of bubble mania keychain-type candy dispensers. These are intended to be an impulse item that someone might purchase at a food store or a convenience store. They are by no means an example of the most sought-after collectible made, but they are likely to be sold on a regional basis. The ones seen here were given to us by our friend Crazy Gary from New Jersey. He was able to find entire sets including packaging. As we said in the fast food packaging and video top-40 countdown, the packaging is often thrown out by the store and therefore makes any item more valuable.

H

Halloween Inflatable
Like the "Let's Party Inflatable", this item was available in retail stores for Halloween. It is Garfield dressed as a witch holding a witch's brew. This item is kept upright by a fan and stands about six feet tall. It was manufactured by Gemmy Industries.

The body has a light inside to make it glow in the dark. They were available in the 2000's and retailed for around $50.

There were quite a few more Garfield inflatables also made. The truth is that I was desperate for something that starts with the letter "H", so here is the winner.

Halloween Costumes

Intended to be Halloween costumes, sadly, some Garfield costumes are worn year-round by some people. The quality of different costumes ranges from basic inexpensive all the way up to professional amusement park quality.

A high quality Garfield mascot costume can be rented from a licensed costume company such as Milestone Production and Events, to be used at certain family-friendly, morally-approved events. They don't want just anybody getting hold of the Garfield costume and using it at an "Adult Club". It would be a public relations nightmare to explain what Garfield was doing at somebody's Las Vegas-style bachelor party. What goes on the Internet, lives on the Internet forever, so it is better that the costume is not in the wrong place at the wrong time.

The Garfield costume attended the 1999 Garfield Gathering. When Cathy and I hosted the 2011 Garfield Gathering we arranged to have the costume at our event also. Pictured above is Cathy wearing the Garfield costume in our living room. We took some pictures and video before we used it for the 2011 Garfield Gathering. Cathy thought it would be cute to get pictures of Garfield admiring her collection. Even though it was 2:00 in the morning of the first convention event and we were completely exhausted and it was hotter than you know what in our living room, Cathy insisted on donning the costume. She, I mean, Garfield, walked around the dining room and living room, played with the slot machines and almost hit the "cash out" button on the smaller slot machine.

Hand-made Montauk Lighthouse Centerpiece signed by Jim Davis

In 2011 when Cathy and I hosted the Garfield Gathering, we hand-made centerpieces for the first night's dinner. They were replicas of the Montauk Lighthouse. I'll go into more detail in the section about the 2011 Garfield Gathering.

Recently, when we went out to Indiana for the world record photo shoot with Jim Davis, Jim was very generous to sign our lighthouse centerpiece. Besides signing it, he also drew a picture of Garfield on it.

Look for our video on YouTube that includes this item as part of our top 40 Garfield collectibles.

Hangers

These two hangers will never touch clothing ever again. They are retired from service. We purchased them from the Paws room at the Garfield Gathering. The first and only time we have ever seen them was in the showroom at Paws, Inc. when we were there for a book signing with Jim Davis. They had probably over a hundred of these with Garfield 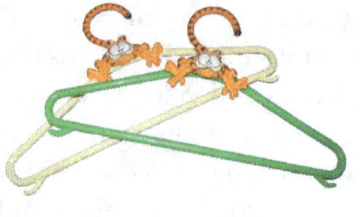 clothing hanging on them. These were probably the same hangers we saw in the showroom.

It is likely that these hangers shown were never available for purchase.

Bonus Story – Book Signing Day

For those of you who are jumping around this book and did not get to the stories about the day we went to Paws, Inc. for the book signing, I decided to insert this bonus photo here because we just referenced the Paws, Inc. showroom while discussing the hangers. Incidentally, if you look closely in the picture, you can NOT see the hanger in the photo.

The showroom and the tour of Paws, Inc. is the same as a Star Trek fan being allowed to visit the production studio of the Star Trek Enterprise. In our world, it is like our living room but much bigger. One of the more exciting parts, as a collector, is to see foreign market items, prototypes, proofs, and regional items that we did not know existed.

This photo is a wide shot of the behind-the scenes of this day. Cathy and Jim Davis were staged at the table. A reporter and photographer from the local paper were asking questions and taking pictures. Also the Paws Inc. in-house videographer and photographer were taking video and photos of the event. Seen in this photo is my video lighting and high-definition professional video camera recording the entire event.

I was also in the wings taking still photos. I always say, if you have a press conference, at least bring your own cameras if the media does not show up. You will have a chance to see my new camera at book signings and other publicity events since it is a good formula.

Now back to the list!

I

Ice bucket

Here is an ice bucket, which was made by Enesco in the early '80s. Cathy just loves Garfield's "Bah Humbug". There are other items that go with it. They were probably all sold separately, but we know there are matching coasters, a serving tray and, hopefully, glasses or mugs. Cathy stumbled across this on eBay one day and has never seen another one. She did get the matching coasters, but nothing else. She has set up a Garfield "bah humbug" search. More on how to do that later in the book.

Inflatables

Several inflatables were made in the likeness of Garfield. You have already seen the Halloween inflatable in the previous section. There were also inflatable kiddie pools, small punching bags, and some Avon soap holders manufactured in the '80s.

Giant Inflatables

Cathy is extremely fortunate to have this very rare piece. We purchased an inflatable that stands about 20 to 25 feet tall and is held up by a high-power industrial fan. Our contacts at Paws,  Inc. were very surprised that we owned this because they believed that they had the only one ever made.

The person we purchased it from paid $5,500 for it in the mid-1980s and kept it in front of his furniture store to attract the attention of passing cars. When he downsized his store to be indoors at a mall, he stored it at his parents' home on Long Island, and later sold it to us. We actually got a great deal on it since he included the industrial fan with it. Normally the fan alone is several hundred dollars.

Movie Inflatable

Stamped clearly on this inflatable is the phrase "Property of Fox Movies." It was a large promotional item that was used in movie theater lobbies to promote the first Garfield Movie. This stands over ten feet tall and even has inflatable sunglasses. We imagine they were supposed to be returned to Fox, but you can sometimes see them for sale on the internet.

Once inflated, the closed bladder system keeps him upright and it does not need fans or pumps to stay inflated.

Let's Party Inflatable

This smaller inflatable has interchangeable signs that Garfield holds and is kept upright with an electric fan. It stands about five feet tall and was available as a seasonal lawn decoration.

J

Jackets

Cathy has several very nice Garfield leather jackets.

She has had most of her jackets autographed by Jim Davis. Some were from the "Garfield Stuff" catalog and others were purchased on eBay.

There were quite a few Garfield leather jackets made. We can personally account for four of the designs, but we are sure many more were available. Some of them retailed for around $1,000 and came autographed by Jim Davis.

Jewelry

There are rings, necklaces, pins, bracelets, pendants, etc. Like any jewelry, you can buy fine jewelry and you can get inexpensive jewelry. Some collectors have solid gold pieces and others have simple, lower-priced items.

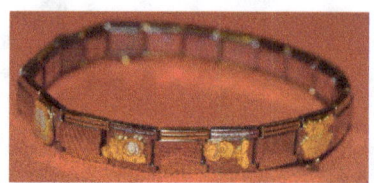

Pictured is Cathy's Italian Charm Bracelet. The links were sold separately and are easy to assemble. There were different Garfield charms that snapped on to the stretchy band, as well as charms for every holiday. They were available around the early '00s and sold for anywhere from $10 - $20.

Jewelry Pin Mold

Every now and then something wanders into our collection that is based around the manufacturing process. This pin mold makes 16 blanks for pins. There is no way that we would be able to produce pins from this old, warn-out mold, but having a piece of

the manufacturing process is often something that most people do not have.

Our research on the pin seems to indicate it is from around 1994, possibly from the company Starline. We do not know exactly how something like this comes on the market. Was it taken out of the company's dumpster? Was it taken from an employee? It is good to know that at least one of these has a good, permanent home as part of a world record.

K

Key Display

Garfield keys and matching key chains were available for both Kwikset and Schlage locks. Anyone can buy the keys, but how many people have the retail key display? There are less in circulation, so ultimately it will be more sought after than just a key or keychain.

The metal frame holds the display backer board and several key blanks and Garfield keychains. The display is a tabletop model, so it was intended to stand on the counter as an impulse purchase. Based on the size of the eyes and the timing of when the keys were all over the Internet, they were being marketed around 2010. Even more recently, Garfield key blanks came out that were not previously available. They retailed for around $7. A bit of security advice: use these keys to give to a neighbor, family member, pet sitter or anyone who needs access to your house. They won't need to write your address to keep with the key. They'll know the Garfield key is for your house.

Key Holder

Several items from this manufacturer have already been mentioned. They were made to look aged and are made from some kind of resin. The face of the lock opens and there are hooks for keys on the inside. They were sold sometime around the late '90s into the early '00s.

Kiddie Ride

We don't know exactly how rare this is, but it makes us laugh every time we look at it. It was manufactured by Durham Industries in the early-to-mid-'80s. The book is family-friendly, so you will have to let your own mind wander. We see it consistently sell for around $100.

Kitchen Items

Talk about a generic category, many Garfield items were

designed to be practical. What can be more practical to a fat cat than kitchen items? This includes salt and pepper shakers, cups, mugs, glasses, plates, serving platters, bowls, cake pans, muffin pans, timers, spoon rests and much more. We will highlight some of our favorites separately throughout this chapter.

Krome Trading Cards

These Krome Trading cards were acquired directly from Doc Davis at the Garfield Gathering with several other items. The piece is an un-cut print. The cards would be separated and sold in packs. They were sold in the mid-90s.

There's a sticker on the back of the frame with the company name S & G Chromium Graphics Inc. Our special collectors piece came framed.

136 | LOVES GARFIELD

Zoomed in

L

Lamp Globe (Glass)

Designed to go over ceiling light fixtures, this frosted glass covered the bulbs and complemented any Garfield room. This item can still be found on eBay but often without the pink nose that acts as the screw to attach the cover to the ceiling fixture.

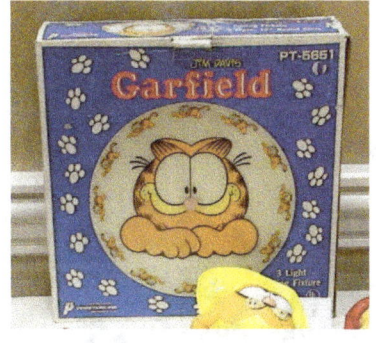

Although we have around four of them, shown here is the one sold at auction at a Garfield Gathering. They usually sell in $50 - $100 range. Many are missing the pink nose, but you can always paint a screw head pink, pantone color PMS176.

Lava Lamp

What comes around, goes around. If it is good enough for the '60s, it is good enough for the '90s. They retailed for $79.95 in the

"Garfield Stuff" catalog. This lava lamp is fun and decorative. Recently, we've seen them sell for anywhere between $50 and as high as $350.

Lithographs

Probably the most notable set of lithographs is the late '90s into early '00s, "Garfield Meets Norman Rockwell" series. The series started out with about six lithographs and has grown by at least another nine. I'm sure these stemmed from the 1997 "Garfield Visits Rockwell" calendar that was available through fine art galleries and in the "Garfield Stuff" catalog. They sold for $395. We've seen many on aftermarket websites. Cathy even purchased one off Craigslist in Florida when she was in town visiting her parents. Each piece is numbered as part of a limited run. They are also signed in pencil by Jim Davis. The pieces are titled (in no particular order):

Garfield's Quartet
How to Diet
The Car Trip
Doctor and Doll
The Shiner
Garfield Rain Out
The Great Frame Up
The Doctor's Office
Moon Gazer
Man at Sea
Self Portrait
Garfield's Vanity
Garfield's Waltz
Coin Toss
The Runaway

They are adaptations of Norman Rockwell's famous paintings from as far back as the 1930's. Paws, Inc. has added Garfield and sometimes other characters into the famous paintings.

M

Macy's Giant Christmas Plush

We have a story to tell you later in the book, but long story short - Cathy has two of these mammoth beauties that she won from Macy's. There were either 300 or 600 of these ever made. We had bought a third one a couple of years ago, but we sold it to a friend for the same price that we paid for it. We wanted to give it a good home and get it taken off Craigslist.

Each Macy's store raffled one to a lucky customer. Some people say a second giant Macy's was also raffled to the store employees. We don't know about that, so that's why we're not sure if there were 300 and only raffled to customers or were there 600 with a second one raffled to employees.

Macy's Parade Water Globe

In 2003, Macy's also had a Thanksgiving Parade water globe that had a depiction of Garfield inside it.

This piece is musical and plays the song, "Santa Claus is Coming to Town." It also takes batteries to rotate the window scenes that appear in the base.

This was advertised as Macy's exclusive collectible water globe and sold for $59.

Montblanc™ Pen Cases and Pen

Very limited-edition Montblanc™ Pens with three different case designs were made for the Garfield collectible market. A major advantage of going to the Garfield Collectors Convention is we were able to purchase them directly from Paws, Inc., the creators of Garfield. Cathy actually purchased one complete case with pen on eBay, and the following year purchased just the two other cases without the pens. One was labeled "sample".

Movie Plush Sample

At the time of filming the full-length motion pictures, "Garfield: The Movie" (2004) and "Garfield, the Tail of Two Kitties" (2006), a handful of prototypes and sample plushes were made prior to full production. Some of these were sold to collectors at the Garfield Gatherings. Others were won at various convention raffles and at the auction. The fact that they are samples makes them more valuable.

The one shown here, that we purchased, is tagged "Prototype" and the ear tag says it was submitted 2/27/2004. Once again, where else are you going to find one-of-a-kind prototypes that were sent directly to Paws, Inc. for approval. The answer is ... the Garfield Gathering. In the picture, it looks like it only has one ear. This is because the left ear is so weighted down by tags and documentation that it can't even stand straight up. You can purchase such items at the Garfield conventions for pretty reasonable prices. Sometimes, they wind up on the internet for double and triple what the person originally paid.

Movie Signage

Just like the explanation of the kids' meal toys signage, movie signage is often thrown out after the movie leaves the theaters. Sometimes signs, posters, and promotional items are rescued and put in the hands of collectors. If you know anyone who works at a movie theater, he can usually get his hands on the items for free since they are just going to throw them in the trash. We have a huge, canvas-like quality poster that our friend's uncle got while he was working at a local movie theater. They made all kinds of cardboard mobile-type hangers, double-sided vinyl posters and paper posters for the first Garfield movie.

We even have a supermarket plastic divider thingy that you use on the conveyor belt to separate your order from the person behind you that was wrapped with marketing for the movie.

The food store graciously gave us the divider that was promoting the June 11, 2004 release of the Garfield movie.

Mugs – Enesco Puzzle Mugs

This set of four Enesco mugs has a design where each one lines up with the one above and/or below it. When fully stacked you have a very expensive unstable structure just waiting to fall over. If you have teenage neighbors with a subwoofer in their car or worse, a cat, we advise you to stack them only two high in two rows or keep them in an enclosed cabinet.

There is much debate on-line that this set is supposed to come with a mug tree stand. This is not true. The wooden Enesco Garfield tree stand does not come with any mugs. It is a separate item by itself. You can use it with any mugs that you choose.

Musicals

Shown is a beautiful example of an older wind-up ceramic musical figurine. It was made by Enesco in the mid-'80s. It plays "I

Could Have Danced All Night". There's a sticker on the bottom that says "Fred and Ginger, Eat Your Hearts Out".

These musicals were also manufactured by Enesco and are made from plastic. The one here revolves and plays the tune "Playmates" It was available in the early '90s and has a matching Christmas ornament without the base.

The musical below plays "We Wish You a Merry Christmas" and Garfield, Odie and Arlene all move. Christmas lights twinkle while the tune plays. This was available in the 1998 "Garfield Stuff" catalog for $45.95.

N

Nachos

A word about food items. You should really open the bags, enjoy the food and wash out the bag or container and store it empty. We've had these bags of nachos, also called tortilla chips, for I don't even know how long at this point. It's not like Garfield is on each nacho. We should have enjoyed them and stored the empty bag. It would certainly take up less space and not tempt insects.

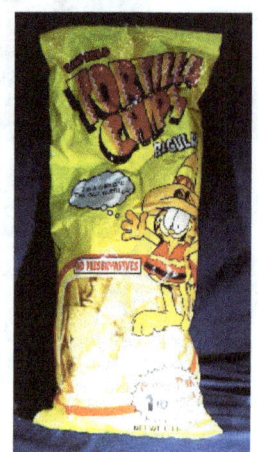

Neckties

There are many Garfield neckties available depicting many holidays, sports and activities. There are holiday neckties celebrating

Valentine's Day, St. Patrick's Day, Easter, Independence Day, Halloween and Christmas. There are neckties with different sports shown on them, like golf and bowling. They are all high-quality ties and can be readily found on aftermarket websites.

My personal favorite necktie is in the top row, third from the left. You barely realize it has Garfield on it. When I wear it to a business meeting and a networking buddy starts to rib me, "What, no Garfield?" I would have to hold it close to their eyes and show the teeny, tiny Garfields. They originally sold between $19.95 and $27.95 in the "Garfield Stuff" catalogs. I purchased most of these in the Paws room at the Garfield Gatherings for a fraction of that price. Some of them are even marked as "sample".

Night Before Christmas

Wicked Cool Toys produced this for Christmas 2014. This plush is a limited edition run with only 1,000 plushes manufactured. There's a cute video on the internet with Jim Davis describing the plush and its accessories. He autographed 10 boxes. Maybe you were one of the lucky ones that got a signed box, making this item even more valuable!

Nutcracker

This wooden Enesco item has old-world charm. It feels like a family heirloom handed down from generation to generation. That's if your family tree started in the early '80s. This one stands about 6 inches tall. There's also a smaller matching ornament to hang on your Christmas tree.

We would classify this as a crossover collectible since there are people who only collect nutcrackers and might have this one right next to their Micky Mouse nutcracker and 30 red soldiers.

Cathy's Mom has a nutcracker collection and this past Christmas, Cathy snuck this one into her Mother's display. I think it took her Mom all of 30 seconds to spot it. Much to our delight, she kept it as part of her display. Since Cathy and I always celebrate Christmas with her parents, it'll be nice to have something else Garfield displayed in their home.

O

Odie In-Basket (really a small pet bed)

As you might imagine, Cathy's collection has spilled over to work and anywhere else she touches. Don't even get her parents started about the items we left in Florida.

Among the many items she has at work is an Odie pet bed that she has re-purposed as her "In-Basket".

Oh My Gosh - What Did You Do to that Pontoon Boat (Way to keep this in the "O" section)

Speaking of Florida and Cathy's parents' pontoon boat, the Garfield Christmas Wire-Frame decorations always find their way onto the decorated boat or her parents' lanai.

Cathy has her hobby and I have mine. I am that guy who synchronizes 5,000 Christmas lights to music on a 14-foot pontoon boat in a gated community.

Look for the full video on YouTube called "Christmas Boat Train"

Office Survival Kit

There's a kit that included file folders, scotch tape, and other office items. There is also a Garfield staple remover. There's tons of Garfield pens and pencils. We don't know what's up with pencils, but we saw a box of eight old-style Garfield pencils sell for what we would consider way too much money on eBay not long ago. Also, Garfield bookmarks with tassels sold for an obscene amount of money on eBay. Now I can't say to look all over your house and get out your Garfield pencils and old bookmarks because you'll make a fortune; it may have been someone who needed a gift for a teacher and was willing to pay top dollar. It could have been a collector who tragically lost part of his collection and was trying to regain the missing items, and money was no object. You never know the circumstances, but we've mentioned several times in this book that ultimately items are worth the amount that you are either willing to pay for or sell an item for.

This item was in the "Garfield Stuff" catalog for $29.95. You will rarely see a complete kit for sale these days, perhaps pieces might show up here and there. We would say this has gone up in value if you can find it complete.

Orange Juice Bottle

Tropicana Orange Juice produced a few hundred glass prototype bottles shaped like Garfield. They were never put into full production, so they may be hard to find. I've seen them sell for anywhere from $50 to over $300 on the internet and at the Garfield convention.

Orange Juice Drink Set

There was a set with a pitcher and four cups made by Enesco. When you look at the eyes it is a perfect example of round eyes which means older, early '80s Garfield. This set is pretty rare to find complete and in good shape. Cathy says, for a cat who likes to sleep-in, it's surprising that Garfield is interested in orange juice since it is a beverage usually consumed in the morning hours.

Oven Mitts

One the best presents that Cathy and I received for our Engagement party back in 1994 was a set of Garfield oven mitts. Over the years there have been several styles available. There's Garfield's café, various Christmas

styles, but the ones we received were especially cute. They were orange with black stripes and had Garfield's face on them. When you opened the mitt, it had "burp" written on the inside. Items like this are definitely more valuable if you keep them in new and pristine condition. Sometimes, it makes sense to purchase at least 2 sets of items, so you can use one and keep the other clean in case you want to sell it or switch out and, dare I say throw away the old grungy one and start using the new, clean one.

P

Pachinko Machine

This item was purchased by Cathy in 2007 from a company in California that refurbishes them once they retire the units from Japanese Pachinko Parlors. The machine actually has some Japanese recordings to talk to players. Surprisingly, the jackpot round sings a song in English.

In Japan, Pachinko machines are treated like slot machines are in the United States. Since gambling for money is illegal in Japan, the Pachinko balls that are won are traded in for prizes or tokens. These items can later be traded in for cash at a location away from the Pachinko parlor.

Our machine is a lot of fun to play. It has the manual stimulus of the balls going through the machine. It also has a computer screen that shows fun animations and bonus games.

Used Garfield Pachinko machines sell for between $250 and $400. They do not come up for sale often, so we would consider this a unique and premium collectible. This is especially true since they were never sold to major retailers. These are special items for the collector who wants to stand out from the ordinary. Paws, Inc. has one in its showroom and the maintenance department built a lovely wooden frame around it.

Pasta Jar

This Enesco ceramic pasta jar has a hinged airtight lid with a silicone gasket to keep the contents fresh. This is a very rare piece. We have only seen it on eBay one time and fortunately it was the one time that Cathy purchased it. It was probably available in the mid-'80s and may have been part of a set.

Pencil Sketches

Art is good. Hand drawn art is better. It is possible to purchase proofs and pencil sketches from Paws, Inc. and other sources. Some sketches are less refined than others. These concept sketches are often rarer since Jim Davis may have roughed out the image for a staff artist to clean up.

The piece shown on the right was purchased from Doc Davis at the 2006 Garfield Gathering. It was used as a proof for the Kennywood ride called "Garfield's Nightmare." The ride debuted at Kennywood in 2004.

We can't know for sure if it was only made for the Kennywood ride since many images are universal and can be used for many types of projects.

Pet Tags and Pet Collars

Bling for your dogs and cats. Since Garfield is the somewhat official spokescat for the feline species, it only makes sense to create accessories for cats and their slobbering archnemesis, the dog. Pictured is a newer pet tag available for machine engraving at chain pet stores. We purchased this one in 2018.

Since our actual dog is a 5-pound Pomeranian, a tag of this size would drag her down like a boat anchor. Our dog is so small that bunnies do not run away when we walk her. They just stare at her and think, "how can you hear with such tiny ears"? We have a smaller tag worn by our dog Zeta that is more her size. It's actually a Garfield charm that one of my clients engraved with her name. Quick  tip: when you're putting your pet's information on his ID tag, be sure to put "needs medication". That may give you a better chance of your pet being returned to you since people will not want to deal with a sick animal.

Garfield was also the spokescat for a pet insurance company in the late '90s and early '00s. In 2010, Garfield was the spokescat for a National Pet Sitting Agency. They had some Garfield marketing materials available for purchase.

There were also various pet collars, leashes, toys, bowls, beds, kitty litter, kitty litter scoops, pet carriers and even a motorized cat toy. Even if you don't have a pet, the bowls are great for snacks or soup.

Pewter Castings

The good news is they are hard to damage since they are a solid cast of metal. The bad news is that they are less than a half inch tall so they are easy to lose. Due to the magic of a great close-up lens, shown here is a highly enlarged photo of these unique pieces. At least shipping costs would be low on these items, but they do have some weight to them since they are pewter. They were produced by Schmid in the early '80s. We're not sure how many different poses were made, but there were at least a half dozen different ones. The number on the bottom is the model number. There's 0701, 0702, etc. Be sure to not mistake these for the Monopoly game pieces!

Phones

Several phones have been produced over the years. Tyco is a major manufacturer of the Garfield phones. Phones include wall phones and table phones. On one phone made by Tyco (middle bottom of photo), the eyes actually open when you answer the  phone and close when you hang up the phone. The phone shown at the top of this photo is rarer since it has a tail. There was another version with no tail. Also shown is a table top phone that spoke several different Garfield phrases when someone was calling, instead of a traditional ring (far left).

Plates

Over the years, there have been several sets of collector plates produced by the Danbury Mint. In our world, as high-end Garfield collectors, we also hold onto the paper birthday plates you buy at a party supply stores. Believe it or not, they might be rarer than the Danbury Mint collectible sets.

A Day with Garfield Plates

Sometime in the '90s, Danbury Mint put out a series of plates called "A Day with Garfield." There are twelve plates in this series.

Dear Diary Plates

Danbury Mint also produced eight "Dear Diary" plates as shown below.

Calendar Plates

In 1999, Danbury Mint made twelve calendar plates. One for each month of the year. The set came with a wooden display with plastic tiles to change the calendar every month. There were some tiles with Garfield dressed for specific holidays. The plate for the month would sit on top.

They originally were sold for $29.90 plus $3.95 shipping and handling for each plate. The plate border and month name are in 23kt gold. Three plates are shown below.

Christmas Plates

Danbury Mint also produced a set of eight Christmas plates.

Plush (Stuffed Animals)

We highly sophisticated collectors refer to stuffed animals as "plushes". It makes us feel older and more serious. After all, who wants to admit that they have a house full of stuffed animals? An entire book can be written based on all the plush Garfield items in existence. We personally have hundreds. They are hard to break and you can pile them into a net or large box.

On the low end of the spectrum there are still active contracts for carnival prize vendors for give-away prize plushes filled with the finest recycled dryer lint and recycled shredded rags. On the higher end of the spectrum is the Steiff Bear, fetching hundreds of dollars.

Shown is the Musical 20-year plush that marked Garfield's 20th birthday in 1998. Garfield is holding Pooky and is wearing a gold-tone commemorative medallion. It plays the song, "Teddy Bear Picnic".

Shown below are a few hundred plushes that we have on top of our television entertainment center. There are hundreds more in storage. I purposely did not crop the picture tight so I could show off our fine cassette deck. Above that is a VCR. Kids and teenagers, be sure to ask your parents and grandparents what a cassette deck and VCR are. They are always looking for a fun way for you to remind them that they are getting old. We would get rid of ours, but we have some Garfield video tapes that might need to be seen again someday.

Possible Dreams Clothtique

Cathy is more of a stickler for details than I am with everything. She just spent over an hour researching the Possible Dreams Christmas items. She's fairly certain that they are a subset of Department 56, but since she's not 100% certain, she doesn't want to put it in the book. So, since I'm okay with wishy-washy details, I told her I'd put it in the book. In the mid-'90s, these Possible Dreams Clothtique figures were released.

The bodies are made from a hard, yet lightweight resin and the fabric is stiffened so that they keep their shape when displayed. They were shown in the "Garfield Stuff" catalogs in the late 90's. They include:

- Countdown to Christmas (not shown) = $42.95
- Return to Sender (set of 2 on left) = $39.95
- Private Stash (right) = $44.95
- Love Me, Love My Teddy Bear (not shown in any Garfield Stuff catalog I have)

Postage Stamps

On July 16, 2010 the United States Postal Service issued a "Sunday Funnies" stamp pane with 20 stamps. On the pane were Beetle Bailey, Calvin and Hobbes, Archie, Garfield and also Dennis The Menace. 80 million blocks were made.

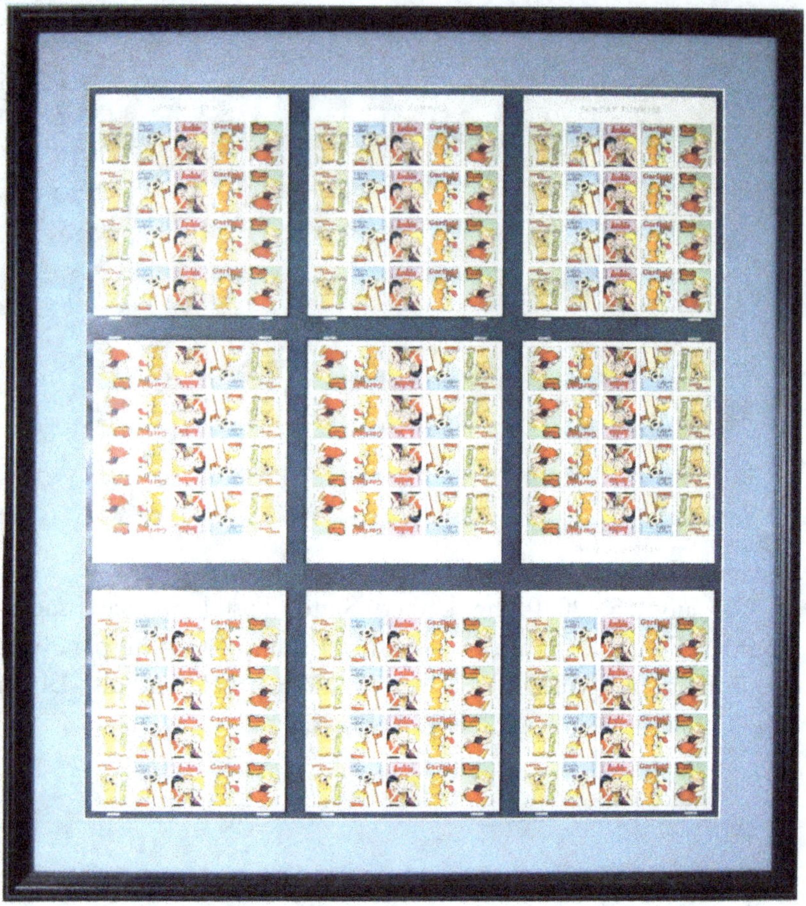

We purchased an uncut press sheet and had ours professionally framed. No offense, but our creditors do not deserve a cartoon stamp. They can get a liberty bell and like it.

Q

Quiet Time Fabric Display

This is not the real name, but we were desperate for something that started with a "Q." This item was only available to libraries.

As one of their public service programs, Paws, Inc. was involved in a young persons' reading program. Several unique posters and decorations were created to make the children's section of the library more fun and "Garfieldey" (I just made up that word).

Among the reading decorations is this soft quilt-like wallhanging with Garfield hugging a book. When libraries moved on to the next popular trend, a few business-minded library employees sold some on-line. That is how we found ours.

Quad Sericel

Normally these sericel images are framed individually, so this one is four times the fun. We purchased this framed sericel with four of the images mounted inside on eBay for a fraction of what they would sell for separately.

We are pretty sure somebody with framing skills made the best of surplus sericels that they purchased on a cruise ship. Either way it is a fun way to present such a somewhat common "limited edition" piece. They were originally commissioned in 1993 for a run of 9500 pieces each. The Park West Gallery found on most cruise ships starts these pieces at $100 at their auctions. That's before any fees, and unframed. Don't think you're going to buy these on the ship for $100 and triple your money once you set foot on dry land. If you like them, buy them, but don't think you'll make your fortune from them. Here's another tip, once someone places the opening bid, just outbid that person one time. Do not get into a bidding frenzy. Once the hammer goes down, if there was anyone else bidding, the auctioneer will usually say "oh by the way, we happen to have more than one of these and we can sell them to each bidder for the last price bid."

R

Race Cars

In 2002, the King of NASCAR, Richard Petty joined up with Paws Inc. for a two-year licensing agreement. Together they produced an entire line of replica #43 race cars featuring the two larger than life personalities. Their slogan was "Grinning & Winning" and show Garfield wearing Richard Petty's signature style cowboy hat and sunglasses. Richard Petty is also featured on the items.

There were multiple-sized cars produced, the smaller 1:64 ratio and the larger 1:24 ratio. There were various quantities available per style so be sure to check the total number of pieces produced of the style you are looking to purchase or sell. Items with smaller production runs will be more valuable since there are less of them available. Lower numbers in the production run also make an item more valuable. But, there can be a tradeoff, if a higher numbered item is in better condition, you may want to consider that one over a lower number in poorer condition. Samples, prototypes and artist's proofs will trump any production number. There were many other items produced like statues, banks, posters, shirts and plushes, just to name a few. These items are great collectibles since the sport of

NASCAR has a huge fan base and Richard Petty is literally the King of the sport. He won a record 200 races in his career! The "Garfield Stuff" catalog featured the 1:24 scale, die-cast metal race car at a price of $65.95.

In 2003, as part of the celebration of Garfield's 25th birthday, Petty Enterprises had Richard's son, Kyle Petty's #45 Dodge Intrepid wrapped with a special Garfield paint scheme. The car was unveiled at the Indianapolis Motor Speedway's Brickyard 400 in August 2003. The paint scheme was designed by famous motorsports designer, Sam Bass.

S

Scales

You can't make fun of eating and overeating without producing a Garfield scale as a reference point. There were several scales made, including one from Tyco, that we have in our possession. Garfield's eyes open and close when you step on and off the scale. Over the years, many have been made for foreign and United States markets. Here are some that were auctioned off at the Garfield Gathering.

If you follow the comic strip, you already know that Garfield does not have a good relationship with his scale. I am sure somewhere out there somebody designed a cursing, sarcastic, talking Garfield scale. Fortunately, in order to keep Garfield family-friendly and child-safe, that item will never see the light of day.

Silver Pins

Made in Mexico these pins are sterling silver. They are regularly available for sale on aftermarket websites. They are marked "925" on the back. This signifies that the piece contains 92.5% silver and the remaining part is mostly copper. These pieces need the addition of the copper to harden the material so the jeweler can produce the pieces with the fine details as shown below.

Silvertowne

A local Indiana licensee is a company called Silvertowne. Silvertowne produces silver coins and bars. There have been many different designs over the years. They produce colorized silver coins in addition to plain silver coins. They manufacture silver coins and bars for many holidays including Easter, Christmas and Mother's Day.

This is a great example of crossover collecting. Some people collect Garfield and other people collect silver. It might be possible that a silver collector has a few Garfields because he thinks they are cute. Cathy has several Silvertowne pieces, and it is only because they are Garfield. Silver can also be a valuable commodity and the value will fluctuate over time. You'll want to buy low and sell high.

These sold in the "Garfield Stuff" catalog for somewhere in the range of $24.95 up to $134.95 for a set of five.

Slot Machines

This is a touchy subject to be discussing as a collectible. Overall, I would discourage the collecting of slot machines since they are illegal to own in certain states. They are also not serviceable. If a board is out of place or the machine stops working, the industry is very guarded about who will be allowed to be given parts or even advice.

Keep in mind that security at a casino is very important. For an electrician or computer engineer to have the chance to take apart and inspect a gambling device like this can compromise the machines that are still in use in casinos.

With that already said, our slot machines do not pay out any money. You need a casino mainframe computer to completely run it. I like to think of ours as expensive video games.

Putting it in context, when only three items out of over 12,000 total Garfield collectibles are slot machines, even the dumbest regulator can figure out that we are not running a casino out of our home.

Excuse our clutter. With over 12,000 items in the house, it gets a bit crowded. On the far left is a large Garfield slot machine. In the middle is a large Odie's Revenge slot machine, and on the right is a small Garfield slot machine.

Garfield Small Slot Machine

The software for the large Garfield and small Garfield slot machines is the same. The one difference is that the large slot machine has an extra bonus-game topper on it. The small slot machine still plays the bonus game, but only on the TV screen at the front of the slot machine. Ours is pictured in the far right of the photo.

Garfield with Topper

On the left of the picture (above) is our large Garfield slot machine with topper. This topper lights up for bonus rounds. Above the bonus topper is a lighted Garfield designed to attract people from across the casino.

Odie's Revenge Slot Machine

Odie's Revenge can be found as small or large. The difference once again is the tall bonus-game topper. Like on most modern slot machines, there is a TV display where the simulated slot machine wheel is, as well as bonus Odie animations. Our Odie's Revenge slot machine can be seen in the middle of the picture above.

Just a quick note that we purchased our slot machines from people who only collect slot machines. The fact that they were Garfield and Odie-themed did not mean that much to them.

Tabletop Slot Machine

A third design that we are aware of is a machine shaped like a table. You can put your drink on top, look through the glass, and play the machine. These were probably marketed to bars and lounges in Las Vegas or Atlantic City.

We did not appraise the Garfield and Odie Slot machines since we do not want to encourage people to buy them.

Slot Machine Glass

There is no law against owning a piece of glass. Since slot machine glass is rare it may be very collectible. You are also bidding against slot-machine hobbyists as well as Garfield collectors, so this makes it even more competitive.

Since glass is fragile, it may ultimately break and become rarer. This is a unique and special collectible since it is not licensed for mass production.

We paid between $50 and $150 for our slot machine glass. I made them both into light boxes so the colors would pop. It was pretty easy. First, build a wooden box that will fit the glass. Next, put a pre-made light fixture in the box to light up the glass.

Glass from Garfield slot machine turned into a light box

Odie's Revenge slot machine glass

Snow Globes

Unlike their cousin the water globe, snow globes contain particulate matter like fake snow or glitter. Shown here is an old Enesco snow globe from the mid-'80s.

Sparkly Wall Hanging

One of my favorite pieces is this older wall hanging that is super sparkly. I don't know if it is rare, sought-after or even "a dime a dozen" but this picture just celebrates Garfield as the center of attention in all of its reflective brilliance.

Spice Rack and Spices

In 1996 Danbury Mint produced a set of 24 spice jars and a wooden rack to display them. Each spice jar was priced at $19.95 and the wooden rack was included with the set. It took a year to send you the entire set and you had two years to pay for it. The total cost came to just about $500.

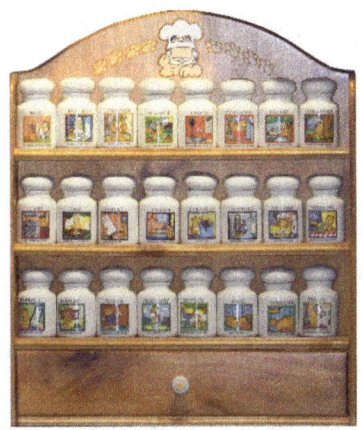

Today the prices range from under $100 to well over $300. You might find the jars without the rack for $100 or you might find a complete set for over $300.

Danbury Mint also made a set of mugs with the same graphics that are on the spice jars.

Salt and Pepper shakers

There have been many, many, many salt and pepper shakers produced throughout Garfield's lifetime. Enesco and Westland pieces are shown below. There were salt and pepper shakers produced for the Christmas and Thanksgiving holidays. The Thanksgiving pieces are popular with Odie looking like a turkey. The ones shown below with Garfield and Arlene depicting the "American Gothic" Pitchfork Couple were produced in the mid-'80s and have been known to sell for over $50. The newer Westland pieces have magnets glued to them to keep them together.

Spirit of '76

We never even knew this piece existed until we went to the 2010 Garfield Convention. It was held in Williamsburg, Virginia and the theme was **Americana**. This piece was one of the items up for grabs at the $5 raffles after the final dinner.

Danbury Mint produced this and it is very rare. It can consistently fetch over $200 if you can actually find it for sale. As pictured, the "Spirit of '76" is a statue in a glass dome depicting Garfield, Odie, and Nermal as a fife and drum band.

If I were to take a guess, I would think that maybe it was manufactured in 1996 to celebrate America's 220th Birthday.

Statues - Factory Entertainment Statue

Ruben Procopio is a famous animator, comic book artist and sculptor. He is best known for his work with Disney and as the founder of the Masked Avenger Studios.

In 2012, he produced this sculpture as a 3D rendition of Jim Davis' dream design of Garfield standing in front of a mirror admiring his big belly. Garfield knows he is a cat of size and does not apologize for it one bit. He loves himself just the way he is!

This is another great example of a crossover collectible. There are many people who collect Disney sculptures, comic books, sculptures of comic figures and there are Garfield collectors. When I was speaking with the President of Factory Entertainment, he was telling me that Ruben Procopio has such a following already that the fact that the piece is a Garfield is merely secondary for those collectors.

Above is the granddaddy of all collectible photos. The Factory Entertainment statue is accompanied by the Steiff Bear (see below) and a Silvertowne coin.

This statue is a limited edition of 500 pieces worldwide. Each one is numbered and comes with a plaque hand signed by Jim Davis. Check the internet for the review Cathy and I did once we received ours. Admittedly, it's a little long because we go on describing the box for probably five minutes, but to be honest, it comes packaged in a really nice box!

They originally sold for several hundred dollars but they do come up quite often on eBay for considerably less.

Star Sleeper

This item made the list because you cannot buy it in stores. You can only get them from medical professionals who specialize in sleeping disorders. Believe me, we tried bribing doctors. The code of ethics is strong in them.

Thanks to eBay, some person with sleep apnea sold out. Long live democracy. To be complete, it should come with a 51 page fun pad included. It has games for kids that revolve around bedtime and sleeping.

Steiff Bear

Believed to be the best collectible of all Garfield plush collectibles is the Steiff Bear. Steiff is a well-known teddy bear company located in Germany. The original price was $255 and it has overall held its value.

Made in 2003, the Steiff Bear is only complete with its 22kt gold plated medallion around Garfield's neck. The medallion denotes the official 25th birthday logo.

Due to the limited number produced and the reputation of Steiff, this piece can consistently cause a bidding war on the internet. It sells between $300 to $500 and sometimes lower if you hit it at the right time.

Statues (25th Birthday)

In June of 2003, 25 statues were revealed to the world during Garfield's 25th Birthday celebration in Muncie, Indiana. Each statue was assigned to a local not-for-profit organization and the decorations were imagined and produced by local artists associated with the charity. Some designs were plain and more traditional, while others were downright artistic or borderline "creepy." Some might just say, "Ugly!" Since beauty is in the eye of the beholder, we will not be outing the 'ugly' here in this book.

Originally, the statues were put up for auction as a fundraiser for the charity. Some were sold and others remained with the charity for display. Slowly, the 25 statues started trickling out into the world.

Cathy and I are the proud owners of "Garfred Rogers." We purchased it from the local PBS television affiliate, WIPB in Muncie, Indiana on the Ball State University campus. They were no longer displaying it in public and we were looking to purchase one, so it was a win-win arrangement.

It personally felt like we were tomb-raiding an Egyptian pyramid. Bringing a hand-painted, one-of-a-kind Garfield collectible from Indiana, the land of Garfield, to New York seemed disconcerting at first. Now that Cathy holds a world record, it feels justified that the statue has a good home.

This statue is probably my favorite piece in the collection since it is one-of-a-kind and has an impressive history.

It is also Cathy's favorite piece, as she was a huge fan of Mister Rogers on TV while growing up. She would hurry home and watch him every day. She even had a special sweater with a zipper that she wore when watching the show. Apparently, it is very hard to find sweaters with zippers and not buttons, so this was a big deal.

Mister Rogers passed away not long before the start of the statue fundraiser. The PBS station that commissioned the statue wanted to commemorate the life of Mister Rogers in their design. It was painted by artist Kip Shawger, an Associate Professor of Theater at Ball State University. The statue is titled, "Garfield Salutes Mister Rogers".

Look for our videos online featuring our top 40 favorite items that we filmed honoring Garfield's 40th Birthday on June 19, 2018.

Suitcases (Garfield Photo Luggage)

Among the favorite items that we own are our Garfield carry-on size suitcases marketed by Mo' Money Associates in Pensacola, Florida. This information was hard to come by. We had to check their privacy policy on their website, www.garfieldphotoluggage.com.

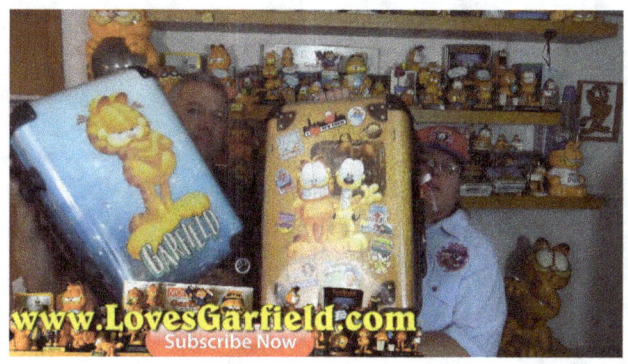

I can finally be very specific about this because the license is still active, and they can be purchased right from the link on the Garfield website. Even so, it feels like knowing the manufacturer's name does not even matter. The people at Paws, Inc. may want to be presenting a unified and consistent brand and unless it is a prestigious partner like the Danbury Mint, which is already known for collectibles, the manufacturer probably does not matter. This makes our job at the Garfield Gathering more difficult when disclosing details about auction items.

What's great about the Garfield suitcases is they are useful. When you are traveling it is a way to show your identity of loving Garfield. Even better, if you check your bags, the likeliness of another Garfield suitcase coming off the carousel is low. But we would not recommend checking these suitcases at the baggage counter. They are the proper size to fit in the overhead compartment on most airplanes.

The photo is from our video series about our top 40 favorite Garfield items. The suitcases were on the video Part 3 #30 to #25. The suitcases were number 28. It shows up in the video right around the three-minute mark.

T

Tail clock
Sunbeam produced a clock in the 80's where the eyes and tail swing back and forth while the clock runs. This clock was styled after another famous tail clock known as "Kit-Cat" clock, first made in 1932. This Garfield clock is a more popular collectible because it's another item that will appeal to more people than just Garfield collectors. It continually sells for anywhere from $50 to $150, depending on if it's new in box and works. As a practical warning, often when the battery runs down, the tail is the first to stop moving, followed by the eyes. Simply replace with fresh, new batteries and it will re-animate.

Thermos Cooler
Ready for a picnic or just to transport a living organ, this old-

school thermos cooler is just like the kind that paramedics use to transport real organs, except that this one has images of Garfield on it. It's from the early to mid-'80s as you can tell from the older-style Garfield featured. This is the only one I've ever seen. Cathy purchased it on eBay several years ago.

Tiny Ceramic set

Be real carful where you put these figurines because they are tiny. Each figure is inspired by an era in world history. The captions appear to be in French, however some are the direct reference to what it represents, such as "Garfield the Kid". Some of the captions are made up words as a ploy to connect Garfield to the original historic character, such as the Egyptian figure "Tutangarfield".

They came in different sizes. The smallest are shown here. Cathy did not pay a lot of money for them so don't go crazy bidding them up. They appear to be made from porcelain, but are surprisingly durable.

Toilet Seats

There were about a half dozen toilet seats produced with Garfield on them. I wouldn't say that they are show-pieces, but if you have a toilet and you are a Garfield collector, you might as well get one. They were available in the mid-'90s. There were a couple of Christmas styles, one blue one with Garfield riding a motorcycle and a couple white ones with Garfield and Odie on them.

Tree Textured Enesco

I'm not sure if these are supposed to be vases. The one on the left is a vase because it is tall and narrow. The ones in the middle and right seem to be too short and wide to be considered vases. If they are mugs, I would think that they might be difficult to hold. I would hate to break off Garfield. These are an older design with round and almost separate eyes. Since Enesco was one of the first ceramic companies, that fact alone makes it an older collectible. These were probably manufactured in the mid-'80s. They are pretty common on the aftermarket websites.

U

Ugly First Talking Plush

You caught me again, here I go adding the word "Ugly" just so I do not have any missing letters. In my opinion, this plush is the thing that causes nightmares. Not only does it have creepy sunken eyes, but it also talks slowly and satanically. At least the one we have does, perhaps our pull string talking mechanism is not working right. This is "Talking Gourmet" and the original retail price was $17.95. There were two other styles produced. This was given to Cathy as a gift.

So why is this featured in the special collectibles section? We already established I was desperate for the letter "U". The second reason is that it is our understanding that this was the first talking plush Garfield ever made. Do what we did, if you acquire one. Hide it behind a pile of cute plush dolls so you do not have nightmares.

Umbrellas

It should come as no surprise that there are also Garfield Umbrellas. Umbrellas are not the most elite of Garfield items, but they are practical and useful. While wearing a Garfield shirt and jacket, why not sport a Garfield umbrella on a rainy day. There are a wide variety produced from child-size to full-size, and with a spring-loaded opening. This particular one was sold in the "Garfield Stuff" catalog for $24.95.

United Feature Syndicate

As we already mentioned, from 1978 to 1994 United Feature Syndicate owned the rights to Garfield. In 1994 the rights were bought by Paws, Inc. the company owned by Jim Davis since 1981.

Just by seeing the words "copyright United Feature Syndicate" you know the piece can date back as far as 1980, when Garfield merchandising first began.

Utensils Set

Enesco made a utensil holder that came with several utensils. The holder itself is ceramic and the utensils stand up inside of it. Our set came with a wooden fork, a wooden meat-tenderizing hammer, a whisk and three wooden spoons. Not sure if they are the original utensils or not; that doesn't matter to us.

When you look at this piece you can see clearly that the eyes are round and separate. This indicates that it is an older Garfield collectible. At a certain point, Enesco no longer had the contract to make Garfield ceramics, so this also lumps this piece as a more sought-after collectible.

Valentines

Russell Stover and other candy companies (Zachary Confections shown above) used to manufacture Garfield Valentines chocolates. Some of the smaller boxes had plastic Garfield figurines on top. The larger boxes would have Garfield plushes attached to them. They stopped producing those sometime in the late '90s. Then they just had Garfield shown on the box, like the ones pictured above. There were many different boxes, plastic toys and plushes to choose from.

Russell Stover also made these smaller boxes with larger plush Garfields holding the candy, like the one pictured on the right. Make sure you eat the candy and just save the empty box. Milk chocolate can melt and make a mess of your shelves. Not to mention, would a real Garfield fan let chocolate go to waste? There were also some large Garfield molded chocolates that were sold in form-fitting plastic. You could save the plastic and use it as a mold to make your own Garfield candies. We never actually tried to, but people said it would work.

A regular attendee of the Garfield Gathering used to work at Russell Stover headquarters, 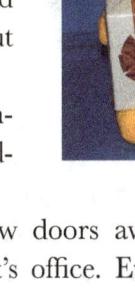 just a few doors away from the President's office. Every year she would set up her desk with a magical Garfield shrine of Russell Stover collector characters and boxes. One day it was made known that Russell Stover did not renew the Garfield license as a business decision. I am not sure if our friend's hunger strike, walkout, or blackmail attempts had any effect on its decision, but it has not made any Garfield candies since.

Van – lunchbox

This is really just another lunchbox, but since we needed the letter "V", I'm calling it Van – lunchbox. It's metal and has Jon driving with Garfield, Pooky, Arlene, Nermal and a random bird flying around  the back of the van. Odie and Squeak can be seen looking out the back window. Apparently, there's a musical version that is more valuable than the one we have. This is another item that has mass appeal because many people collect lunch boxes with any theme on them.

Also shown here is a red Thermos lunchbox. This is another crossover item since somewhere out there are collectors of just lunchboxes that might even have Garfield in their collection. People collect all sorts of things, and lunchboxes are popular. There were many different styles of plastic Garfield lunchboxes produced from the '80s well into the '90s.

Vitamins

In the dawn of Garfield's popularity, an entire suite of personal care items was created, including Garfield soap, Garfield toothpaste, Garfield combs and brushes, Garfield shampoo and Garfield vitamins.

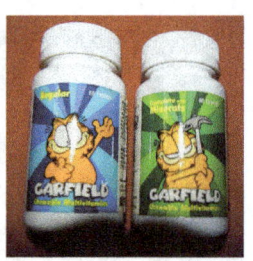

A true fan could wake up hearing his Garfield alarm clock going off, while wearing Garfield pajamas, uncover his Garfield sheets and comforter, get out of bed and turn on his Garfield lamp. He would open his Garfield curtains, put on his Garfield robe and Garfield fuzzy slippers and head to the bathroom for full Garfield toiletries. Finally, take your Garfield vitamins with water from a Garfield cup and you are ready for the day. In the spirit of Garfield, a true fan would go back to sleep and stay in bed all day.

The Garfield vitamins were distributed by Menley & James Laboratories Inc. Our bottles expired in 1995 and 1996 so we are guessing they were made in 1994. We know of regular vitamins and vitamins with added minerals.

Video Games

Over the years, there have been several software packages made for different game platforms. We have a Game Boy Garfield game as well as a WII game. There are many cell phone apps and even some floppy disks that help children learn math and reading.

Paws, Inc. is a multimedia company, so it should not be a surprise that they commissioned or created interactive experiences to keep up with the times.

VHS Tapes

Attention millennials, VHS tapes are those plastic rectangular things that your grandparents have laying all over their house. They have been replaced by the DVD, the Blu-Ray and the Digital Download. In simple terms, a VHS tape was the way that people would record their favorite television shows to watch later. You could also buy VHS tapes of your favorite movies.

Back in the day, people would go to video stores and rent VHS tapes. If we did not return them re-wound, we would be fined a dollar. No, we did not ride dinosaurs to school ... that was your grandparents. The first Garfield movie that was released in 2004 was the last Garfield available in the VHS form.

W

Wallpaper

They made actual Garfield wallpaper for papering a room. Even though we own several rolls, we covered our hallway with Garfield contact paper also known as Garfield shelf-liner. Unlike wallpaper, shelf-liner is self-adhesive, so we just had to peel and stick.

As a licensed realtor, I am trained to advise you not to cover your walls with Garfield wallpaper or shelf-liner. It is a real turnoff to potential buyers. The likeliness of another high-end Garfield collector in your area house shopping is slim to none. While I am giving home staging  advice you might also want to put your amusement rides and giant plush Garfield in storage until you get a serious offer.

Watches

As the husband of a Garfield collector, I can certify that the best thing about watches as a Garfield collectible is the fact that they are able to be worn every day and are more refined and subtle. Watches give a Garfield presence without overwhelming your appearance. Cathy is lucky to work in a very casual environment, so she can wear her Garfield baseball caps and t-shirts to work every day. I try to be more subtle and I may wear a Garfield tie and watch to a networking event. I always tell Cathy that I can work her Garfield world record and the fact that we foster dogs for North Shore Animal League America into any conversation with anyone in under five minutes.

194 | LOVES GARFIELD

70 More Watches

Invicta

Around 2016, Invicta watches came out with a really nice line of watches. At the tail end of 2017, Cathy managed to catch Invicta at a weak moment during an awesome sale. Following are some of the nice watches Cathy essentially "stole" from www.Invicta.com. Also pictured are some watches that Kohl's carried in the early to mid-'10s that were produced by ewatch-factory.

Just a quick note if you have any Odie watches. Some Odie watches run backwards. These timepieces actually rotate counter-clockwise. Make sure you mention that to the person changing the batteries. We've almost given more than one jeweler a heart attack when they put in the new battery and the watch starts working backwards!

Smart Watch Graphics

The times are changing and traditional watches are being worn less and less these days. Technology has taken over and integrated cell phone devices called smart watches are becoming more popular.

There are many designs of Garfield graphics to choose from that make your smart watch look like a smart Garfield watch. We would list the devices they are compatible with but the cell phone industry is changing so fast that this book would be obsolete before it is printed.

A smart, pun intended, Garfield collector would only buy a smart watch that has Garfield designs available even if it is an unpopular watch with bad technology. We have our priorities.

Water Globes

Like its cousin the snow globe, a water globe does not have any suspended pieces in the fluid like simulated snow or sparkles. Following is a fun assortment of water globes.

The one on the far left is my favorite water globe. It was produced in 2003 by United Media. It is a tribute to the Macy's Parade held annually on Thanksgiving Day in New York City. Inside the dome are a few miniaturized replicas of parade balloons including Garfield. This is a great example of an item created for the mass market that can be considered a Garfield collectible just because it has a Garfield in it.

It is another example of a crossover item. Somewhere there is a Charlie Brown collector purchasing it because Charlie Brown is in it. The piece also has a built-in music box and moving pieces. It is battery-operated and wind-up.

Other cross-over characters in this water globe include "Angelina Ballerina", "Little Bill", "Mr. Monopoly" and "Raggedy Ann", whoever they are.

Weird Ceramic Bank

We are not too sure if this item is made as a licensed collectible or was just the failed project from a junior high school student. At first when we got it with a collection that we purchased, we thought it was a fake. We almost threw it out, but eventually a few more just like it started to show up online.

It is likely made from a ceramic mold and hand-painted by someone to look like Garfield. This is a perfect example of "do not do anything unless you know what it is." In the video countdown Cathy and I made for Garfield's 40th birthday, we featured this as a mystery item. On the video comments somebody offered to buy it from us. Since we did not know if it was sculpted by George Washington or just a cat mold painted to look like Garfield, it was a bad idea to sell it.

If anyone knows anything about this item, please drop us a line.

Cathy thinks it might be made from paper mache although it does have some weight to it.

Window Shade

This beauty looks great in any room. What makes it most useful is that while it is easy to cover your walls with shelves of collectibles and Garfield pictures, how do you cover that unsightly spot without Garfields called the  window? You guessed it ... with a Garfield window shade. Now the entire house can be wall-to-wall Garfield.

Wine Bottle Toppers

These were sold in the "Garfield Stuff" catalog for $19.95. They also sold matching cocktail forks and little spreader knives.

World Leaders Figurines

Available in 1999, in Asian markets only, P&G produced a set of figurines in a yellow box. It's called the "Coolest Cat in History" and there are 20 pieces in the set (plus the box). Garfield is dressed up as important figures from world history. The set includes four artists, four scientists, four adventurers, four leaders, and four thinkers. Such examples are Van Gogh, Albert Einstein, Christopher Columbus, George Washington and Abraham Lincoln to name a few.

This set was not made for the U.S. market, making it much harder to find in the United States. When we met Jim Davis in Muncie and toured the Paws showroom, even Jim was surprised that we had a set of world leaders. Another collector, Jo Boom Boom, owns two sets of this special piece. It regularly sells for around $90 without the box and closer to $150 with the box. The box is nice because you can use it to display each figure. Be prepared for higher shipping charges since you don't want the box to get crushed in transit.

What's with the cluttered photography?

If you were touring our home, what you see is what you get. Many of our photographs are presented in their native environment. Most of them are unobstructed, but in the case of the world figures piece, it is somewhat obstructed.

We want to give you bonus items that are not in the listings. We also want to prove that it is in a home setting. Anyone can cherry-pick nice Garfield items from eBay and claim them as their own. And finally, and this is a free tip, we have learned the hard way that the more times you handle collectibles, the more likely it is that you will break them. That is the reason we do not dust very often.

World of Golf

An amazing sculpture with lots of Garfields playing golf makes Danbury Mint's World of Golf look like a stunning masterpiece. A major problem is that it is very fragile with a very high break rate.

When it is brand new, you are lucky to get it out of the box without snapping off a feature. If you buy one that is not in the original box, you are in for a world of breakage. We know from personal experience. Cathy bought one on eBay that was wrapped in bubble wrap, but the seller put the wooden base on top of the piece so it broke while in transit. If you do find one in its original box, be very careful to read the instructions explaining how to unpackage the piece. Unpackage it and place it on a shelf that is enclosed to keep it from getting damaged. We've seen these sell from under $100 to a couple hundred dollars depending on the condition. Of course, this piece is very popular with Garfield collectors who enjoy golf and they may be willing to pay closer to the couple hundred dollars price.

X

X Who are we kidding, our publisher told us we need every letter filled in. If anyone knows about a Garfield Xylophone please let us know. For the rest of the letter "X" we are cheating by denoting size and description.

X-rated kiddie toy
(see "Kiddie Ride")

X-Large inflatable
(See Inflatable)

Xylophone
Wow! Cathy googled it and, yes, there is a Garfield xylophone. The image is licensed, so you all need to Google it but, when we are wrong, we say we are wrong (You see what I did? I mixed in a little "Dirty Dancing" movie quote there). There actually was a Garfield xylophone. To be legit, Cathy did try to purchase it, but there's a

minimum order quantity, so unless we sell them to Nancy to put in everyone's registration packet at the next convention, you'll either have to check it out yourself or take our word for it.

I can't help but think that some unscrupulous graphic artist has laid a trap for some desperate author documenting Garfield items to be stuck at the letter "X" and spring their trap for a copyright lawsuit. Bullet dodged. Google it yourself.

Y

YABA Bowling Patches

In 2002, the organization, "Young American Bowling Alliance" licensed Garfield's image to make a series of bowling patches. We got our hands on most of the leftovers and put some on a bowling shirt or two.

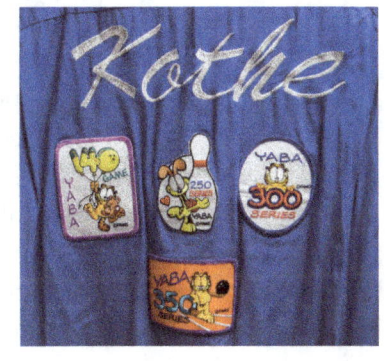

The embarrassing part is when we wear it at a bowling alley nobody knows we are Garfield collectors. They think we are proud of our "140 game" or our "300 series". Remember these are kids' patches. Everyone gets a participation medal.

On the other hand, since we only go bowling once a year as part of our "forced family fun" after Thanksgiving, we are so bad that it is a good thing we purchased the patches because it would have taken us a while to earn them.

Youth Patch / Yacht Patch (Regatta)

While we are on the patch theme, with the YABA patches above, the Boy Scouts of America issued a Garfield patch called the Regatta. You caught us ... Regatta starts with "R", not "Y", but we have plenty of "R's" in this book so to make an honest person of me, let's also call it the Youth Patches. In fact, in 1999, Garfield was licensed as a donation by Jim Davis and Paws, Inc.  to be used by the Boy Scouts of America. In the press release, Jim Davis was quoted to say, "The Boy Scouts are as American as lasagna. Garfield and scouting make a purrfect team." No, that is not a typo ... It's a pun.

Besides the Regatta patch there were many other patches and items available; mugs, t-shirts, jackets, plushes, plastic banks, keychains, snow globes, paperweights, pins, magnets, bookmarks, just to name a few. You can still find these items available for purchase on eBay and other aftermarket sites. The prices  range from $1 and up, depending on the item. The jacket is pictured here.

Yard Ornaments

Around 2014, there was a surge of Garfield planters and Garfield yard statues made by Woods International. Some of them had solar lights and would charge throughout the day and light up at night. We removed all the batteries from the solar ones so they wouldn't leak any chemicals since we were not going to display them outside. At the time they were easily found at stores like Tractor Supply Store. Since there were not a lot of Tractor Supply Stores in the suburbs of Long Island, New York, we delegated to friends in more rural areas to purchase as many as they could.

The second wave of the "gold rush" was when the stores clearanced them at ridiculous prices. It turns out that some of them said "Copyright Disney". If you were paying attention to the book so far, Garfield is a copyright of Paws, Inc. I do not know who was angrier, Disney or Paws, but they probably clearanced them at rock bottom prices before they were recalled. What store wants to pay for shipping twice on heavy statues? In the stamp collecting world, that mistake would make the item worth thousands of dollars. In the Garfield world, it's just a footnote.

Yo-Yos

The term Yo-Yos is apparently not a registered trademark so we can definitively say that there are Garfield Yo-Yos in existence.

The one pictured here is Copyright 1978, 1981 United Feature Syndicate Spectra Star (Made in China) This one was distributed by Avon Products in 1981.

Yarn

Latch hook kits come with all the little pieces of yarn necessary to complete the piece. They were all the rage in the mid-'80s. There were several Garfield latch hook kits available with Christmas themes. Cathy purchased three Christmas kits directly from Doc Davis at our first convention, which was Christmas-themed. I would recommend trying to purchase completed ones so you don't have to spend hours working on them yourself.

There were also crochet patterns available to knit Garfield sweaters and to make your own plushes.

This is a very fitting spot for another very special tribute. Back in November 2014, Florence Bartolett passed away. She was Nancy Vega's mother. Nancy is the organizer of the Garfield Gatherings. Her Mom was an essential part of the Garfield Gatherings. She would spend countless hours knitting Santa hats to decorate the Garfields that would be given out to each attendee at dinner. Or if the theme called for another prop to be knitted or sewn, she was always up to the task. Some of her creations fetched hundreds of dollars at the auctions.

Z

Zipper Pulls

We have been using little metal charms as zipper pulls. Since Cathy and I each own similar clothing like we are twins, it is an easy way to tell our jackets apart. They can also be used as jewelry charms for necklaces, bracelets and earrings or keychains.

Zodiac

What's your sign? You look like a Libra. Over the years there were zodiac tote bags, clothing, mugs, bookmarks, trading cards, Enesco figurines, and even zodiac night shirts. So, when the moon aligns with the stars, Garfield will be there, too. Don't forget to check your horoscope.

Zombie Items

There was a time when zombies and vampires were all the rage and yes, there are licensed Garfield Zombie items. According to an interview with Slate, the one regret that Jim Davis has was licensing the zombie items because they were gnarly and did not help the brand. Cathy does own Garfield Zombie trading cards. I can't say they are an important part of the collection. These were included with other items that we purchased at the 2017 convention.

NOT IN OUR COLLECTION (THE WHAT AND WHO)

I always say, "Give credit where credit is due." Cathy might have the world record but by no means does she have everything ever made. That would be impossible.

This section of the book is also a reminder that Cathy's collection, as impressive as it is, does not symbolize that she is better than other people. There are some amazing items out there that we do not, nor will we ever, own and you can be impressed  with yourself that you might have collectibles that even the world record holder does not have.

This section contains items that we do not have but deserve to be in the book. Fortunately for us, we have a network of Garfield collectors to rely upon, such as from the Garfield Gathering auction. We also have some items that deserve a mention because they are just plain outlandish. We will start with the Odie-colored, once-owned by Jim Davis Cadillac.

Cadillac Owned by Jim Davis

We should have probably given this item its very own chapter because in our life, hunting this car has been a lot like the book *Moby Dick*, the story of the great whale that keeps getting away and the hunters obsessed with catching it.

Somewhere around 2008 we saw a listing on the Internet about a yellow Cadillac that was previously owned by Jim Davis being sold. At the time the price was affordable, between $1,500 and $2,000 if our memory serves us. We could easily afford that, but it would probably cost double that to either drive out to Indiana and drive it back or have a car carrier company pick it up and transport it to Long Island. After all, what were we going to do with an Odie-yellow, land yacht of an automobile from the '80s? That would have been a sign that we have gone overboard with this collecting thing. It should be noted that this all took place before we did go overboard with this collecting thing as evidenced by holding the world record for Garfield collectibles.

Cadillac photos with permission from Earlywine Auctions

Fast forward around eight years and Cathy and I were reminiscing about the Jim Davis Cadillac. I commented that it is the only item that I regret not purchasing. You see, I have a theory that the best available Garfield collectible is the item that is so completely ridiculous that people start to doubt your insanity.

Since having a 600-pound coin-operated amusement ride in our living room was not cutting it for the shock factor, the Cadillac would probably do the job.

Here is the amazing part of this story. When I mentioned to Cathy that I regret not buying the Cadillac, she pulled out her smart phone and did a quick internet search. Would you believe that the very same car was to be put up on the auction block that very weekend? It was the Thanksgiving weekend in 2016. The car was on the block and this time we would at least pretend to try to purchase the car. After all, what are the odds of us thinking about it and it becoming immediately available for sale?

To add insult to injury, at the time of the auction, Cathy and I already owned four cars for just two drivers. We had her car, my car, the Jeep we use to tow the boat, and a Saturn we never got around to donating. The Cadillac Coupe Deville would make five cars and since they did not exactly make them small in the '80s, it probably would not fit in a modern parking space. We would end up being "those people" at the back of a parking lot taking up two spaces. There is nothing practical about this car.

The 1984 Cadillac Coupe Deville weighs 3,935 pounds. This

weight is not necessarily modern safety equipment; it has a body so solid that when you get in an accident you hose off the interior from the dead driver and sell it as "slightly dented". This car was a survivor of the days when people did not think about gas prices and only thought about trunk space.

Speaking of the trunk. This trunk could fit five dead bodies in it at one time. I don't mean skinny people. I mean five full-size overweight adults. You might even fit some golf clubs with the people in the trunk.

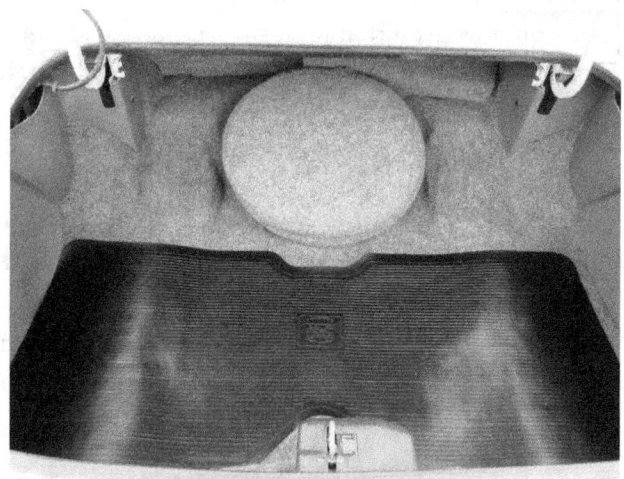

The more research that we did about the car the more it seemed to be a bad idea. The auction house was suggesting that it might fetch between $8,000 and $14,000. Our research indicated that its Blue Book value was $600 to $1,500. We saw the same type of car selling on Craigslist.com for between $600 and $2,500.

The engine in this car is somewhat hysterical. You would think that a V8 engine that takes up the entire engine compartment of a land yacht would be a powerful street rod. It turns out that the V8 was rated between 100 and 130 horsepower. I just Googled it and our Saturn has the same amount of power and weighs a thousand pounds less.

According to Wikipedia, this Cadillac model year was more concerned about gas mileage than horse power.

The red flags kept piling up. We paid for a "Carfax" report and found out that there was never a reliable odometer reading. The first entry was in 1999 when the reading of 55,000 miles was suspect due to a crack or possible roll-over. Since the odometer did not go past 5-digits, it was likely that it already flipped past 100,000 miles by the time the 1999 entry was recorded.

At the time, Cathy and I had a good relationship with Paws Inc., the creator of Garfield. We still do. We could have called the company, asked for Gary, who maintains the cars, to see if he remembers the Cadillac, but we did not want anyone to know the car was for sale again. I guarantee they have more money than we do. All we could have done was assume the mileage was not accurate.

So, with these warnings and red flags piling up, we did the obvious thing. We put a bid in on the car. Since we were going to be at a concert at the time of the auction, we pre-registered and put in a standing maximum bid of $3,500. And waited for the day of the auction.

On the day of the auction, our contact at the auction house called us when the car was up for bid. He said, "OK, it's coming up the ramp to the auction block. There's one bid, there's another bid, oh, you're outbid". We were outbid within seconds! Despite higher bids than us, the reserve was not met and the car was not sold at the time of that auction. Like Moby Dick, our great white whale, we all lived to meet again someday.

L.E.D. Spinner Plush

In the 2017 Garfield Gathering auction, these two L.E.D. Spinner Garfields were featured separately in the auction. Each sold for hundreds of dollars.

I have to say, next to the Pachinko machine and the slot machines, these are among the coolest things I have ever seen. The propeller on the front spins at an exact speed while Light Emitting Diodes (LED's) light up by a computer sequence and spell out phrases.

I believe these ones spell out, "Happy Halloween". On line at the collectors' Facebook page, someone had one that spelled out, "Happy Birthday".

Not in Our Collection (The What and Who) | 215

Furry Tail Series

Get it ... "Furry Tails". Sort of like "Fairy Tales". In 1989 there was a hardcover book published, *Garfield's Furry Tails*. It took five popular fairy tales and put a Garfield spin on them. They included:

1. Garfield and the Three Bears
2. Little Red Riding Odie
3. Garfield and Penny Henny
4. Garfield and Sleeping Beauty
5. Garfield and the Beanstalk

There were hundreds, if not thousands, of plush Garfields made and the Furry Tail Series is among the rarest. We can't say if there were fewer of them made, but when they come up for sale, they usually sell for much more than your average plush. It helps if they have their hang tags and are in excellent condition with all their accessories. Included in the series are:

**Goldilocks / Big Bad Wolf
Mother Goose / Little Red Riding Hood**

Thanks to Tricia Lazrovitch, we can show you some of the plushes from the Furry Tails Series. She also provided the picture of the Frog Prince below. Some of these are extremely rare and really good finds.

The Furry Tails series plushes were produced by Dakin. The stories have also carried over to an animated Garfield cartoon.

In the stories, Garfield and friends hijacked the plot line of popular fairy tales with a twist. Instead of porridge, Garfield stole lasagna from the three bears.

Shown here is the frog prince. As I write this, there is one for sale on eBay for $125 without the tags and with some blemishes.

The Garfield as the Big, Bad Wolf comes up for sale quite often, as does the Goldilocks plush and Little Red Riding Hood. The Frog Prince is very rare and Mother Goose is pretty rare. There is also a beanstalk Garfield, Little Bo Peep Garfield and Ole King Cole Garfield.

We should also mention that many times they are missing pieces like the Mother Goose book, the spoon on Goldilocks, Little Red Riding Hood's basket or Little Bo Peep's staff. If you see one for sale and the price seems too high, make sure all the parts are attached and the hang tag is not missing. You can scroll through Google images and get a good idea of what accessories should be included.

Disclaimer about facts throughout this book

It should be noted that Garfield collectibles are the ultimate chicken-egg dilemma. In other words, some Internet genius who probably has a photographic memory and is not afraid to use it, will immediately call me out for not being fully factual.

I envision him saying something like, "The plushes were out long before the book or cartoons came out." In fact, as I am writing this, Cathy is telling me that her research is showing that the plush came out in 1981.

The truth is that the reason that we are wishy-washy on the dates is that nobody really knows. In fact, our contacts at Paws, Inc. tell us that they had a professional historian who is also a cataloger and database expert come in, and it would likely take thousands of man-hours to figure out the details on all their vendors, samples, inventory, and archives.

If Paws, Inc. doesn't know everything that they have and where their items came from, we don't stand a chance figuring it out by ourselves. For this we apologize. Cathy has the largest documented collection in the world but since she purchased most of the items online, it is better not to pretend when it was made and who made it for what reason.

Cathy collects what makes her happy. She's not concerned about the manufacturer information. She's not expecting to make a fortune from her collection.

Paper Towel Holder

Part of the same series as the CD holder and other antique-looking statues, the paper towel holder is a beautiful piece. Like its counterparts made by the same company, it is art with a purpose. Some collectors are proud to hang this on their kitchen wall to hold their paper towels.

The one shown is from the auction at the Garfield Gathering. Somebody from our group might be reading this book and saying, "That's mine, I won the auction."

Pedal Car Fire Truck

This is a beautiful metal piece. The one shown was sold at auction at the 2009 Garfield Collectors Convention in San Antonio, Texas. The truck pictured here was bid on and won by Gary, a volunteer fireman in New Jersey who is an avid collector.

When Gary bids on Garfield fire department items, failure is never an option. Money is no object. Much to everyone's surprise, during the 2017 Garfield Gathering, Gary deliberately backed down from a Garfield fire department item. When I asked him why he let it go, he said that the other bidder was with another fire department and he wanted to respect the other fireman. He knew it was going to a worthy home.

The Garfield fire truck is almost four feet long and could function as a child's toy if it wasn't so rare and beautiful. These types of cars are very collectible by people other than Garfield collectors and can be quite expensive. If you have one, take very good care of it to make it worth top dollar. Even in bad condition, it can still be worth a decent amount, but the purchaser will have to put some money into it if they want to restore it to mint condition.

King Garfield

Even Cathy does not have one. You do not see this huge plush very often. Most of the time it comes up for sale it is in Europe or Australia. There was one as part of the $5 raffles at the 2007 Garfield Convention in West Palm Beach, Florida. Cathy was hoping to win it but knew if she did, we'd have to buy him a plane ticket to get him home. We know of only a few in the United States and this one belongs to a regular attendee of the Garfield Gathering and the co-host of the 2015 Garfield Gathering. Photo courtesy of "Thinks she is a princess," (in her mind), Jo Boom Boom Herrman. You would think I made that up, but that is how she wanted the photo credit.

This plush weighs at least 40 pounds, stands almost five feet tall, and is almost three feet wide at the base. It is probably larger and heavier than the giant Macy's Garfield from the 25th Birthday raffle.

The asking price is workable but shipping it cross-continent is expensive for something so large and bulky.

Lasagna pan

Of course, there was a Garfield lasagna pan manufactured. If you look at the size of the eyes on the lasagna pan, you can see that they are small and separate. This indicates that the pan is one of the earlier Garfields made. I'm sure it was a no-brainer to the folks at Paws early on when they were first marketing Garfield items. The fact is it is usable and breakable; many of them are either worn out or broken. When this item comes up for sale, which is not often, it can easily fetch good money. The average selling price online is around $400. Be sure to pack it up well before shipping or another one will be lost to time.

Race Car Suit

For years, we would see somebody trying to sell the Kyle Petty NASCAR 2003 Brickyard 400 race-worn driver fire suit on eBay. It came up for sale many times but was never bid on due to the high starting price. This clearly is a great piece to have, but apparently nobody wanted it at the starting price of almost $10,000.

Wine Bottles (Hand-Painted)

As a charity fundraiser, hand-painted wine bottles from Paws, Inc. were used for annual charity auctions that Jim Davis was involved in. The wine bottles were auctioned off to raise funds for charity. Every now and then, a bottle will come up for sale aftermarket. The starting price is usually a couple hundred dollars, but we have yet to see any of the empty bottles sell. This is an indication that it was priced too high. A true value cannot be established if there are no corresponding buyers at the asking price. It still is a rare and nice collectible if you can get one.

10
NOT RARE (THE WHAT)

You can't have a book on Garfield collectibles without dispelling some myths about what might be valuable. Below are some of the more popular items that sellers often insist are rare and hard to find. Don't believe the hype.

Chia Pet Garfield

In popular culture there are two ways that you know you are somebody. Either Weird Al Yankovic parodies your song or they make a Chia Pet in your likeness. Yes, there is a Garfield Chia Pet. First made in 2002 by Joseph Enterprises in San Francisco, California, this item is not rare, but sure is a benchmark in popular culture.

Massager

This item is evidence that eBay sellers will describe anything as rare. We have found that this item is one of the most un-rare Garfield items available. First, they were originally available at a discount store.

Second, to add insult to injury, we paid $2.99 each for

ours. Cathy and I purchased every one available at the discount store to re-sell at the Garfield Gathering.

We initially tried to sell them during room-hopping for five dollars. By the end of the weekend we were trying to give them away with any purchase and people declined. They did not want to waste the space in their suitcases.

McDonald's Mugs and Happy Meal Toys

In the mid-'80s, the set of four glass mugs with activities such as canoeing were a dime a dozen. There are thousands of these out there, so if you get a dollar for each consider yourself very lucky.

Not Rare (The What) | 223

There were also Garfield "Happy Meal" toys that featured Garfield driving a jeep, riding on a scooter, a skateboard and a moped. There are thousands of these out there and many times they do not have all the parts. I've seen just the Garfield and not the jeep more time than I care to mention. Now that might work for you if you need Garfield in a sitting position wearing a safari type hat. Otherwise, these are not very valuable, unless you can get the signage with them. Packaging and signage always increase the value of just about any item.

On the other hand, the set of four McDonald's checker-board mugs are much harder to find. They were only available regionally. They have either a red, yellow, green or blue checkered background and feature just Garfield saying one of his "Garfisms". Cathy's cousin who lives in Pennsylvania was able to get the set for Cathy. You don't see them anywhere near as often as the others, but I wouldn't pay too much for them - under $20 for the set, including shipping, is more than enough.

On the other hand, there were Garfield tall drinking glasses available at McDonald's that are a bit rarer. They were another series of four and show Garfield in a sailboat, riding on a bicycle, on a skateboard and in a car. We've seen these sell at the convention auction for close to $100. Cathy had never seen them before so when we got home, she started her search for them. Several months later was able to pick them up for a considerably lower price on eBay.

"Sericels" – from Cruise Ships

Prices are all over the place. These cells are less rare because the auction houses that sell them seem to have a lot of inventory.

Because cruise ships overhype them, people immediately assume they can get more for them on land. They are all over eBay for much less than you can get on the ships.

Once the cruise line auction department realized Cathy and I were not your average Garfield collectors, we purchased a set of six unframed cells for $150. Not $150 each. $150 for all six. They were selling for $350 each, framed, at the ship auction.

Many Garfield Plush are Not Rare

There are quite a few Garfield plushes that are popular and

sought-after, but most of them can be purchased for only a few dollars online.

Garfield Books are Not Necessarily Rare

Garfield books with the comics inside are fun to read, but they are very abundant. Paws, Inc. has been selling books from the beginning and they are very popular. It is great to get a full set of your own for your bookshelf, but I would not use them as an investment.

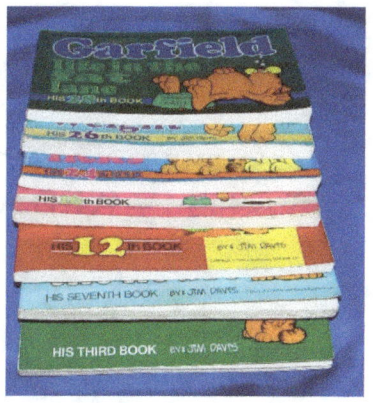

Others such as the leather-bound 20-year book, the leather-bound 25-year book, 30-year, 35-year, and Season's Eatings are better items to collect.

11

GARFIELD IN THE HUMAN WORLD (THE WHO AND WHERE)

Obviously, Garfield collectors are human but the direction of the book that we are about to move in involves what people do or can do in the real world to enjoy Garfield.

Garfield collecting can be a social activity. For others it is a private activity. If you are a Garfield collector who does not share the experience with others, you might consider some of the more social activities around being a Garfield collector.

Comic Con

For the record, neither Cathy nor I have ever been to a Comic Con, so we had to gather this information via friends and good, old-fashioned research. Paws, Inc. will often attend a Comic Con to promote what is going on in its world. Jim Davis attended the Denver Comic Con in 2018 to promote Garfield's 40th birthday book. Apparently, Jim does his appearances a little differently than others. He pre-signed several hundred books, and you could purchase as many books as you wanted. You were then able to take a "selfie" with Jim Davis. You could take as many pictures as the quantity of books you purchased. Jim has realized that no one really cares to watch him sign his book; everyone wants a photo with him now. It helps to keep things moving at a quicker pace.

Gocomics.com

Gocomics.com is a licensee that has the rights to distribute Garfield comic strips via the internet. You can sign up for free and have the daily comic strip delivered to your email address. You can go to their website and search through old comic strips. You can even purchase any Garfield comic as an archive-quality print. That would make a great birthday present for anyone born after June 19, 1978. Imagine getting the Garfield comic strip that appeared in newspapers on the day you were born, or as an anniversary gift for the special Garfield loving couple!

Factory Entertainment

Factory Entertainment created a licensed Garfield statue designed by famed artist Rubin Procopio as previously mentioned in this book. The original design was created by Jim Davis, the creator of Garfield.

Factory Entertainment also offered several Garfield statues called "shakems" on their website in the early '10s. They produced an exclusive Garfield shakem for the 2012 San Diego Comic Con. It's a limited edition of 500 pieces produced.

Facebook Groups

There are several social groups that revolve around Garfield collecting. There are numerous other generic groups about Garfield, but not necessarily targeted to collectors. We would recommend joining and following the various groups. Below is a small sampling of the available groups.

Garfield Facebook Group

Moderated by Paws, Inc., the parent company to Garfield, this group has millions of followers and is generically about Garfield. They regularly post a Garfield comic strip or picture. They may announce a special sale on original artwork or other Garfield items. They'll introduce new Garfield games and apps.

Garfield Collectors and Collectibles Group

One group that Cathy and I are members of is a closed group specifically for Garfield collectors. The rules are more rigid to keep the group positive and targeted to Garfield collecting. People post Garfield items they just acquired or items they would like to get more information about. Be sure to put NFS (not for sale) on your post unless, of course, you are looking to sell your items. If that is the case, please, please, please post photos. You can describe an item in detail, but like the saying goes, "a picture is worth a thousand words." You might not realize that something is missing from the pieces, but the picture will show that something is missing.

I must admit that I feel like an actual celebrity posting in this group since Cathy has the world record and we are so actively involved with a lot of collector activities. The best part is, unlike real celebrities, we can have a normal life and not get followed around by tabloid media photographers.

Book Signings

Often when a new book is released, Jim Davis may go on a book tour to help promote the project. In 2003, when he was promoting Garfield's 25th birthday book after the cruise, I was amazed at how many fans came out of the woodwork in Huntington, New York at the world famous "Book Revue" bookstore. I have never seen any of those people at the collectors' conventions.

Plays / Special Events

There have been several plays produced around the Garfield character. We have been to a few children's plays for the holidays. In 2015, there was a play called "Garfield: The Musical with Cattitude". It was shown in several playhouses around the country. It was unique in that you could see the faces of the actors portraying the characters. They were not wearing the very large costumes with the huge head covering masks, so they could be more limber in their actions and clearer in singing. Unfortunately, Cathy and I did not get to see the show, but Cathy did purchase a banner advertising it at the 2013 convention.

Earn a Visit to Paws, Inc.

There was a not very well-known program that could get you access to a special tour of the headquarters for Garfield. There was a credit card program from Commerce Bank (Garfield Credit Card) that allowed you to earn enough points to get a tour of Paws, Inc. You needed 50,000 points to get the tour. The tour included a handful of Garfield gifts and a tour of the facility.

Cheryl, one of our collector friends, has been on the tour at least three times thus far. Having been at Paws, Inc. several times ourselves, I can testify that it really is a highlight in the collector experience.

LOVES GARFIELD

Prior to the publication of this book we discovered that the benefit is no longer available to credit card holders so do not run out and apply for the Commerce Bank credit card. After a long "round-and-round" phone call between customer service and the rewards department I discovered that the program no longer exists.

Cathy got the Paws tour the hard way by getting the world record. A press conference was arranged, including a "meet and greet" with Jim Davis, the creator of Garfield. Previous visits to Paws for Cathy and myself were because of our heavy involvement in the multimedia for the Garfield Collectors Convention called the Garfield Gathering.

Garfield in the Human World (the Who and Where) | 231

Inside the showroom of Paws, Inc.

12

THE GARFIELD TRAIL (THE WHERE AND WHAT)

When you are a high-end Garfield collector, it is not uncommon to consider Indiana as a great place to visit. Jim Davis grew up in the Indiana area and when his professional efforts started to pay off, Jim chose to build his headquarters in Indiana.

In the mid-2000's, the idea to erect Garfield statues in the towns making up Grant County in Indiana was developed. It was thought that it would raise tourism to the area as Garfield fans would flock to Indiana to drive the "Garfield Trail". Over the course of about five years, ten statues have been placed around the community. There is also  another statue, not part of this group, but worth mentioning. It's a Garfield chainsaw carving displayed at a local golf course. If you do make the trip, be sure to contact the Grant County tourism office, as the locations may change or a statue may be taken down for maintenance.

This section has the classification of "Where and What."

The "Where" is obvious because the Garfield Trail is a group of geographic locations. It is also classified as "What" because when you find them, they are some big statues. In a way, a custom-made fiberglass Garfield statue would be the ultimate collectible. The Garfield Trail is made up of one-of-a-kind statues that are shared with the community.

Get a Map

You can download a map of the Muncie Trail at the Marion / Grant County Visitors Bureau website:

http://www.showmegrantcounty.com/grant-county-attractions/garfield/

They are located in City Hall at:

505 West 3rd Street
Marion, IN 46952
www.showmegrantcounty.com
(765) 668-5435

When we were in town, the Muncie Visitors Bureau was helpful to us in getting around the area. At the time, they also had one of the 25th Anniversary smaller Garfield statues in their office.

Muncie Visitors Bureau
3700 South Madison Street
Muncie, IN 47302
www.visitmuncie.org
(765) 284-2700

Cell Phone Audio Tour

There is a cell phone audio tour. Call (765) 997-7034 to hear more about each statue. Following is a list of each statue that corresponds to the number on the tour. If you:

Press 0 you will hear a recorded overview of Garfield
Press 1 for "Paws for Thought" in Marion, IN
Press 2 for "Speedking" in Swayzee, IN
Press 3 for "College Bound" in Sweetster, IN
Press 4 for "Dr. Garfield" in Marion, IN
Press 5 for "Duffer" in Marion, IN
Press 6 for "Worldly Cat" in Van Buren, IN
Press 7 for "Gone Fishin'" in Matthews, IN
Press 8 for "Cool Cat" in Fairmount, IN
Press 9 for "Firefighter" in Jonesboro, IN
Press 10 for "Glass Blower" in Gas City, IN
Press 11 for "Scream for Ice Cream" in Upland, IN

Next are photos of the statues in no particular order. Be sure to look at the map and visit the statues in a more logical order if you are in the area.

Cool Cat - Fairmount Historical Museum

This Garfield statue is in front of the Fairmount Historical Museum. The museum is primarily a tribute to James Dean, but it also has a room devoted to Garfield and his creator, Jim Davis.

It is tough to give a strong endorsement for the museum considering we have more collectibles in our bathroom. To be fair, since

Cathy does hold the world record, that is probably an unjust comparison.

The museum is devoted to James Dean, not necessarily Garfield, so if you are a James Dean fan, you will probably be more impressed.

If I recall, they even had James Dean's motorcycle.

The address is:

Fairmount Historical Museum
203 East Washington Street
Fairmount, IN 46928

Did we mention we had more collectibles in our bathroom? Here are some of them.

Dr. Garfield - Marion General Hospital

With a stethoscope in one hand and ready to help the sick, this Garfield statue welcomes visitors to the Marion General Hospital. Hopefully, it is a short visit to the hospital because who wants to stay in a hospital?

According to Wikipedia.com, the hospital employees raised money to have the statue made for them. Wikipedia said the statue was unveiled on May 11, 2007.

Just like the James Dean Garfield statue and like most of the larger statues on the Garfield Trail, this statue is right out in the open. It is a very easy photo opportunity to walk right up and get a picture with Dr. Garfield.

The address to the hospital is:

Marion General Hospital
441 North Wabash Avenue
Marion, IN 46952

Speedkings - Swayzee Elementary School

This statue is dressed up for the local High School basketball team. According to the Chronicle-Tribune.com reprinted article provided by the Marion / Grant County Convention and Visitors Bureau, the number 9 on his shirt represents "the number of overtimes in the record setting game against Liberty Center in 1964."

This statue is also accessible and a great Garfield photo opportunity. The address is:

405 S Washington Street
Swayzee, IN 46986

College Bound - Sweetster Switch Trail and Depot

This Garfield is standing in front of a train car in Sweetster. The train car is a restored red train caboose. The train and statue mark the beginning of a three mile long nature trail. Parking is right near the train and statue.

Decorated with old fashioned baggage carts and suitcases, it is reminiscent of the days the rails ruled the transportation world.

238 | LOVES GARFIELD

The following information is from www.traillink.com:

Parking and Trail Access

To access the starting point at the Garfield statue in Sweetster, follow Interstate 69 to County Route 18 and travel west for 12 miles through the town of Marion to Sweetster. Turn left (south) on N. Main Street and drive 0.25 miles. The trailhead is before the railroad tracks. Look for the Garfield statue on the left by the retired rail cars.

To access County Road N 700 West from downtown Sweetster, take Main Street north to State Road 18. Turn left and follow SR 18 west for 2 miles. Turn left onto County Road 700. The trailhead is on the left just before the railroad tracks.

To access County Road N 400 West from downtown Sweetster,

take Main Street north to SR 18. Turn right and follow SR 18 east for 1 mile. Turn right onto County Road 400. The trailhead is on the right just before the railroad tracks.

Worldly Cat - Van Buren Public Library

Garfield is holding popcorn since Van Buren is apparently the popcorn capital of the world. Dressed up like the Van Buren High School Aces, Garfield holds a globe in his right hand.

The address is:

Van Buren Public Library
115 S 1st Street
Van Buren, IN 46991

Gone Fishin' - Matthews Public Access Site Next to the Cumberland Covered Bridge

This statue shows off the comedy of Jim Davis with a cartoon fish in the net and a smile on his face. Behind him is the beautiful Cumberland Covered Bridge. The local creek is a boat launch site as well as a popular fishing spot.

This statue is my personal favorite. The creek is beautiful. The covered bridge is an amazing back drop. There is also nothing like the sound of running water. The address is:

816 South Wisconsin Street
Matthews, IN 46957

Upland: Scream for Ice Cream

What can be better than a photo opportunity and a meal followed by homemade ice cream? Conveniently located on the property of Ivanhoe's Restaurant, you can go inside and have a good meal. Inside the restaurant, they embrace the Garfield Trail with some pictures of other locations on the Trail. The address is:

979 South Main Street
Upland, IN 46989

(In front of Ivanhoe's Restaurant)

Marion: Paws for Thought

This statue is located behind a fence by the Garfield Garden Trailhead.

Of all the statues, this one was the most uninviting. It was buffered by a steel fence and you needed a zoom lens for a photo opportunity. It seemed to be cast from the same mold as the "Garfred Rogers" that is in our living room. The area is nicely landscaped with a giant paw print.

According to their website, if you want access to the statue you need to call the Community Foundation of Grant County at (765) 662-0065 during their business hours.

Jonesboro: Firefighter

The firefighter statue is right in front of the Jonesboro firehouse in Jonesboro, Indiana. This was one of the latest statues to be placed. We were not able to see it in our 2009 trip, but we did see it in 2014. The address is:

414 South Main Street
Jonesboro, IN 46938

Duffer – Marion

Inside the clubhouse of the Arbor Trace Golf Club is a handmade chainsaw carving of Garfield. It is extremely well done and really shows off the talent of the artist who made it.

As an interesting fun fact, this statue was not part of the original Garfield Trail. We found it thanks to the internet in 2009, and it was not listed on the map. Over time, it was added to the Trail.

The people at the golf club were very friendly. They were also very proud of their statue. The address is:

Arbor Trace Golf Club
2500 E 550 N
Marion, IN 46952

13

THE GARFIELD CRUISE (THE WHO AND WHERE) "IT'S ALL ABOUT ME AT SEA IN 2003"

Cathy here. I just want to interject with some other details before we jump into the itinerary for the cruise. For as long as I can remember my parents would go away for their wedding anniversary every year. It's something that Rob and I have worked hard to be able to do for ourselves as well. Just about every year, we have managed to take a vacation to celebrate our wedding anniversary.

In 2002 we booked a Disney cruise for our eight-year anniversary. Wouldn't you know it, not long after we submitted our final payment for that trip, we received a solicitation in the mail for Garfield's 25th Birthday cruise. What?! – a chance to meet

Garfield and Jim Davis, the creator? No way would I miss an opportunity like that! But, it was another cruise and the same exact itinerary we were taking with the Disney cruise only 6 months before the Garfield cruise. I did stop and think about it for all of about 30

seconds that we shouldn't go. But, no way, this was too good to pass up and we booked the trip right away.

The mailing had given us a good idea of the events that would be held onboard. There would be a meet-and-greet, theme parties and autograph signings throughout the entire cruise. So, I immediately started planning out our wardrobe and had to order new T-shirts and lounge pants for the pajama party. We had to have our lounge pants professionally hemmed so we wouldn't trip over ourselves. I gathered up items that I thought would travel well to have Jim Davis autograph for me.

I brought metal license plates and signs, the Monopoly board from the Garfield Monopoly game, the scrapbook that was included with the purchase of the custom acrylic and some small specialty books. I also brought the largest Garfield plush that I had at the time. I rubber banded suction cups to his hands and feet, so we could suction cup him to the doors to our veranda onboard.

We had the largest Garfield "Stuck on You" on the ship! Jim signed him for me on the last night of the cruise! I'm so glad we went; it was an amazingly unforgettable experience!

In May of 2003, as part of the Garfield 25th birthday celebration, there was a Caribbean cruise with over 400 Garfield attendees in the party. Or as I like to put it, 200 Garfield collectors and their husbands or travel partners. The cruise was with Holland America aboard the "MS Zuiderdam." It was for 7 days and 6 nights.

In attendance was Jim Davis, the creator of Garfield, along with his wife Jill, who is Senior Vice President of Licensing at Paws, Inc. Other notable passengers included Doc, Jim's brother, who was the inspiration for Jon's brother, "Doc Boy," a character in the comic strip, Kim, the company publicist, as well as other family members.

The Garfield Cruise (the Who and Where) "It's All About Me at Se... | 245

Welcome Aboard Party

Our first event was a welcome aboard cocktail party. This was the first time that we were meeting the other Garfield fans. Jim Davis entered the room, greeted everyone and thanked us for joining in the birthday celebration. All the fans in the room surrounded Jim, listening and talking, but the moment the people in the Garfield and Odie costumes came into the room, the collectors left Jim like cockroaches with the lights turned on and surrounded Garfield and Odie.

Let's think about this for a moment. On one side of the room is the brains of the operation, the founder, the creator, the writer, and the owner of the entire enterprise. On the other side of the room is what could have been two busboys dressed up in Garfield and Odie costumes. This proves they are Garfield fans because any normal person would have stayed with Jim Davis. Once the excitement of meeting Garfield and Odie died down, people went back to lining up to meet Jim. He was extremely gracious and took his time talking with each person in the room.

Cathy and me, sporting our new shirts acquired just before the trip

Jim Davis, Garfield, and Odie

On the cruise, there were fun-themed signs and other decorations. One of the best was, "Garfield's Top Ten Reasons to Indulge on this Cruise" (shown below). Jim presented the Top Ten list during the cocktail hour.

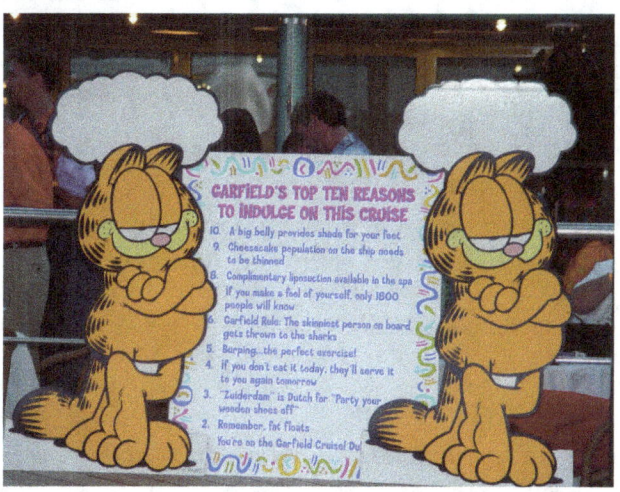

Garfield's Top Ten Reasons to Indulge on this Cruise

10. A big belly provides shade for your feet.

9. Cheesecake population on the ship needs to be thinned.

8. Complimentary liposuction available in the spa.

7. If you make a fool of yourself only 1800 people will know.

6. Garfield Rule: The skinniest person on board gets thrown to the sharks.

5. Burping… the perfect exercise!

4. If you don't eat it today, they will serve it to you tomorrow.

3. "Zuiderdam" is Dutch for "party your wooden shoes off."

2. Remember. Fat floats.

1. You're on the Garfield Cruise! Duh!

Day One - First Port: Key West

In Key West, the big event for the day was the scavenger hunt. The group was broken up into teams and sent out to collect items and complete fun challenges. We were given Polaroid cameras and had to photograph our entire team completing the challenges. The scavenger hunt sent us all over the island. It took hours and was a lot of fun. In the end, our team did not do too well, but we later found out that the winning team rented one of those funny looking electric cars to drive all over the island. So, at least we got our exercise for the day!

Cathy and I did not know it at the time, but on our team was Nancy Vega and her husband, Manny, who are the original organizers of the Garfield Gatherings. We have since become good friends with Nancy and Manny, and these days, Cathy and I help out with the Gathering website, audio-visual presentations, auction items, some games, and I act as the auctioneer and game show host for a few events.

Fun Story "Kritter Patrol"

While running around Key West, the group ran into some people selling T-shirts out of their car trunk. It turns out that they had "Kritter Patrol" Garfield and Odie shirts left over from an event. When they saw many of us from the cruise dressed in Garfield clothing, they decided to run home and get their leftover inventory. Their instincts were right, and they sold every Kritter Patrol T-Shirt.

My research seems to indicate that Kritter Patrol is a not-for-profit organization that spays and neuters feral animals. We believe Paws, Inc. donated the artwork to help the cause.

Day Two – At Sea

It was a Monday, so there were no activities scheduled in the morning. We were encouraged to sleep in.

Mama Leone's Lasagna Lunch

Of course you couldn't have a Garfield cruise and not have a lasagna luncheon. Garfield and Odie were wandering around and you could have your picture taken with them. There were special napkins on the tables and signage around the room with an Italian theme.

Chalk Talk

Jim Davis had what they called a "Chalk Talk." It was an intimate meeting with the group where he was on stage with a large pad of paper on an easel, some permanent markers, and his stories. We learned how Jim got

into drawing and cartooning as a small boy on the farm. We learned about the predecessor to Garfield, Gnorm Gnat. (The G isn't pronounced.) And we learned about the early days before Garfield exploded into what it is today.

You Call that a Cat?

During the Chalk Talk, a man from the audience stood up and started playfully heckling Jim. The man said things like, "You call that a cat? You really think your cartoon is any good." With this group, those were fighting words.

Jim calmly called him out and said to the man, "If you think you are such a good artist, why don't you come up here and show us what you can do." The man accepted the challenge and took the marker. Jim continued to give his Chalk Talk presentation. Within five minutes, the man drew the comic character "Dagwood" from his comic strip "Blondie."

At that time, Jim Davis announced to the group, "Ladies and gentlemen, let's give a warm welcome to my good friend, Dean Young." He was apparently secretly traveling with the group as a guest of Jim Davis. Up until the Chalk Talk staged set-up, nobody knew who he was. (Except Cathy had seen the man having lunch with Jim earlier at the lasagna luncheon, so she leaned over to me when she saw who was heckling Jim and said, "Oh, this must be a put on. He was having lunch with Jim before"). He was the son of the founder of Blondie who went on to take over for his father and run the company. It seems that the cartoonist community is pretty small and very close to each other.

The Garfield Cruise (the Who and Where) "It's All About Me at Sea... | 251

Dean Young presenting Jim Davis with original artwork of Blondie and Garfield together

Dean Young then presented Jim Davis with a very special 25th Birthday present for Jim and everyone at Paws, Inc. It was a framed drawing of Garfield with Dagwood and Blondie.

How Jim Davis Met Charles Schultz

Jim Davis used to be very good friends with the renowned Charles Schulz, the creator of the comic strip, Peanuts. In fact, during Chalk Talk, Jim Davis told the story of how he and Charles Schulz met while they were both working at an animation studio. In 1982, Charles was working on the latest Peanuts project and Jim was making the very first animated Garfield television special, "Here Comes Garfield".

During the animation session, Jim was getting frustrated because Garfield did not look right. Jim wanted Garfield to stand on just his back paws and dance during the open credits, but Garfield looked ridiculous trying to stand up on his tiny, little back paws. Somehow, Charles caught wind of his frustration and came over to help out. Charles explained to Jim that a cartoon character needs to shape shift and morph depending on the scene. When Garfield stands up, you need to draw his feet ridiculously large to support the torso. When Garfield is lying down like a cat, you need to shrink the arms and legs to be more catlike. Charles Schulz actually drew the first picture of Garfield standing!

From that day forward, Jim Davis and Charles Schulz became very good friends.

Flash Forward – Another Cartoonist Story

Since I am already talking about cartoonists and how well they get along, it reminds me of a story told to us by Jim Davis when he and Cathy got together for a photo opportunity around Cathy's world record ceremony.

In the hour or so in Muncie, Indiana, Jim told us a story that a television company had the idea to follow him and other famous cartoonists around for a reality TV show. The idea was quickly squashed because the production company did not like the fact that working cartoonists were close friends, got along really well and respected each other's work. The entire episode would not be industry-related fighting. Instead, it would be a bunch of cartoonists getting along beautifully and complimenting each other the entire time. Apparently, getting along is not a winning formula for a reality TV show.

Day Three – Cozumel

Today we had a "movie marathon" where they showed a bunch of Garfield cartoons in the main theater. One of which is Jim's favorite television special, "Garfield in Paradise".

At night, this was the big "Garfield Garb" dinner. Everyone put on their best Garfield clothing and had dinner in the main dining room. This is when Jim was wearing the t-shirt celebrating the artwork "Grande Odalisque" painted in 1814 by Jean Auguste Dominique Ingres.

Day Four – Grand Cayman

Jim had several autograph sessions throughout the cruise. Cathy would take a few items to each one. By the end of the trip, he signed everything that she had brought with her and even some things she picked up on the trip. He signed menus, napkins, all kinds of things. He was always very kind and extremely gracious. Jim Davis should be sainted. He signed hundreds, if not thousands, of items and posed for hundreds of pictures.

Even after the event was supposed to be over, he stayed until there was no longer anyone waiting on line. He joked that he could only see a little out of one eye from all the camera flashes going off and he was no longer able to move his fingers from all of the signing.

Jim Davis autographing Cathy's album included with her custom acrylic

Day Five – At Sea

These were the best days of the cruise because no one was going ashore; they always had a bunch of activities for the Garfield fans. The day started with the PJ party and character breakfast. Everybody met at a private dining room dressed in Garfield pajamas for the Garfield Pajama Party. That was a sight for sore eyes. Four hundred fully grown adults and a handful of children dressed up in lounge pants, pajamas, sweat pants, long shirts as tops (with no pants), and other hard-to-forget outfits.

Cathy and me at the Pajama Party with Garfield and Odie

The winner for both best male costume and best female costume were two men from California dressed in their wives' Garfield negligees. These guys were not small and their wives were small so the men looked like stuffed sausages in drag.

That is something that is very hard to un-see. I blurred their eyes to protect the should-be embarrassed.

Cooking with Garfield

The next event of the day was a cooking demonstration with Jim Davis, Garfield, and Odie. They were promoting the recent release of a Garfield cookbook, "I'm in the Mood for Food". I'm sure Jim doesn't spend a lot of time in the kitchen since the recipe they chose to make was popcorn balls. After the demonstration, Jim sketched Garfield drawings on the apron and chef's hat he was wearing. The apron and chef's hat were later auction items at the Garfield auction. If my memory is correct, they ended up fetching over $600 for both. At that rate, I'm sure a used Jim Davis napkin would have gotten at least $100.

The Garfield Auction

The final Garfield event for this already action packed day was the Garfield auction. The organizers brought onboard a whole bunch of Garfield collectibles for a private collectors' auction. Since we were already on a cruise ship that employed an auctioneer for the art gallery, they just used the ship's auctioneer for the Garfield auction.

I will never forget how badly the auctioneer underestimated our group. Her opening line was, "We wanted to give you all the opportunity to get Garfield items below the usual retail price." As soon as she said that the room burst into spontaneous laughter.

The auctioneer did not have any idea why we were laughing. Cathy and I were not so sure why everyone was laughing so hard either. This was our first exposure to a Garfield collectors' auction. We all soon figured it out when a $100 gift certificate to use for items in the "Garfield Stuff" catalog sold for $120. This is a piece of paper entitling you to spend $100 on the Garfield website selling for $20 more than its face value. The bidders rationalized this crazy purchase since it came in a leather Garfield checkbook cover.

For the entire auction, every item fetched hundreds and sometimes thousands of dollars. Later, discussing the cruise with Nancy Vega, the organizer of the Garfield Gathering, she admitted that she too was in disbelief. One of the items that sold for over $100 could have been purchased that day on her website www.NancysPlushToys.com for only $50. And she had experience with this crowd from past Garfield conventions!

I remember thinking after the fact that the smartest thing to do at the time of the auction was to go on the internet, specifically eBay, and bid on those items. After all, the top 200 collectors in the world were all busy on a ship at a private auction. But if you've ever been on a cruise, you know how expensive WIFI can be, so it probably would wind up being cheaper to stay at the auction on the ship. Cathy did get to raise her auction paddle at least once, but thankfully, did not win any of the items.

We were amazed at how much some of the items sold for. Some of the more notable items were several different prototypes of the Macy's 25th birthday plush that was available for the holiday season later that year. They sold for at least $350 up to $750. I've never seen any of them for sale and am not even sure exactly what they look like any longer. But that's an example of an item that may get into someone's hands who had no idea what you paid for it and who just thinks it's any old plush, and may sell it for a fraction of what you paid.

Doc Davis helping with the auction

Day 6 – Half Moon Cay - Holland America's Private Island

The day started with Garfield's Private Birthday Bash. The party was brought to the island and Garfield and Odie were all decked out in their beachwear. The cruise line has a private island, Half Moon Cay, in the Bahamas and we had a barbeque at one of the pavilions with games, trivia contests, and in the spirit of Garfield, more food.

Hey Lady. . . We've Given You All We Got.

When Cathy was at the party, she ended up taking hundreds of pictures of the Garfield and Odie costumes. While everyone else took a handful of pictures and moved on, Cathy was there for what must have felt like forever to the poor performers in the hot costumes. I'm sure there are only a handful of poses you can do in those costumes and they ended up doing them all for Cathy. This trip was right around the time that digital cameras were coming on the market. I remember Cathy being so reluctant to make the switch from film to digital, but I can only imagine how many rolls of film we would have gone through on this trip if I didn't convince her to make the switch.

Take Everything Even if it is Nailed Down

The collectors were voracious. We tried to get our hands on everything and anything Garfield. Not just the pens to write with, but the packaging, the wrapper, and the box the Garfield Pens came in.

The organizers were giving out pens for one of the Garfield trivia games. Some people would take a pen, pocket it and raise their hand that they needed a pen. There were boxes and boxes of Garfield pens, so I think some people were trying to get a complete set!

Cathy and I scored horribly on the trivia contest. We were all given consolation prizes. I think they were running out of prizes so they started taking down the birthday decorations and giving them out as prizes. We got a Garfield mobile, and when we were walking back to the tenders to go back to the ship, we ran into Jim and he signed our cardboard Garfield. We have had it hanging in our living room ever since.

Farewell Reception

This was the final event on the cruise. It was the most formal party to celebrate Garfield's 25th Birthday. It was held in one of the lounges on an upper deck. There was a Garfield ice carving, a huge sheet cake with pictures of the very first Garfield comic strip. Jim thanked everyone for coming on the cruise and promised he would do it again for Garfield's 50th Birthday! Garfield and Odie came out dressed up in sparkling tuxedo jackets and Garfield had a sparkling Happy Birthday sash across his chest. This was the last chance to win Garfield items and they had door prizes for everyone. I remember Cathy winning a set of marbles. Thankfully, something small and easy to pack to bring home.

Odie and Garfield dressed for success

Day Seven – Return to Port Canaveral

All packed up to go home. We had acquired many new Garfield treasures. We got t-shirts and pins with the 25th Birthday cruise logo on them. We bought beach towels with the logo on them. We kept menus and napkins from the lasagna luncheon.

We left the ship and ran into Jim one last time in the warehouse where you collect your suitcases that were taken off the ship earlier that morning. He was busy gathering his family's luggage and Cathy saw him. She went over to him and thanked him for organizing and coming on the trip. Even though he was busy, he stopped what he was doing and thanked her for being such a loyal fan and coming on the trip. They both said what a blast it was!

We would never have thought that that would wind up being our first encounter (of several more to come) with Jim Davis and the folks at Paws, Inc.

14

THE GARFIELD GATHERING (THE WHO, WHERE, AND WHAT)

Why Go to the Garfield Gathering?

First ... it helps if you are actually a Garfield collector. We assume this fact is obvious. Otherwise, you would be on vacation with a bunch of people who dress funny and talk too much about a cartoon cat.

I was skeptical at first. Cathy dragged me to our first event. Some town in the middle of Pennsylvania that I never heard of is usually not my idea of a vacation. A vacation is going someplace familiar such as Lake George, New York, or perhaps Orlando, Florida. You can never go wrong with Disney and other Orlando parks.

Looking back now, it is the randomness of somebody else picking the location for you that actually stretches our comfort zone. We would have never seen Pigeon Forge, Tennessee or San Antonio, Texas if it weren't for the fact that this is where the next group of people volunteered to host. We slowly learned that every city or town has something fun to do nearby.

"It is the Only Week of the Year that I Feel Normal."

When Cathy and I checked in to the first Garfield Gathering that we attended, the woman at registration said to us, "This week is the only week of the year that I feel normal." All year long people are saying things to us such as:

- "Don't you have enough Garfields?"
- "Why don't you sell some of them and make some money?"
- "Nobody collects Garfield anymore."
- "You are not going to be able to move around in your house."
- "Don't they just collect dust?"

There is a group called "Blind Melon" who made a rock video for the song "No Rain" where a girl is dressed up in a bumble bee costume. In the beginning of the video, she is made fun of, ostracized, ignored, and made to feel awkward. Towards the end of the video, she discovers a group of people all dressed up as bees. They dance and celebrate and she finally feels whole.

Like "Bee Girl" in the Blind Melon video, we are surrounded by people who have the same hobby, collecting Garfield. We don't have to explain, justify, or apologize to anyone in attendance. We can just buy, sell, and talk about Garfield with like-minded people in a nice vacation environment.

Every Gathering has…

I do not want to be redundant and mention the same types of events again and again. Every Garfield Gathering always has similar events. The events might include a dinner with games or other types of activities as mentioned below.

Opening Dinner

The first night is usually a dinner. It may or may not have a theme. The dinner often features a welcome message from Jim Davis. There are videos of personal collections playing, as of the 2009 event. The dinner features games to win Garfield items as well as raffle prizes.

A Major Get-Away (or 2 or 3)

There is always at least one group outing outside of the host hotel. It's usually a day trip to the most popular local attraction. We've been to several amusement parks, aquariums, river cruises, shows, and a zoo - just some of the examples.

Room Hopping

There is room hopping. This is when you can read a room list of attendees who are selling Garfield items and buy items right out of their rooms. Room hopping is usually open just after the dinner and can extend into the wee hours of the morning. There can be a dozen or so rooms to see, and you never know what you will find. It's a fun way to meet people and get caught up with people you haven't seen since the last convention.

Sale and Swap Meet

Some people who don't want to sell out of their rooms can buy tables for a trade-show-like event where they can sell Garfield items. Tables are very reasonable and if you have a lot of stuff to sell, you can purchase multiple tables. Some items are used and some are brand new. Cathy and I have taken a table at several conventions and usually sell new items. Occasionally, we may sell used items that Cathy bought as part of a group of items and are duplicates to things she already has. It's nice to make a couple bucks and help to defray the expenses associated with traveling to the convention. At the end of the event, there is usually a raffle.

Raffle Items

Winners are drawn for Garfield items at many of the dinners and events. There is the normal $1 raffle most of the nights, and there is a $5 raffle for premium items on the last night following the auction. Included in the raffles are items that are specific to that year's convention theme. There may be large plushes dressed up as witches for a Halloween theme, or elves for a Christmas theme. There are also items with that year's logo on them. They can be drinking glasses, towels, chairs, etc.

Closing Auction

The last night is a banquet dinner and live auction. Premium auction items are usually rare items only available in foreign markets or samples and prototypes. The last night also features the $5 raffle drawings. There are about a half dozen high value items that can be won. The first person chosen gets to pick the item he wants first, the second person gets to pick the second item and so on until all the items have been won.

Who hosted the First Convention?

There is some minor and fun-spirited controversy as to who hosted the first Garfield Gathering and where it was. The good news is that the people who are the possible "firsts" are all friends and it doesn't matter to them who the first really was.

The technicality is that the first convention was not called the Garfield Gathering. There was some overlap between who the key people were and who led to whom.

1993 Gary Skinner and Sherry Skinner's Get-Together - Indiana

Gary Skinner and his wife Sherry are good friends of the

Garfield community, both inside and out. Gary is a very high-end collector from the beginning and he even went so far as to have a business that exclusively sold Garfield items. If Gary cared, he could have probably beaten Cathy for the world record.

Prior to the first get-together, there were three or four Garfield collectors' clubs that frequently communicated by mail, and every now and then, had a long-distance phone call with each other.

When the clubs found out there was going to be a "Garfield Fun Run" in the Muncie, Indiana area, they decided they needed to be a part of it. Gary already had a good relationship with Paws, Inc. so he arranged to get special privileges for the collectors when they were in the area of the Fun Run.

In 1993, with some help and the permission of Paws, Inc., Gary hosted a small group of collectors in Anderson, Indiana. The base of operations was the basement of a church where they exchanged information, sold, traded items, and had other activities.

He was asked to keep it under 40 people since this had never been done before. One can admit that this was the first collectors' convention. Looking back now, part of keeping it small resulted in some bonus surprises.

The collectors were given a private tour of Paws, Inc. To a Garfield collector, this is like a Christian visiting Jerusalem and even getting to meet Jesus. Yes, Jim Davis was there.

Other activities included a pizza party. Some local businesses donated door prizes for the group and the cherry on top of the ice cream sundae was a dinner at Vince's, a restaurant that was owned by Jim Davis - and Jim covered the entire tab.

Gary Skinner – Inside and Out

I said earlier that Gary was a friend of the Garfield community both inside and out but I never clarified what that meant. Since Gary lives in Indiana, he was one of the people that can just pop in to Paws, Inc. and interact with people. He was never an employee of the company, but over time, he became a very trusted liaison to the collectors. Paws knew he would represent them well and he was often their semi-official delegate at the convention. He also brought items from Paws to sell for them.

The Missing Links, Bob and Gretchen Gibson

Bob and Gretchen Gibson were in attendance at the first get-together with Gary and Sherry Skinner. They were part of the Garfield clubs and collectors community.

In the years in between 1993 and 1999, the groups continued to get together. We apologize in advance for these details being omitted from this book. This is not because the events were not significant; it is simply because Cathy and I started getting involved in 2006 and were only able to recreate the folklore from the people who still attend.

Many of the original collectors and organizers no longer attend or have since passed away, so we were not fortunate enough to have met them. The foundation that they built has led up to the Garfield Gathering as we know it today.

1999 Nancy and Bob - Denver, Pennsylvania (The first "Garfield Gathering")

Gary had the first Garfield Collectors get-together, but the Garfield Gathering as we know it today started in 1999 at a home in Denver, Pennsylvania. It was the home of Gretchen and Bob Gipson, mentioned above. They even managed to get the official Garfield costume from Paws, Inc. Many of the people who attended this event still attend today.

Nancy and Manny Vega and Gretchen and Bob Gipson were the original primary organizers and they have put together future events for years to come.

The Garfield Gathering (the Who, Where, and What) | 267

Fun Fact – Bob Gipson also wrote a book about Garfield collectibles.

Nancy also has a business which is a great place to purchase Garfield items: www.NancysPlushToys.com.

The Structure of the Group

Around 2009, Bob and Gretchen took more of a back seat, while Nancy and Manny continued to be the primary organizers. Other people picked up the slack, such as Jubilant Joy, Tony Capuano Jr., Barbara and Romeo Basconcillo, Pat Wade, Phyllis and Bill Clayton, and Jerri Berry, to name only a few.

A "Host" is the official person - or people - of the current year who take on the responsibilities of being a local contact and organizer for that year. There is always a small army of people helping set-up, doing registration, manning games, selling tickets, holding up auction items, and other vital functions.

Since 2009, Cathy and I began to take on new roles helping the event by running audio-visuals, hosting games, and helping find and organize auction items. Prior to us, Barbara and Romeo Basconcillo took on the responsibility of collecting the auction items.

2000 St. Louis, Missouri - Tony

Anthony (Tony) Capuano Jr. hosted the 2000 Garfield Convention in St. Louis, Missouri.

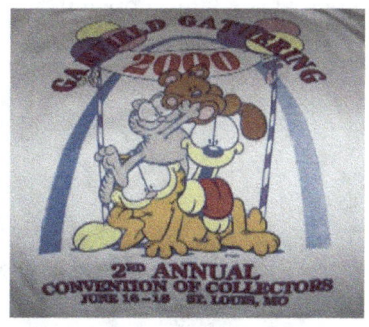

Tony has always been very involved in helping out with the conventions. He helped with ordering and selling the shirts for the events. Tony was also one of the more technology-savvy attendees.

The still photos shown for the 1999 convention were taken from live video that Tony provided to me in later years.

Jim Davis sent a great video to open up the 2000 convention.

Sadly, in January 2015, Tony passed away from complications after a tragic car accident. He was struck by a truck in a parking lot and never recovered from his injuries. He has been missed very much at the latest conventions.

Tony and his mother. She loved to join him at the events.

2001 Pittsburgh, Pennsylvania - Janice Bunch

This gathering was hosted by Janice Bunch. Besides the usual activities, such as eating, eating and eating, 2001 featured a fun getaway trip to Kennywood Amusement park in West Mifflin, Pennsylvania, which is very close to Pittsburgh.

As you can see from the banner below, Kennywood is one of the amusement parks that had theming for the Garfield family of characters. This is an obvious spot to hold a convention.

I am sure the attendees of the event were even more enthusiastic than the children at the amusement park when watching the Garfield-themed shows and posing by the Garfield games.

The Kennywood 25th birthday banner shown here was produced in 2003, a little after the 2001 convention. The banner was purchased by us years ago. Probably a resourceful employee put it up for sale or perhaps the amusement park arranged the sale themselves.

2002 Des Moines, Iowa – Barbara and Romeo Basconcillo

Des Moines, Iowa is one of the few locations that repeated as a location for hosting. This usually happens when the host is an insider who picks up the slack if nobody volunteered to host the upcoming event.

At other times hosting is repeated if the location is worthy - such as in Hershey, Pennsylvania where the fun is built in.

According to a fun Facebook post, when we crowdsourced some details for this book, it was recalled that the events in Des Moines included a pizza dinner Thursday night, a zoo as an outing and possibly a trip to the botanical gardens.

2003 Muncie, Indiana – Paws / Gary Skinner

2003 was a special year for the Collectors Convention since it was Garfield's 25th birthday year and Paws, Inc. headed up the planning for the entire event. People who attended that year said that the entire town was involved one way or another. Restaurants were selling more lasagna than ever before since that is Garfield's favorite meal.

One of the big events and highlights for the collectors was a tour of Paws, Inc. For a collector, this is like telling Trekkies that the event will be held on the bridge of the Starship Enterprise.

According to my sources, one of the dinners was also a dance with a live band. The Garfield and Odie costumes made appearances all over town.

Another event in Muncie that some Garfield collectors also attended was called the "Fat Cat Walk-a-Thon." I believe it was a fundraiser for an animal charity. The usual sale and swap meet took place, as well as room hopping.

We have a copy of The Star Press newspaper that reveals the entire weekend agenda:

Friday June 20, 2003 "Garfield's Escape the Daily Grind Day"

- 9am: Fat Cat walk/run for business executives at the cancer center at Ball Memorial Hospital
- 10am to 7pm: Garfield marketplace, live radio remote - downtown and surrounding area
- 11am to 2pm: Lasagna lunch at participating downtown restaurants
- 11am to 8pm: Vendors, inflatable games, face painting, clowns, dunk tank – downtown
- 1pm, 3pm and 5pm: "A Cat for All Seasons" planetarium show – Central High School

- 8pm to 11pm: "The Furr Ball", casual dance with the Marlins – Horizon Convention Center

Saturday June 21, 2003 "Garfield's Family Fun Day"

- 10am to 4pm: Food and gift vendors downtown, street entertainment, coloring contest and Garfield marketplace; "Fat Cat Car Show" – downtown
- 10am: "Big Fat Hairy Birthday Parade" and "Garfield on the Town" art projects, both downtown
- 11am and 2pm: Cartoon workshops by Paws Artists – Horizon Center
- Noon to 6pm: Muncie Astronomy Club offers peek at the sun through high-powered telescopes during summer solstice, Central High School
- 1pm, 4pm and 5pm: A Cat for All Seasons, Planetarium Show – Central High School
- 5pm to 7pm: Concert featuring ETC. Band – Downtown

Reveal of the 25th Birthday Statues

10am Saturday was the first time the world laid their eyes on the 25 unique Garfield statues that were all poured from the same mold and painted by different community artists.

Photo provided by Tony Caputo Jr.

Most of these statues are still owned by local community businesses and not-for-profit organizations. Some are in private collections. Cathy and I are proud to own the "Garfred Rogers" statue that was made by the local **PBS TV** station to memorialize the famous Mr. Rogers.

This was taken back when we had less stuff

These statues have slowly been scattering in the wind like dandelions. We could have posted a chapter on each statue and where it is now but many of the facts are unknown, like ours, in a private home; we would probably not want some authors to print where we live and where to find us. There are several pages written online such as in Wikipedia that are more dynamic than a book. Check our website www.LovesGarfield.com. This, too, is a dynamic home of Garfield content.

2003 Caribbean Cruise

Chapter 13 is devoted to the 25th birthday cruise. If you did not read that chapter, now would be a good time to do so. We'll wait for you to come back. Be sure to bookmark this page so you know where to come back and continue reading. Please don't  Odie ear the pages in the book, creases like that are not necessary and can lessen the collector value of the book.

2004 Hershey, Pennsylvania – Nancy and Manny Vega

You guessed it. How can there be an event in Hershey, Pennsylvania without going to Hershey Park? Nancy and Manny Vega were the primary organizers and it was pretty close to their home.

Since Nancy, the organizer, loves Garfield Western items, the event theme was, predictably, Western.

2005 Bristol, Connecticut – Pauline Chung

The main event was a day at Lake Compounce Amusement Park in Connecticut. At the time, it was one of only a few amusement parks that were themed with Garfield. As you can imagine, for Garfield collectors this is a very big deal.

Cathy and I did not attend the convention, but we did go to Lake Compounce several years later.

2006 Williamsport, Pennsylvania – Patti Aikeley and Susie Caskey

This was the first convention that Cathy and I attended. The main event was a chartered riverboat cruise aboard the Hiawatha

Paddlewheel boat on the Susquehanna River followed by a barbeque.

I remember it was raining, but since everything was covered, it was still a good day out. We took a trolley ride to where the boat was docked and the barbecue was under a covered pavilion. A couple renewed their wedding vows that afternoon.

Left to right: Susie, Doc Davis and Patty. Doc is presenting a thank you gift for hosting. Photo Courtesy of Patti Aikeley

The theme of the gathering was Christmas. Christmas in June. One of the themed events was a pajama party. Believe me, you do not want to see grown adults in their PJ's. I will spare you the photos. I will also spare our fellow attendees the embarrassment. Santa was there and gave everyone in attendance a gift.

During the barbeque, Marge and Chuck renewed their vows at the event.

Midnight Madness

Doc Davis and Gary Skinner were at the event representing Paws, Inc. They were selling out of their hotel rooms hundreds of rare and collectible items at a really fair price.

On Saturday night, some more stock came out of the cargo trailer and it was dubbed "Midnight Madness." Wow … prices started at free and went up from there. All of the attendees of the event were squeezing their way into the rooms. We even spilled out into the halls.

It was close, but we almost got thrown out of the hotel for making so much noise. From that event on, future hotels were advised to put all the collectors together, so we would not disturb other hotel guests.

Cathy purchased a barbecue acrylic from Doc Davis

Doc Math

When Doc Davis used to attend the Garfield Gathering, there was a phenomenon known as "Doc Math". "Doc Math" was what happens when Doc Davis added up all of the purchases that somebody made in the official Paws, Inc. (Garfield corporate) room. "Doc Math" was very generous. If you had $1,000 worth of merchandise that you were ready to purchase, Doc Davis would only charge you $600 for everything.

In contrast, for a few years, Doc's daughter, Sherri, would do what most people would call "Math". There have been many attempts to teach her "Doc Math" but apparently, she has an accounting degree and "Doc Math" does not work for her. We would lovingly badger her about "Doc Math" and she might eventually break down and give us an extra discount.

2006 was also when Doc Davis retired from Paws, Inc. and decided to take some time off from the Garfield Gathering. He could not keep away and joined us again a few years later. Photo Courtesy of Patti Aikeley

Competition for 2007

Throughout the weekend, the people interested in hosting the convention for the following year campaigned for their area and proposed events. I remember Michigan, West Virginia and West Palm Beach all being contenders. After the votes were tallied, it was announced that West Palm Beach had won the bid to host the 2007 convention.

2007 West Palm Beach, Florida – What a zoo!

2007 … What a zoo. No, literally. We went to the Palm Beach Zoo as our major outing. It was a fairly nice facility. There were interesting animals, and we walked around in small groups and at our own pace.

Having been to West Palm

Beach many times, we still managed to find some fun things to do on our own, like the amphibious Duck Boat tour of the city.

As usual, we also had dinners, raffles, room hopping, sale & swap meet and the auction.

2008 Pigeon Forge, Tennessee – Pat Wade

We have never been more impressed with a city than we were with Pigeon Forge, Tennessee. We were expecting just a day at Dollywood Amusement Park, but we were given an entire city of amazing tourist attractions. This was a Las Vegas for families. Cathy and I like to arrive a day early in case we run into any delays while traveling. We drove to Gatlinburg and rode up a chair lift to catch the scenic view of the Smoky Mountains. We rode go-carts and saw an IMAX movie. It was a great trip but, we couldn't understand why people had to blow their horns when driving through tunnels. We live on Long Island and have driven through several tunnels to get into New York City. No one has ever blown his horn the way they do in Tennessee. But looking back now, I guess that's why there's so many signs all over when entering the tunnels here to NOT blow your horn. I've Googled it many times and it seems there is no real reason why people do it.

Dollywood

The main events for the Garfield convention were a day at Dollywood followed by the Dixieland Stampede dinner. It was so much fun. Dollywood is a world class amusement park and the dinner was fabulous.

Since Cathy and I had now attended a few conventions, we felt that it was time to toss our hat into the ring and try to win the bid to host the 2009 convention. Also offering to host 2009 was a family from San Antonio, Texas. Our theme was, "Stay in New Jersey and Play in New York City." Cathy and I found a hotel on the river in New Jersey that was right next to a ferry terminal that goes straight to Manhattan. Knowing that we were up against San Antonio, Texas, we prepared a slideshow and had pamphlets showcasing the possible activities in New York City. Although we lost by only three votes, we learned several valuable lessons and developed new ideas that were used from that day forward. We had become friends with the couple that won the bid and told them some of the ideas we had to enhance some of the events. They liked the ideas and we collaborated with them to implement some of our ideas at the 2009 convention.

Lead with Your Strengths

They say to "lead with your strengths." My strengths are in website design, graphics, technology, and video production. This is because I own a website design and video production business. In the past years at the Garfield Gathering, we observed that the only audio-visual used was a microphone. With our ideas, that was all about to change. We were going to drag the Garfield Gathering into the 21st century.

AV Ideas

By simply adding a computer, projector and screen to the festivities, we opened the event up to an entire world of interactive fun and new games. It just so happened that I own several laptops, projectors, a twelve-foot screen and a 1,000-watt sound system, so there were no added costs involved. Sure, you could rent all of these items from the hotel, but the charges can be quite high.

Collections Video Idea

Cathy and I observed that the prior gatherings only appeared to be Garfield clothing conventions. This was because people were so space conscious of suitcase and car sizes to bring home their new purchases that they would never consider bringing pieces to show and share. Some people had photo albums and flip books, which probably gave us a new idea.

We asked attendees to email me photographs of their collections (and a photo of themselves) and I would add the face and name to the photo and create an audio-visual slideshow of their collections. We would play the photos on a continuous loop while people were getting seated and mingling before the night's dinner.

Welcome Message and Paws, Inc. Tour

Cathy and I were planning a trip very close to where Paws, Inc.'s headquarters is located in Muncie, so we called and pre-arranged a tour of their facility. We were hoping that we would get to meet Jim Davis again and maybe even get him to record a welcome message to show to the collectors at the upcoming convention.

Our contact gave us a tour of the entire Paws, Inc. facility and I was able to film it. The idea was to capture the tour so other collectors could also experience what they have inside Paws Inc.'s main office. Some collectors had already been to Muncie for the 2003 convention but, Cathy and I did not attend any convention until 2006. So, it was a real treat for us to have a private tour of their facility.

While we were being shown around, the man himself, Jim Davis, came walking down the hall. He said hello to us and asked us why we were in town. I told him about the convention and that we were filming so other collectors could see the inside of headquarters. I asked if he would mind saying a few words to the collectors. He smiled and said, "Sure, have you seen Mona Pizza yet? We said no, so he took us around the corner to the art piece titled "Mona Pizza" and filmed a welcome message. He was great. In one take, he welcomed everyone to the convention and told us about some new ideas coming up over the horizon.

"Mona Pizza" was a painting created for the 2007 Garfield calendar, "Fat Cat Masterpieces". Each month of the calendar showcased a world-renowned piece of art, but with a Garfield twist. "Mona Pizza" was a nod to Leonardo DaVinci's painting "Mona Lisa".

This video of all the footage we captured at Paws, Inc. was edited and shown for the first time at the 2009 convention in Texas. We played it before the dinner on the first night when people were getting seated. The collectors were very excited to see behind the scenes of the offices and studios where Garfield is produced.

Statues Video, Muncie Tour, and Muncie Children's Museum

Indiana is less known for tourism and more known for farming and growing corn so it is funny to find out that Cathy and I scheduled extra vacation days in the area to sightsee. As I already outlined in chapter 12, Cathy and I took extra time and drove from county to county to film and photograph the Garfield Trail. For months before the trip, Cathy researched everything and anything Garfield-related so we wouldn't miss anything on the trip.

The Garfield Gathering (the Who, Where, and What) | 285

Cathy feeding Garfield some great homemade ice cream.

At the time, the Muncie Children's Museum also had a large exhibit that featured Garfield. We were given permission to film and photograph anything except visiting children.

The drive to Muncie took about 15 hours but it was well worth it. We stopped along the way at the Rock and Roll Hall of Fame in Ohio. We stayed overnight at Cedar Point Amusement Park and even made a quick stop to the famous house featured in the timeless classic, "A Christmas Story".

2009 San Antonio, Texas – Stuart and Ronan Harrison

I believe the temperature in Texas was the hottest of any year that Cathy and I attended. It was over 100 degrees outside every day we were there. I guess it doesn't really help when the convention always takes place in June, around Garfield's birthday. We can thank Jim Davis for that. Couldn't he have been inspired to release Garfield in February? I  guess we would be complaining about snow if that were the case! When we were at Sea World for our outing, people were fighting over who got to sit in the splash zone. That is where the Orcas swim past the audience waving and drenching everyone in the first couple of rows completely with water. Salty, yet briefly refreshing!

The theme for San Antonio, Texas was, "Remember the A la Mode." The logo was custom-made by Paws, Inc. depicting Garfield eating ice cream in front of the historic Alamo fort.

Observation Trivia

Since we had so much video footage of everything we had seen in Muncie, we came up with a new, fun game to play after one of the dinners. We played about a 10-minute video and then asked several questions based on what the collectors just observed. Frankly, the game was very hard and very cruel. Cathy and I would not have known the answers except for the fact that we had the answer sheet. You had to really pay attention to the tiniest details in the video to get a perfect score.

River Walk

A very popular attraction in San Antonio, Texas is the River Walk. It's a city park with walkways all along the banks of the San Antonio River. It's located one story below street level. There are restaurants and shops along the way. You can access the River Walk from multiple stairways and ramps. There are pedestrian bridges that cross over the river. You can even take a tour boat around the river. It's a definite must-do if you ever visit San Antonio.

Remember the A la Mode

As mentioned above, the slogan for this convention was "Remember the A la Mode" and had Garfield holding a multi-scoop ice cream cone as the graphic. This was, of course, a reference to the famous "Remember the Alamo" slogan. We took a tour of the Alamo fort. The tour guides were passionate about getting the message out about the bloody history of this famous battle zone. What remains of the fort was surprisingly small and it is hard to imagine being under siege in the middle of nowhere before they built the multiplex movie theater and the shopping mall next door. Despite the modernization of the area, the tour guides made sure the message of the soldiers' sacrifice was understood loud and clear. It is very hallowed ground and extreme respect should be practiced when visiting.

Sea World

There is so much to do at Sea World. It has great shows, rides and attractions. We are not going to step into the middle of the captivity controversy when it comes to orcas, also known as killer whales. In 2009, Sea World was in full-show operations with trainers actually entering the water and interacting with these massive creatures. The shows were breathtaking and inspiring.

Cathy and I are unofficial enthusiasts of hair-raising roller coasters and Sea World boasted quite a few. They were tall, fast, and action-packed. I'm sure they've added many new things since we visited. This is the largest Sea World park of several locations around the country.

At each group meal at the host hotel, using my laptop and projector, we would play a video that I edited of a Garfield related subject. Sometimes it was the Garfield Trail, other times it was the Muncie Children's Museum or perhaps our first trip to Paws, Inc.

Games after Lunch

To change things up from our usual trivia questions and word search games, the organizers decided to have some relay races outside the hotel. This turned out to be a pretty bad idea.

I mentioned earlier that one reason people love Garfield was that he hates exercise. I hate to generalize since there are probably a few world-class athletes who like Garfield but, overall, our little group does not take well to running and physical activities.

During a relay race, there were two people who were injured.

One person had a twisted ankle and another person had a sprained elbow.

Right after the person injured her ankle, Crazy Gary came over and started feeling her leg. She seemed a bit surprised at first; luckily, I was there to tell her that he was a trained EMT. Once the identity confusion was cleared up, his recommendation based on the assessment was to go to the hospital. His instinct was right because she came back in a cast.

From this day forward it was decided that the group should formally stay away from physical races and other similar activities.

2010 - Another Trip to Muncie

One of the great reasons to attend the conventions is to find out about the availability of Garfield items that you may not already know about. When we met Jo at the 2006 convention, she told Cathy about the Pachinko machine. When we got home, Cathy immediately set up an eBay search for a Garfield Pachinko machine. After many months, one came up for bid and Cathy was able to snatch it up.

At the 2009 convention we were talking with some people and they said the Garfield slot machines were being phased out and you could find them available for sale. I put a shout-out on our website, if anyone was selling a slot machine to please contact us. A guy in Michigan contacted us in the late winter in 2010 and said he had a Garfield slot machine available for sale. He didn't want to ship the machine because it could be a little temperamental and he wanted to make sure that everything worked. So, we asked him if he could wait until the weather was a little nicer and we would plan to drive out and pick it up.

We did some research and figured that if we were already going to drive to Michigan, Muncie Indiana can't be that far out of the way. We reached out to our contact at Paws and arranged to meet and film Jim again. This time he knew we were coming, so he had more information ready to give the collectors as part of his welcome message. He also filmed a goodbye message for us to show at the last night of the convention.

2010 Williamsburg, Virginia – Rick and Dawn Paxton

Because this is such an historic area filled with a rich American heritage, our theme for this convention was Americana. Our logo featured Garfield and Odie dressed in Colonial garb with Odie playing the drum.

Busch Gardens --- Williamsburg, VA

Our grand outing in 2010 was to Busch Gardens Williamsburg in Virginia. Just like Sea World in San Antonio, Texas, the roller coasters were world class and the shows were fun.

Colonial Williamsburg

The convention hotel was located close enough that some collectors also visited historic Colonial Williamsburg. This historic town consists of many colonial buildings and re-enactments of the era.

Sadly, in 2016, Dawn passed away after a long bout with cancer. She has been sorely missed at the conventions.

The Garfield Gathering (the Who, Where, and What) | 291

Rick and Dawn Paxton with Garfield. Jubilant Joy was in the costume.

2011 Long Island, New York – Cathy and Robert Kothe (hey that's us!)

2011 was the year that Cathy and I hosted the Garfield Gathering. This was such a major highlight of our Garfield-centric life that we gave it its own chapter. The next chapter is all about the year that we hosted.

15

2011, THE YEAR WE HOSTED THE GARFIELD GATHERING (THE WHO, WHAT, WHERE, WHEN, WHY AND HOW TO)

In 2011, Cathy and I hosted the Garfield Collectors Convention on Long Island, New York. We supersized the event to include more of everything: more multimedia, more games, more events, and more Garfield licensees. We even got custody of the official Garfield costume for the week. Many people say it was one of the best conventions ever.

The 2011 New York Logo

Usually the logo for the convention is picked out from pre-made Garfield stock art and modified to fit the event. Our logo was actually conceptualized by Cathy and myself, while Paws, Inc., the parent company of Garfield, stylized it to be perfectly Garfield and cartoonish.

We went back and forth with Paws, Inc. over the logo for the convention. They wanted something that represented New York City. People were suggesting that we use Garfield with a big apple or Garfield dressed up as the Statue of Liberty.

Cathy and I wanted something that characterized Long Island, specifically. If you know anything about New York, you know that it is HUGE with very distinct differences across each region. There is upstate New York, the five boroughs of New York City and Long Island. Each area has a very different atmosphere. So, we wanted people to know that they were coming to Long Island. Long Island is a suburb of New York City, miles away from the downtown area and very pretty. Long Island is a destination known for its beaches, lighthouses, boating, and fishing. What better landmark to feature than the Montauk Lighthouse.

Backing up a little, in 2008 when we were campaigning to host the 2009 convention, we only lost by only three votes. We learned from some people that they had concerns that New York City is a scary place and they might get mugged. Everyone who knows modern day New York City would realize that Disney purchased it and it is now the backdrop to endless Disney Broadway productions based on old cartoons. New York City is now like the crazy college friend who got married and coaches little league while driving a minivan. Nothing to be scared of there. While hosting on Long Island, we needed to distance us from the city and the lighthouse was just the thing.

I took a photograph of the Montauk Lighthouse and made it

cartoony. I put a stock photo of Garfield and friends in front of it and submitted it to Paws.

An artist at Paws had the even better idea of making Garfield climb the lighthouse like he was King Kong and the 2011 Logo was born.

I bartered my life away to get the costume, get a licensee, and get a professional auctioneer. We took what we liked most about past conventions and did more of it. If giving away the centerpieces from the dinner tables was a highlight of usually only the last night's dinner, we made a centerpiece for each group meal and gave each of them away.

Speaking of centerpieces, Cathy and I made replicas of the lighthouse in Montauk, New York. It took us about 90 hours to make 18 lighthouses. They were cut from quarter inch plywood. We hand painted them. The centerpieces were designed to collapse so people could pack them in their suitcases to travel home. The lighthouse had a battery-operated tea light candle on top in the dome and lit up. Shown is a lighthouse on the table with Tina and her mom. We met Tina and Trish at the Texas convention and it turned out they live on Long Island. We have since become very close friends with them and get together very often to show off our new items.

The reason we made the centerpieces replicas of the Montauk lighthouse was because the logo depicted Garfield scaling the Long Island landmark. Then we affixed a Garfield plush animal to the centerpiece and it was ready for the first night's dinner.

Later in 2014, we had the lighthouse signed by Jim Davis when we were at Paws, Inc. for the world record book signing and photo shoot. See the alphabetical listing for more details in chapter 8.

Attention to details was the key to us hosting the 2011 convention. At two locations where we had events, Adventureland Amusement Park and the Atlantis Aquarium, we convinced the parks to stock the carnival games and claw machines with Garfield plushes.

The Request for Proposal – In General (How To)

I said there would be some "How To" in this chapter and if you are considering hosting a convention you should start with a "Request for Proposal". This is a document that is distributed to your local visitor's bureau and describes the event and what to expect. Hotels can create a quote based on the description or simply choose to pass on submitting a bid.

Part of our Request for Proposal was disclosing the fact that some in the group are big eaters and we don't ever want to run out of food. We ran out one year and we never want that to happen again, even if they had to charge us more money to guarantee sufficient food.

We also disclosed that room-hopping could be loud and distracting. The hotel should try to keep our group together on the same floor and not around other guests.

Another piece of the Request for Proposal was the need for a conference room or a storage room. This space insured we were not leaving inventory in trailers and cars. It also gave organizers a staging area where we could set up centerpieces and get together for logistical meetings. The room had to be near our event rooms and easy to get to.

The Request for Proposal for the 2011 Event

When Cathy and I knew we were the winning bid, to choose a final winning hotel to host the convention, we wrote up a Request for Proposal describing the event in detail. As I already mentioned, the Request for Proposal contained all of our requirements. It outlined the predicted number of attendees and the types of events we needed catered at the host hotel.

At first, I personally called and emailed the event managers at all of the hotels that I thought would be large enough and had the proper facilities (ie. Banquet rooms). Eventually, we discovered that the Long Island Visitors Bureau had a distribution list to forward the RFP to every hotel on Long Island.

The best part was that the winning hotel came from the Long Island Visitors Bureau list and not from the original hotels that I handpicked.

The Hyatt Hotel in Hauppauge, Long Island was and still is a five-star facility with a world class golf course, tennis courts, indoor and outdoor pools, hot tubs, and plenty of catering space. They were easy to work with and they took really good care of us. Ironically, Cathy and I had stayed at this hotel the night of our wedding, but we both completely forgot about it and were very happy that they contacted us. Everyone in attendance was very impressed with the hotel.

The hotel alone was an experience that attendees would not forget. Since it was such a nice facility they really felt like they were on vacation. Thanks to the RFP, they found us and we were able to do business. Knowing that Jim Davis is an avid golfer, Cathy and I were hoping that maybe the golf course on the property would entice him to come to the convention, but unfortunately he did not attend.

The Notebook

Once we knew that 2011 was going to be on Long Island, Cathy and I carried a paper notebook everywhere we went for brainstorming new ideas to make the event better than ever. Everything was written in the notebook. Some ideas were good. Some were stupid. Some ideas actually saw the light of day and were implemented. But, make sure to write everything down. One stupid idea could lead the way to a great idea. We fixated on making the event better than ever and carried that notebook everywhere we went and just kept coming up with ideas and details.

Game Ideas --- The Price was What?

Cathy had a great idea to keep track of items that sold on eBay during the year leading up the convention that were either really expensive or really undervalued. We called the game, "gBay – The Price was What?" The game was inspired by eBay.com, an online auction website where people buy and sell items. It is on eBay.com where Cathy picks up most of her collectibles as do other collectors, so everyone would be very familiar with the format.

On eBay.com, items are occasionally sold for a ridiculously high price or a criminally low price. On the higher side were a few packs of Garfield scratch-and-sniff stickers that sold for over $300. On the low side would be a rare Enesco figurine that sold for a little over a dollar. It was probably worth over $200.

We designed a practice round, ten official rounds, and a bonus round. Each round highlighted a different item.

I hosted the game. I would display a picture of the item on PowerPoint with the price covered up. I would then read the description out loud. Next, I asked people to write down their guesses. Everybody was asked to stand up. Three more slides would slowly reveal the selling price. As people were eliminated they would sit down. The person closest to the selling price, without going over, would win a Garfield prize.

The gBay creation was such a big hit that we continue to make and host the game every year.

2008: Promise to Doc

In 2008, when we were bidding to host the 2009 event, Doc Davis, Jim Davis' brother and the inspiration for the Garfield character, "Doc Boy," was at the event. I asked him to say a few words on camera. He pointed out that he was a bit apprehensive since it would show favoritism over the Texas bid. I assured him that even if we lost the bid we would implement the audio-video ideas at the Texas event.

Even though we lost by three votes, we kept our promise to implement all of the multimedia ideas in Texas. The family hosting Texas loved the ideas and they were the first to have all of the technology at their event.

2011: The First Year of Multiple Events

One observation that Cathy and I made about past events was

that several times the activities were held in the evening only. That would leave people to have free time to figure out what they wanted to do during the day. We wanted to change that so people would always be doing some kind of event.

The Atlantis Aquarium

In Riverhead, New York, out on the east end of Long Island is the Atlantis Aquarium. This was the perfect choice for our official major get-away activity. It had enough to do and see in an afternoon. It had catering space for lunch and indoor areas in the event of rain. It was reasonably priced and it was not too strenuous for older individuals or people who were out of shape.

The way the aquarium priced its entrance fee, it was actually cheaper to buy a season pass than to pay for two visits. Cathy and I purchased season passes to the aquarium about a year before the event and we were able to go back a few times to take pictures, video and gather fun facts for trivia questions and games.

On the day that the Garfield Gathering went to the aquarium, people were able to walk around on their own and see whatever exhibits they wanted. We had a catered lunch in their event room, and brought in a couple of sheet cakes with the 2011 Garfield Gathering logo printed on them. We had bought little fish bowls that were battery-operated, so it looked like their fishes were swimming around. We printed the 2011 convention logo on clear labels and stuck them to the side of each fish bowl. We played some games after lunch and then people were able to go back and see the rest of the exhibits and shows. The Atlantis Aquarium in Riverhead, New York was very accommodating and everyone had a great time.

Adventureland (Optional)

For the 2011 event, we created an optional, un-official event for people who were looking for something to do. In our area is a small amusement park called Adventureland. Adventureland has free parking, free admission, and plenty of things to do. There was an arcade for people who wanted to play games. People could also purchase a pay-one-price wristband or buy individual tickets to go on the rides. Adventureland even agreed to stock the claw machines and a Whack-A-Mole carnival game with Garfield prizes. (See below for the full story)

We found out who wanted to go to Adventureland and made sure they had transportation to the park. It was a great way to spend the afternoon while other people might have taken a train into New York City to see the sites or go to a beach or do any other activity that they may have been interested in doing. Some people were big fans of "Diners, Drive-thrus and Dives" and wanted to find the location featured on the show. In January 2011, Food Network had featured Pitstop in Merrick on their show "Diners, Drive-thrus and Dives".

Catch the Moment Licensee

When we were planning the 2011 event, I was contacted by a new licensee of Paws, Inc. called "Catch the Moment." It is a professional photo company that goes around and helps major sponsors with photo booths at events.

At first, I consulted with "Catch the Moment" to get them up to speed on the Garfield world. Later, we all decided they would set up at the 2011 Garfield Gathering Sale and Swap Meet so people could have their pictures taken with Garfield. They created a package with different poses, and using their technology, they would put you in the picture with Garfield. They set up a green screen and would have you sit or stand in a specific pose depending on the background that would fill in the final production photo. You could be driving an ice cream truck with Garfield hanging off the back, riding a rollercoaster with Garfield, serving lasagna to Garfield. We wanted something very specific to Long Island also, so you could give a high-five to Garfield in front of the Montauk Lighthouse.

Behind the scenes of Catch the Moment

After the software does its magic

The Garfield Costume

Another premium feature Cathy and I provided at the 2011 Garfield Gathering was the use of the official Garfield costume. Only at the earliest conventions did the fat cat himself make any appearances. Then it became much too costly to rent the official Garfield costume. Since I was bartering my life away to put 2011 over the top, I figured we had nothing to lose, so I contacted the rental company Milestone Event Services. I promised them video footage to display on their website. We only had to pay the shipping charges. Since I film for a living, I was I was able to provide high-definition video footage to the rental company in return. I joked that between that and other barter arrangements, I sold my soul to make the event more of a success.

Garfield Goes to the Prom

In another ballroom at the host hotel, a high school prom was taking place. When the teachers and chaperones found out that we had Garfield, they asked if he could make an appearance at the dance. He was a big hit.

After he danced with the kids for a little while, all of the teachers posed for a picture with Garfield outside the banquet hall.

The Lighthouse Centerpieces

It is customary to have a unique table centerpiece that matches the theme of the convention. Cathy and I decided to woodwork hand-made lighthouses that look just like the Montauk Lighthouse in the logo.

Words cannot describe the number of hours we put into the

project. They were made out of 1/8-inch plywood and were custom fit to an octagonal base. The outside was painted white and red. The windows were painted gray. The light globe was an upside down plastic champagne glass that Cathy painstakingly painted with black nail polish. Cathy wound electrical tape around the bottom of the globe fixture and lined the side with car pinstriping tape so they would look like exact replicas of the Montauk Lighthouse. We affixed a decal with the 2011 Garfield Gathering logo on it. Nancy provided the Garfield plush to attach to the sides in order to look like the logo. We put a fish bowl with a battery-operated fish swimming in it on the base platform.

I joked that no two were alike since I could not cut a straight line.

Centerpiece Giveaway at Every Meal

Prior to 2011, it was customary to give away the table centerpieces at the end of the last dinner. It was Cathy's idea to have a different centerpiece for every meal and give them away immediately after that meal. The idea caught on and the more recent conventions also have separate centerpieces for each meal.

Stock the Claw Machines

Another fun idea Cathy and I had was to arrange with the Atlantis Aquarium events department and with Adventureland to stock the claw machines in the casino with Garfield plush.

One of the licensees had the authority to produce amusement park stuffed animals. You need to have a carnival license to buy from them. Since both the Aquarium and Adventureland already had an account with them, it was easy enough to get the items.

To make sure the Aquarium and Adventureland were not stuck with un-won Garfields, we agreed to purchase any un-won items at the end of the event. The interesting part was that Adventureland did not have any un-won items. Throughout the weekend, other park visitors were asking for the Garfield plushes as their prize.

The Aquarium had left-over prizes so, as promised, we bought the un-won portion from them. This was a winning proposition for everyone since our friends all purchased a complete set of the left-overs and they are proudly featured in their collections. In this group, getting more Garfield items is not a hardship at all.

Our set of left-over claw machine plush

Promote it with Video

As I already mentioned, part of my business is video production. Fortunately this gives us a competitive edge when it comes to marketing and adding value to the event.

We made a video to show off the hotel, the aquarium, and Adventureland. We put this video on YouTube and posted it on social networks and the Garfield Gathering website.

Driving on Long Island

Knowing that many people attending the convention were from more rural areas than Long Island, we wanted to produce a video that would explain how to get to and around Long Island. It was semi-animated and showed the airports, bridges, and tunnels in the area. We warned about rush-hour traffic and promoted a smaller airport in Islip, New York that was very close to the host hotel. The hotel even ran a shuttle van to and from the airport.

Pull Another Favor for School Buses

One of our best friends is the controller of a major area school bus company named "We Transport." He was able to pull a favor with the management of the company and get us school buses at cost to transport the group to the Atlantis Aquarium in Riverhead. This kept the cost down and assured that everyone had safe transportation to our outing.

Pictured here are Bret, from the bus company, and his daughter Abby. It is a tradition for Garfield Gathering hosts to drag along a friend or two to the convention, so they can see just how crazy we are. This is the ultimate fish-out-of-water moment, but we believe they had fun. Liz, Bret's wife is probably taking the picture.

Rudy the Auctioneer

If I were going to sell my soul for the event, I might as well go big or go home. I personally bartered with a professional auctioneer; he would provide his services and I would provide professional finished videos of the event and of his company.

Rudy, the owner and the auctioneer, was a great example of how to do it well. He sat down with me ahead of time to find out more about the group. He asked about people and personalities. He came up with a short comedic monologue that we could relate to that would break the ice.

Rudy even made up a funny bit with one of the organizers. He got up on stage and started to rant about President James Garfield. The organizer ran up and whispered something in his ear. He then acted surprised and said "It's a CAT: Garfield the cat." Everyone laughed. Later on, when I became the auctioneer for the group, I follow Rudy's example. It's easier for me since I was part of the group and knew many of the people.

Our Only Regret: the Diner Claw Machine

Looking back now, there was one tiny regret that we have that would have been a fun detail for the event.

On the morning of the last day of the event, some of the insiders, such as Nancy and Manny, invited Cathy and me out for breakfast at a diner not so far from the host hotel. I found out that the diner was a very popular spot for attendees to grab some food when they were hungry.

By the front door of the diner was an amusement claw machine with stuffed animals in it. If we knew about the diner claw machine we would have asked to stock it with Garfield plush toys just like the Aquarium and Adventureland. That was our only regret.

16

LIFE AFTER HOSTING THE GARFIELD GATHERINGS CONTINUED (THE WHO, WHAT, WHEN, WHERE, AND WHY)

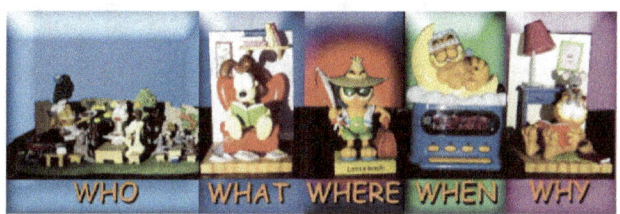

Cathy and I like to think that after we went really big in 2011, the following years took some pages from our playbook. This was especially true for 2013 and 2015. In fact 2015 was co-hosted by friends of ours who admittedly are very competitive. Nancy hosted the event in 2013 and she also went big.

2012 Des Moines, Iowa – Barbara and Romeo Basconcillo

The gathering in 2012 marked the first time the event returned to a repeat city. The 2002 event was also held in Des Moines, Iowa and hosted by Barbara and Romeo. The theme this time around was Halloween and our outing was a bowling trip.

We Lost our Auctioneer

In 2012, two days before the auction, the organizers found out that the auctioneer was not coming. I was not actually in on the meeting, but I assume the conversation went something like this:

> "Oh no! What are we going to do? How are we going to find a new auctioneer on short notice? Who has a big mouth, never shuts up and likes the attention. Hey, what about Robert? We should ask him."

I had already been the game show host for a couple of games that Cathy and I made up, so they knew I was not afraid of public speaking. Suffice to say, I have been the auctioneer ever since. What I may lack in actual auctioneering skills, I make up for by knowing the people in the group.

We had previously hosted in 2011 and the auctioneer that we used was a video client of mine, Rudy. We bartered video production for his services, so it was a win-win arrangement for everyone.

In 2011, Rudy took the time to ask about the group and he wrote a few jokes that they could relate to. Unlike other auctioneers who just treated it like a regular auction, Rudy personalized the experience and made a connection with the group.

Learning from Rudy, I decided to take the time and write a funny opening to set the stage for the auction. In 2012, with only a day to prepare, I did not have the luxury of time. In the following years, I would sit back and observe the group and hope something really funny would happen.

Events included a Halloween costume contest. Any time you ask full-grown adults to dress up like kids, madness will ensue. One man's wife had a hobby of doing stage and monster makeup. She dressed him up as a woman. It took me a while to realize it was actually a guy under there. I would have blurred his face below but I think he was wearing a plastic mask with make-up so nobody would recognize him anyway. Cathy and I killed two birds with one stone since we had to pack light for this trip because we had to travel by airplane. We wore our bowling shirts for the bowling outing and wore them again as our Halloween costumes!

2013 Myrtle Beach, South Carolina - Nancy and Manny Vega

The 2013 event took place at an oceanfront condo complex in Myrtle Beach, South Carolina. Nancy knew of this private time-share community and knew that they rented out units when the owners were not using them.

They had a private catering building that was ours for the entire event.

The downtown area of Myrtle Beach was an attraction by itself. It had plenty of things to do and was a great contrast between the city downtown and the relaxing timeshare with its private beach.

Knowing that there was so much to do in Myrtle Beach, Cathy and I decided to make a weeklong vacation of the trip. We stopped at King's Dominion Amusement Park in Virginia for two days on the way down. We watched fireworks from the top of its observation deck. We continued to Myrtle Beach and saw fireworks displays every night we were there.

Room Hopping Turned to Room Driving

The complex was very big and we were spread out all over the place in private condominiums. In past years, the farthest you would have to go for room hopping was an elevator ride and a short walk down the hall. This year, you either needed a car or comfortable shoes to get to other people's rooms for room hopping.

It was actually a lot of fun, as having an entire condo was much better than a regular hotel room.

River Cruise

One of the fun activities was a river cruise on a tour boat with a catered meal. The river was scenic and they even had a specially sculpted Garfield cake.

What a beautiful cake contracted for the river cruise

Western Variety Show

We attended "ONE", the show at the Alabama Theatre. It was a wonderful show that featured comedians, dancers and singers. The entertainment was excellent.

2013: The End of Meeting Annually

It was decided in 2013 to only meet every other year starting in 2015. The space gave the organizers a chance to have a life and go on other vacations. It was also intended to provide the attendees with a gap, so they can save up and look forward to the next event in two years.

Cheryl, me and Jo before the 2013 auction. They went on to host 2015.

2015 Kansas City, Missouri – Jo Herrman and Cheryl Rogers

Added a day

Due to the two year gap in between events, it was decided to start the Garfield Gatherings on Wednesday night instead of Thursday night and have more activities. We already raised the bar on Long Island and again in 2013, so why not formalize the bigger, better event and spend an extra day?

Our Clique Hosts Again in 2015

I joke that the event can be a little "cliquey." In other words, once you make friends you tend to hang out with them the most.

One of the first people we met at the Pennsylvania event was Jo Herrman. It was her first convention too, and we hit it off right from the start. Along with a small handful of other people, a clique was born.

Jo was one of the co-hosts of 2015 along with Cheryl Rogers, who joined our clique a few years later. Jo and Cheryl both lived in Kansas and volunteered to run the event together. As the auctioneer and game show host, this was especially good for me because I could mess with Jo and Cheryl more than just a random host that Cathy and I do not hang out with.

We started the formal events with Jim's welcome video and two tribute videos in honor of two dear collectors who passed away during the year. To lighten the mood, I hosted a presentation of rejected logos for the convention.

We Found Her Hot-Button and Just Kept Pressing It

As it turns out, when you grow up in Kansas you either embrace the "Wizard of Oz" movie or you become violently sick of it. Jo Herrman, one of the co-hosts, was beyond violently sick of it. What are friends for? A good friend will push your buttons as often as possible for as long as it is funny. To me, it was always funny.

Wizard of Oz Strike #1: 2013 Event

I started early. When we knew 2015 was going to be in Kansas, I incorporated Wizard of Oz jokes and sound bites into the 2013 auction monologue and event.

Wizard of Oz Strike #2: Get Jim Davis in on it

To help get Jim Davis up to speed before recording the welcome video message, I usually send a file telling about who is hosting, where the event is, and other fun facts.

In the 2015 list of notes I stated, "Go heavy on the Wizard of Oz jokes." Jim said some fun and clean things like, "There is no place like home." "There is no place like home." "Oh did I mention there is no place like home." Intertwined in his Welcome message.

Wizard of Oz Strike #3: The Dorothy Shirt as the Game Show Host

Since nobody wants to see a middle-aged overweight man in a blue and white dress, I opted to wear the subtler blue and white checkered button-down shirt while hosting the gBay game show. In the event, it was too subtle; I pointed out the shirt and mentioned the Wizard of Oz.

Wizard of Oz Strike #4: The Munchkin Suit

On the last night, as the auctioneer, I came out wearing an adult size, "Mayor of Munchkin City" Halloween costume. This was far from subtle. This was about as subtle as a sledgehammer to the head.

Looking back now, a Munchkin suit with a large round cutout for the stomach and tails for the rear-end is actually a pretty flattering cut for an overweight person like me.

Worlds of Fun and Oceans of Fun

Kansas City, Missouri has an amusement park called Worlds of Fun. The weather was nice and we had a reserved space at a barbecue area where our group met for lunch.

The entrance fee also included admission to the water park next door owned by the same company. My group did not go over there, but others had a very good time and the water was a great way to cool off.

Hallmark Tour

The Hallmark Card Company has its headquarters in the area. Part of the facility is a Hallmark Visitors Center. The group was pre-arranged for a movie and a self-guided tour.

Pictured is our good friend Gary with the Hallmark welcome sign. As we may have already mentioned he likes being called "Crazy Gary".

Gary is a EMT. In other words, he works on an ambulance and provides medical services. His services have come in handy for many games. Our group does not do well with physical activities.

Coming up, in the "Games after Dinner" section you will find out why it is helpful to have a paramedic in the group.

Mall Time

Across from the Hallmark tour was a pretty large shopping center. We were given free time to eat and shop. It was a great chance for me to buy more Wizard of Oz props and photograph Wizard of Oz items. It seems Kansas fully embraces the Wizard of Oz.

Aquarium and LEGOLAND

After the mall, we went to the aquarium that was connected to Legoland. The aquarium was pretty nice and we only saw the gift shop of Legoland. Much to my surprise, they did have the double-decker couch from the Lego Movie.

Games after Dinner

Cheryl and Jo came up with some interesting, to say the least, games for the event. The theme for this convention was food, specifically barbecue.

You might not know that Kansas City is the barbecue capital of the world.

Cheryl and Jo had teams of people stand about 15 feet away from one team

member who was holding a trash can. Each person had to hurl a piece of fruit into the trash can, but the kicker was that the person holding the trash can could not move. Needless to say, there were some bruises and ice packs handed out before the end of the night.

The Final Dinner and Auction

As mentioned earlier, I dressed up as the Mayor of Munchkin City from the Wizard of Oz. The entire auction opening can be seen on my YouTube channel.

2017 – Asheville, North Carolina – Jenny Abels and Deanna Hass

Back in 2013, it was decided that the Garfield Gathering would go from every year to every other year. As a result, events would be held in odd years: 2013, 2015, and 2017. While the 2019 event is scheduled to be in Hershey, Pennsylvania. it was announced in 2015 that the 2017 Gathering would take place in North Carolina.

In June of 2017, collectors assembled for the Garfield Gathering in Asheville, North Carolina. Our hosts were Jen and Deanna. Just as a personal aside, I knew that Jen and Deanna were going to be a lot of fun because in 2015, when they were announced as hosts, they were wearing overalls and had their teeth blackened to make it look like they were missing a tooth or two. If you recall, I prided myself in pushing Jo and Cheryl's buttons with the "Wizard of Oz" jokes. By wearing stereotypical "hillbilly" clothing, they were telling me that I can't press their buttons but we are going to have a lot of fun.

Asheville is known for the famous Biltmore Estate, which is

billed as the largest private home in America. The Biltmore was one of our day trips organized for the event.

The theme for the year was Christmas. This was decided since there are many Garfield collectibles available for Christmas and wouldn't it be fun to have Christmas in June?

The Hosts --- Jen and Deanna

Jen and Deanna were co-workers years ago and have remained friends. Deanna is a Garfield collector, and in the words of Jen, "I carry Deanna's bags." In other words, she is not a Garfield collector.

Since the event was made to be every other year, an extra day was added on to the convention. The event now runs from Wednesday through Saturday night.

Wednesday – Opening Lasagna Dinner and Games.

Wednesday night was the first official event of 2017. Since Garfield loves lasagna, the dinner was lasagna.

While people were getting seated and getting their food, a video loop was playing with images of some of the attendees' Garfield collections. This was a tradition that Cathy and I started in 2009 at San Antonio, Texas. Prior to the event, people would email a bunch of photos from their collection and I would put it together as a slide show. It is a great way to show other attendees the Garfield environment that they live it. Given the fact that many of our collectibles weigh hundreds of pounds, it is a realistic way to play show-and-tell.

We opened with a welcome video film of Jim Davis specifically for the group. The event is not run by Paws, Inc., but they are friends of the organization and make the organizers' jobs easier. For one thing, since Garfield is a legally licensed and protected character, it is important to be granted the permission from Paws for the logos and other imagery during the event.

The welcome video from Jim Davis is a great way for the group to connect remotely with Jim and to find out what is new with his company. We are often told what is being worked on before the general public knows about it.

Deanna and Jen did a fantastic job of coming up with games and puzzles for the group to participate in.

Thursday Event – Train Ride

During the day, we were bused (or drove) about an hour away to a restored train terminal in Bryson City where we had a private train car waiting for the group. The train rode along a river's pass between residential homes, wooded areas, and scenic cliffs. Lunch and cold drinks were included as part of our tour.

At the half-way point which was two hours away, the train would stop, people could get off and walk around, while other passengers could stay on the train. For some passengers this was the end of the train ride and they would return to the train station  by whitewater rafting on the river. Insert your own "Deliverance" joke here and if you have never seen the movie, don't bother.

After a one-hour stop, the train returned on the same tracks to the station. In the spirit of Disney, we got off the train and exited through the gift shop.

Thursday Night – Ugly Sweater Contest and Dinner

Who thought of this one? Sweaters in the summer. Looked good on paper, but I sweat enough just tying my shoes. This was going to be a problem. In the "hillbilly" spirit, I made my sweater sleeveless to help with the air circulation. Come to think of it ... hillbillies are not so dumb after all for not wearing sleeves in the first place. I get it now.

For those who missed it the first night, we had the collections video loop playing again when people were getting food and eating.

Since it was a hit in 2013, Cathy and I researched facts about the area and presented a video, "North Carolina Fun Facts and Rejected Logos." This was an unofficial, insensitive way for me to do more hillbilly jokes and poke fun at some of the collectors as a group.

The night was closed out with more games and the ugly sweater contest being judged. I don't want to sound bitter, but my sweater was so ugly that homeless people would not even take it from me on a freezing day.

If you thought my sweater was ugly, Cathy's was much worse. She started with a cute penguin sweater and ended up in something only to be seen in Martha Stewart's worst nightmare. Like mine, she had battery-operated Christmas lights all over her outfit, but in the spirit of ugly, she made it so the wires showed on the outside. She wore icicle lights as a necklace and LED chasers around the penguin added a touch of class to help encourage people to have seizures. Her hat contained her Smartphone which played a cell phone app of a Christmas fireplace, while it crackled from the simulated burning yule log.

If the rules called for a "disturbing sweater contest," we would have taken first and second place. We may not be crafty ... but we can do "Ugly."

Friday – The Biltmore Estate

Call security - here comes the Garfield Group! This ragtag group of collectors also enjoyed the tour of the Biltmore Estate. We took the group photo and then had about an hour and a half to take a self-guided tour of this massive home. Apparently, inheriting 12 million dollars went a long way in the 1800s. This house boasts dozens of bedrooms, an indoor pool, one of the first bowling alleys in the country, over 40 bathrooms, and over 40 full-time servants.

The feedback from Cathy was that it would be a great place to display our Garfield collection. We are out of space in our house.

After the tour, we had a really nice lunch at the Biltmore's catering facility. The food was excellent!

Friday Night Pajama Pizza Party and Ice Cream Social

The theme of Friday night was a pajama party. The only word to describe this would be "disturbing." Garfield sleepwear is not known for being worn out in public, but in the spirit of not being afraid to embarrass ourselves, we rocked it. Just a bunch of mental hospital out-patients hanging out in their pajamas eating pizza and ice cream and playing games. It makes you wonder what the high-school reunion group that took up the rest of the hotel thought of us.

Jen came up with some really fun and unique games this year. For one game, each team of people picked one person from the team to be wrapped in toilet paper and given a carrot and black hat to look like a snowman. Another team game involved blowing up green and red balloons and stuffing them in a pair of pantyhose that another team member was holding up to look like reindeer antlers.

Saturday Auction and Bah Humbug Sweater Dinner

That's right. More winter clothing in the summer in the southern part of the United States. I swear that there were "hillbillies" making fun of us.

The auction is probably the toughest night for me, being the auctioneer for the group since it accidentally fell in my lap at the 2012 convention. Unlike the hired auctioneers who we used in the past, I pride myself on doing a short comedy intro solely based on funny or notable things that happen in the current convention. Being real close to the river where the movie "Deliverance" was filmed is just the bonus plan for writing jokes. I will spare you the details but the actual opening can be found on my YouTube channel. If a picture is worth 1,000 words, a video is worth 1 million words.

Some proceeds from the auction go to the hosts' animal charity of their choosing.

2018: 40 Years of Garfield

The year this book was first published was within the year celebrating Garfield's 40th birthday. It was an exciting year with renewed energy from people on the Internet and the Garfield community.

A 40th birthday book came out with past birthday comics and art made from Garfield fans. Jim Davis even went overseas to celebrate a multi-city mall tour in Hong Kong. It was probably the same group that contacted us to see if they could borrow some of our collectibles. We will tell you more about that in Chapter 21.

Even Cathy and I got in on the act, releasing more videos about Garfield in one year than in all previous years combined.

2019 Garfield Gathering – Hershey, Pennsylvania

It was determined that the 2019 Garfield Gathering will be held in Hershey, Pennsylvania. This will mark 15 years since it was in Hershey for the 2004 event. Nancy and Manny Vega will act as both the organizers and the hosts of the event.

Jen and Deanna did such a great job planning the games that they will be helping out in 2019.

Cathy and I will continue to help out wherever we can. We help find auction items, host some games, and I act as the auctioneer.

The theme will be chocolate. That will be a fun theme for the stomach. I wonder how chocolate pairs with lasagna?

Traveling to Conventions

It's funny that we started going to the conventions in 2006. We were able to drive to Williamsport, Pennsylvania, so we didn't give any thought to the items Cathy purchased at the convention. I always tell Cathy that I'm in the 96th percentile for mechanical aptitude and I have great spatial perception and can pack a Mini Cooper with everything from inside a jumbo jet. Then in 2007, the conventions started moving to places that we had to fly to: West Palm Beach, Florida, Pigeon Forge, Tennessee, San Antonio, Texas.

Now that we were flying, Cathy had to be extremely careful of the items she would purchase and the raffle prizes she could win. One year the King Garfield Plush from the second movie was a $5 raffle item. I know how badly Cathy wanted to win it, but if she did, we would have had to purchase a plane ticket for him to fly home with us! Finally, in 2010, we decided the drive to Williamsburg, Virginia would not be too bad. We drove down in the largest vehicle we owned, a 1994 Jeep Grand Cherokee. The air conditioner was broken, but we wanted the capacity to bring our loot home.

We couldn't get any closer in 2011 - when we hosted on Long Island - and just to celebrate how close it was to our home, the last night Cathy bought every pair of slippers they had left in the Paws room. She wanted to bring home the biggest box, just because she could. Then we wound up having to fly again in 2012. We drove in 2013 and made a whole vacation out of the trip. Back to flying in 2015, but able to drive in 2017. We were planning on driving the Jeep again in 2017, but felt that it really wouldn't be a good idea. It had well over 150,000 miles on it and we just thought the trip through the mountains would be too much for it. Glad we didn't, because it gave up the ghost shortly after we got home from the trip. We are very excited to be able to drive only about four hours to Hershey Park in 2019. Anyway, since we have driven to Muncie and so many other places, it's not a big deal as long as we have a reliable car and great music.

WHERE TO BUY GARFIELD ITEMS (THE WHERE, WHAT AND HOW TO)

Garfield has huge recognition and popularity and yet, as a collector, it is not so easy to find Garfield collectibles in stores. This chapter will help you find Garfield merchandise.

Some Stores are (or were) Garfield-Friendly

Strangely, as recognizable as Garfield is, many major retailers such as Target, Wal-Mart, Sears, K-mart and others will rarely have Garfield items.

Unfortunately, most popular stores do not sell many Garfield items. If you are lucky, you might find Garfield greetings cards, Garfield Christmas ornaments, or perhaps the occasional stray clothing item such as a T-shirt or pajamas. Overall, many major retailers are not very Garfield-friendly.

Smaller Stores – Not so Much Either

When my wife and I ask smaller gift shops if they have anything Garfield for sale, owners tell us that nobody collects Garfield anymore. They are ignorant to the fact that Garfield is still a children's cartoon on major cable networks. Younger kids of today don't really know what a comic strip is, but they do watch the TV show "Garfield and Friends".

Spencer's – Not Garfield-Friendly Anymore

There was a time when Spencer's Gifts was very Garfield-friendly. They sold at least a dozen Garfield items. Some of today's best collectibles were sold at Spencer's - such as the lava lamp, the Tyco phones, the fish tank and many animated Christmas plushes.

Thrift Stores / Antique Stores – Hit and Miss

Many Garfield collectors have a lot of luck going to thrift stores and antique shops to find Garfield items. The advantage is that often times thrift stores are not aware how valuable an item may be worth. You can pick up a Garfield phone for $5 or a Garfield cookie jar for $20. These items normally sell for much more money.

The disadvantage of thrift stores is that you end up driving all over the place and you may not find a single item. You can ask the store employee to take your name and number in case they get any Garfield items in stock.

Tip: Make friends with other collectors of different items such as Disney or Betty Boop, and make sure they call you if they find a Garfield item for sale when they are out shopping. In return, you will call them if you find what they collect.

Garage Sales – Hit and Miss

Like thrift stores, it is unlikely to find Garfield items at garage sales. For some collectors, this is a hobby in itself. Cathy finds you can cover more ground in less time using the internet.

Thank God for the Internet

Although big box stores at most might only stock Garfield greetings cards, the internet has more than made up for it with an abundance of places where you can find Garfield items both old and new. Every now and then, Google "Garfield" or "Garfield merchandise" or a specific Garfield item you are looking for and you may be able to find out new information. You can set up a Google search for a specific item and you will receive an email when the search term has been found.

Nancy's Plush Toys – Very Garfield-Friendly

www.NancysPlushToys.com is a website owned by Nancy Vega, the primary organizer of the Garfield Gathering. As a high-end collector herself, she is always looking to represent current Garfield product lines from licensees.

Café Press – Garfield-Friendly

www.CafePress.com is a custom print shop where you can choose from thousands of designs to be turned into clothing, mugs, cups, bags, hats, and other items. Café Press has contracted with Paws, Inc., the parent company of Garfield, to provide on-demand printing based on hundreds of Garfield comics and graphics.

Tip: Get on their mailing list and wait for a sale. They are always running discounts and promotions.

CraigsList.com

A popular website for local classified ads is www.Craigslist.com. We have purchased entire collections because we learned about them on Craigslist and were able to meet the seller and see the items for sale.

There are many scams that are done on Craigslist, so in-person cash sales are a good idea. You get the items for sale and the seller gets cash. Chapter 17 will go into more detail about Garfield items and Craigslist.

Other Popular Websites

The following are some websites that either specialize in Garfield items or have a large selection of Garfield items:

Garfield.com

www.Garfield.com is the official site for Garfield. It does not necessarily sell items directly, but it does give clues to finding new licensees and retailers to work with.

GarfieldCollectibles.com

www.GarfieldCollectibles.com is owned by Paws, Inc. and is a great place to purchase collectors cells, Jim Davis sketches, and other rare, one-of-a-kind or unusual Garfield collectibles.

Retail Stores Websites

Many popular retailers who do not sell any Garfields in the store might actually have Garfield items on their website. This is because online items are often delivered by unrelated fulfillment houses and not the stores themselves.

eBay – So Much to Say it has its Own Chapter

eBay is such a great source for buying and selling Garfield collectibles that we devoted an entire chapter to it. See our next chapter, "eBay – The Granddaddy of Garfield Collectible Websites."

18

EBAY --- THE GRANDDADDY OF GARFIELD COLLECTIBLE WEBSITES (THE WHERE, WHAT AND HOW TO)

Most of Cathy's collection has been purchased on eBay.com, the largest online auction website in the world. There are several ways to purchase items on eBay:

Auction

Like any online auction, you bid against other eBay users and the highest bidder wins the item. Please remember that most of the time the item will become available from another seller, so do not  get caught up in the frenzy. Unless you need something for someone's birthday soon, try and be patient because Garfield collectibles will almost always be sold by several people at different times. In a way, you are not competing against other users, but actually competing against your own willingness to get the item. When you reach a number that is too high in your mind, just stop bidding.

Buy-it-Now

Sellers on eBay have the option to set a price where the first bidder can outright purchase the item without completing the entire bid period. If the first bidder chooses to "buy-it-now," they can pay a pre-set higher price and immediately win the auction.

Many times, sellers who set up a buy-it-now often are selling many copies of the same item. Look around and see if the item is being sold in another auction. You may be able to win it at a lower price by being one of the only people to bid on it at a lower bid price than the buy-it-now. If it seems like the seller has several to sell, play around a little and try to win the first few at a lower opening bid before you go right to a buy-it-now and pay a higher price.

Best Offer

Some auctions on eBay allow you to make an offer directly to the seller. If the seller accepts the offer, he ends the auction prematurely and you are declared the winner.

Cathy tends to low-ball her offers and the sellers might actually accept them or other times they make counteroffers. The offer is always lower than the buy-it-now price. If a seller has many of the same items for sale he might agree to the offer since he plans on selling in volume.

Watch Out for Shipping and Other Fees on eBay

You need to be aware of all of the fees that the seller is including before you bid. The seller is supposed to disclose any fees and costs associated with any item for sale. Items may or may not include shipping. If they do not include cost of shipping, a seller may set it up as a flat rate or may require a bidder to contact him for an estimate before submitting a bid.

Shipping and other fees could double or triple the cost of an item, so be sure you know what you are getting into.

Padded Shipping

Since eBay collects fees based on the final selling price, many sellers pad the shipping and handling charges. Although this is frowned upon by eBay, it is a common practice.

If you do bid on an item with padded fees, add up all of the fees before you bid. Factor in the total cost, not just the bid price, or you will be shocked to find out the final cost you agreed upon. Read each description carefully and if you do not understand the fees, do not bid on it.

Insurance

Paying for insurance is usually the responsibility of the buyer. Sellers do not always offer insurance. When they do, find out the cost before you bid on the item. Insurance is a good idea to take if the item is fragile, rare, or expensive.

Even with insurance, you can lose out. We purchased a fragile golf item, paid for insurance and it arrived broken. The post office first reneged on the insurance, then they kept the item while the claim was being processed. During that time, they lost the item and the claim, and eventually they paid us half the selling price because that was all the supervisor was able to offer to close out the lost year-old claim. Hopefully, this was the exception to the rule, but looking back now, we were better off keeping the item, gluing the broken pieces back together, and not filing a claim.

Currency Rate and International Shipping

An item might look like a good price, but often times if it is being sold from another country, you may be responsible to pay international shipping, money conversion fees, and currency rates.

Items sold to people residing in the United States should be listed in U.S. dollars. If something is not in U.S. dollars and you live in the United States, you should think twice about bidding on this.

On the other hand, Cathy has purchased items from China in U.S. dollars, including free shipping, and the cost was exactly what she expected. You don't always have to be scared of international transactions. Be sure to read the description. Send a note to the seller if you have any concerns. He can provide a shipping quote or even tell you that he does not do business outside of his own country.

President Garfield...Again?

A funny thing always happens when searching on eBay. Your results will be fairly accurate, but you may run into a few stumbling blocks along the way. For example, anything related to former President James A. Garfield will be reported in your search. Andrew Garfield, an actor from one of the "Spiderman" movies, will also mess up your search. You might run into some of his autographs or Spiderman collectibles. In New York, Craigslist might add in more nearby results outside of Long Island. There is a city called Garfield, New Jersey.

Fun Fact: Getting back to President Garfield - Garfield the cat was actually named after Jim Davis's grandfather, who was actually named after President Garfield. So, in a way, the mixed search result was inevitable. It could have been worse if he named the cat "Ford." If he did, you would get the search results of every Ford car for sale as well as Ford memorabilia and President Ford collectibles. Anything involving "Francis Ford Coppola" the writer, producer, and director, would also come up in the search results.

Andrew Garfield...Really?

Just when you thought President Garfield items were obstacles, you also get bombarded by Andrew Garfield items. Andrew Garfield is the actor who starred in some of the recent Spiderman movies.

Let's hear from Cathy

We apologize in advance, but you are about to hear from Cathy some of the things I just told you. Sure, we could have combined it as a joint-effort chapter, but the next section is specific to what Cathy does and in what order when she is on eBay. If you picked up the book and went right to this section, it could stand-alone.

Tips on Buying Garfield items on eBay (Written by Cathy Kothe)

I have been a member of eBay since 1999, long before high speed modems came along. I used to wait, not so patiently, for the page to load trying to guess exactly what Garfield item was going to appear based on the seller's description. Back then, the download speed was incredibly slow, and the lines would download ever so slowly one line at a time!

My husband was thrilled when we had the opportunity to get high speed internet access. He was even more thrilled when it was me who insisted on getting it as soon as we possibly could. It wasn't him begging me to upgrade. It was me telling him to get it installed as quickly as possible. We were the very first house on our block with high speed internet access. It was awesome! No more playing "guess the Garfield item", the entire page would download completely in a matter of seconds, not minutes!

I had a fairly decent Garfield collection before the creation of eBay. I must admit that eBay has helped my collection grow by leaps and bounds. It's helped me to get items that I would have never even known existed. It's made the world smaller and hundreds, if not thousands, of Garfield items well within my reach.

Early on, I made my fair share of mistakes on eBay. I certainly paid too much money for some items. I didn't read descriptions carefully enough on some items and I received some things that were much smaller than I expected or were missing pieces.

I learned to read descriptions very carefully and not to be afraid to contact the seller to ask questions. Size does matter! Everything seems larger when you look at the photos sellers place on eBay compared to what ultimately shows up on your doorstep.

Tip #1: Read Descriptions

Read descriptions very carefully and look for phrases like, "from a smoke-free home"; "from a pet-free home"; and "played-with condition". If these phrases are not included in the description, ask before you bid. I've received more than my fair share of stinky, smoke-ridden items because I didn't ask. The good news is that there are ways to clean and rid items of the horrible smell.

Tip #2: Set Up Automatic Searches

If there are key items that you are looking for, set up an automatic eBay search for those items. You will receive a message from eBay every time an item with the description you are looking for is listed for sale. Sometimes it will not be the same exact item you want. For example, I have a Garfield kiddie amusement ride but I get notifications practically every day for a Christmas ornament or mug or some other item that has "ride" in the description. It's not a big deal for me to just delete those e-mails.

I don't want to be too specific with my key words because a seller might not call the item the same thing I would. Sellers might not know a Dakin from a Fine Toy plush. They just see a Garfield dressed as a pirate. Don't even get me started on the sellers who don't know Heathcliff from Garfield. Not all oranges cats are created equal!

Tip #3: How to Start Searching

I like to start my eBay search as generic as possible. I have found over the last couple of years that Andrew Garfield screws up my eBay searches more than President Garfield does, darn that Spiderman!

I find you need to pull out certain words to reduce the number of items listed to a more reasonable number. In the search you can remove words so I subtract out:

- And Marks (clothing that has nothing to do with Garfield)
- & Marks
- Andrew
- President
- Spiderman

That usually knocks out a couple thousand items. If you find that you are seeing a lot of non-Garfield items just re-do your search pulling out the most common word that you see in the title of the item. Make sure it's not going to remove a Garfield item that you may be interested in. For example, you may not want to remove President from your search if you're looking for Garfield running for President items. But you may want to search for Garfield president and remove James from the search results.

If there are specific item categories that you are interested in, you may search several times using those key words:

- Garfield mugs
- Garfield shirts
- Garfield Christmas
- Garfield pens

I usually start my eBay search with just a generic "Garfield" search. I then sort the items to see the newly listed items. On several occasions, I've been able to snag an item early on with a "buy it now" before it's seen by more people. So, I continue to scroll through the items until I see items that I've looked at on a previous day.

Tip #4: Sort by "Ending Soonest"

Next, I sort the items by "ending soonest". That way I may be able to successfully bid on an item that has gone unnoticed or is listed for a reasonable price. Yes, I have been the victim of those darn last-second snipers more than I'd like to admit. I get so upset when I've been outbid by only a couple of cents or a dollar, but the truth is, you really don't know what price they were willing to pay, so the purchase price may have only gone up by fifty cents, but maybe they were really bidding up another fifty dollars, you'll never know.

About "Snipers"

I don't use sniper software so I'm not real familiar with it. Honestly, I don't know exactly how it works or why someone needs it. If you really want an item and know how much you want to spend on it, just enter your highest bid and eBay will do the work for you.

When bidding you have to at least have an idea of how much you are willing to spend on that item. The worst thing I've ever done was to get so caught up in a last-minute bidding war, when I spent way more than I originally wanted to on an item.

Tip #5: "Watch" Don't Bid Yet

I try not to bid on an item until the last hour or so. I always click to watch the items I'm interested in, but I don't bid on them until the end. If the price has gone up higher than I even wanted to spend, I don't even bother bidding. If I'm still interested in the item, I'll place my bid in the final hour and walk away. Now you can even have eBay send you a text message so you don't forget to bid on an item.

Tip #6: Enjoy the Surprise

I try not to watch the item in the last couple of minutes of bidding any longer. It's a pleasant surprise if I win the item and I'll admit I'm bummed about the items I've lost and really wanted. But the truth is, there's a good chance that item will come along again. It may take weeks, it may take years, but there's usually always another chance. With that said, I'm actually thinking of an item that I missed out on a few years ago over the Thanksgiving weekend. It was a Garfield neon lamp. It sold for somewhere around $150 which was definitely more than I wanted to spend, but I have not seen another one up for sale since. Speaking of which, I should take my own advice and set up an eBay watch for that item. I'll be right back …

Tip #7: What Comes Around, Goes Around

Unless it's an item that you really want and it's super unique, I would put it on your watched items list and keep an eye on it. Some sellers just keep automatically relisting the item and don't adjust the price or the shipping charges. Don't be afraid to contact the seller and let him know you are interested and how much you are willing to spend. If it's not a crazy request, you never know, they may lower the price and make it a buy-it-now auction so you can seal the deal and get the item on your terms.

Tip #8: Home Country or International?

I used to only search for items within my home country, the United States, but after talking to my good friend and fellow Garfield collector, Trish, she convinced me that it's not an issue to get items from other countries. I always thought the shipping would be astronomical or the currencies would be a problem. You must make sure that you read and understand how long it might take to receive an item, but as long as you are OK with the terms, there should be no issue with the purchase. That has helped me to find some of the rarer, sought-after items that are hard, if not impossible, to find in the United States.

Tip #9: Use PayPal When You Can

Since most sellers accept PayPal for purchases, you are always covered if you don't receive the item or it's broken in transit. I know people complain about the fees all the time, but don't be fooled into buying something outside of eBay's protected environment.

Tip #10: Be Aware of the Total Cost

"Hey, that's a great price for that item" - until you look at the shipping charges. As I understand it, years ago, eBay increased their fees so sellers were getting around that by lowering the starting prices on their items; but increasing the shipping charges to where it would easily double or triple the price of the item. Don't be afraid to ask the seller if they can charge you for the actual shipping rate. They may knock off a couple dollars especially if they started with very high shipping charges.

Tip #11: Combine Shipping

Most sellers will combine shipping on items. Be sure to contact the seller if you are interested in several items where the auction closing dates are days apart. Some sellers will wait until you are all finished buying and send you one combined invoice for everything. I've asked sellers if they would combine the items I'm interested in into one lot, so I can complete all my purchases with that seller in one transaction. Some sellers will not do that but will wait a week or so until all the auctions are over and set up all your winning items in one transaction.

Tip #12: Consider Insurance, Pack it Right

If an item is extremely fragile, offer to pay a couple more bucks to make sure they don't skimp on packing materials. Also, make sure the seller insures the package for the full amount you paid. I've had more than one shipment of ceramics come in completely broken because the seller only used newspaper and no bubble wrap or peanuts. I got my money back but it's not worth the hassle, let alone the once nice pieces that are literally now in pieces.

I said it before but it's worth repeating: be sure to read the descriptions carefully. Most sellers will be honest and upfront about damage because it's only going to hurt them more in the long run with negative feedback. Look for key words like:

- Chip – a small blemish usually removing the paint from part of the item
- Crazing – small, hairline cracks in ceramic items
- Re-glued – ask for more details, sometimes you can't even notice while other times there are chips left and it's not a good repair.
- Smoke-free home – if you don't see this and you are buying plush or clothing, ask the seller if they are smoke-free or not. Sometimes they won't know because they bought the item in a thrift store, but they can tell you if there's a strong odor or not.
- Pet-free home – if you don't see this and you are buying blankets or sheets, ask the seller if he is pet-free or not. It may not matter to you if you have a pet also, but it may, depending on how you plan to use the item.
- Scratches – ask for more photos of the item. You may be able to buff them out or they may be in a spot where you won't see them on the item when displayed.

Now these issues might not deter you from wanting the item. Sometimes you can get a great item for a great price because there's some damage to it. If it's not too visible and it won't bother you, it can be a great buy. If you are unsure of any information, ask the seller for more details and more photos. Many times the seller doesn't know enough about an item to know that it's missing pieces.

Be especially careful when bidding on Danbury Mint items. Some of them have many pieces that can easily break off and you won't know it until you get the item and unpack it.

I find that you need to be careful what time of year you purchase certain items. Close to major holidays, like Halloween, Christmas and Easter, people will list items for sale with a higher starting bid because they figure they can get more money for an item that someone will want to use as a decoration for that holiday. I have no problem buying Christmas items in May because they are usually priced cheaper, and people will pass over the item because the holiday is too far off to even think about.

Tip#13: Read Feedback

Check the sellers' feedback and only do business with sellers who have close to 100% positive feedback. Be warned if you are bidding on a fragile item and the feedback is less than 100%. Read the comments regarding negative feedback. Did the items show up broken? Were they not packaged carefully? It that's the case, don't bid. Set up an automatic search for the item and wait for a more reputable seller to offer the same item.

Tip #14: How Many are For Sale?

When you are on the fence about an item, search eBay to see if there are others listed. You may see the same item priced lower, ending sooner or in better condition. Buy the one that you like the best and at the best price.

Tip #15: Don't Believe the Hype

Beware of "RARE". I'm sure you've all seen people list items as "rare" or "vintage" and it turns out be a mass-produced Garfield McDonald's mug or some such thing. Don't get me wrong, there are some truly rare Garfield items out there, but chances are pretty good that they're not the items listed on eBay by some random person. Especially if they don't even have Garfield somewhere in their user name!

What really is a "vintage" Garfield item? "Vintage" is one of those words that sellers toss around to make you think they are rare and valuable.

It is clearly defined in the automobile world that a classic car is older than 25 years old, but there really is no definitive line in the sand that determines the right age to call a Garfield item "vintage". The oldest a Garfield collectible can date back is from 1978. To get really technical, merchandising did not start until the early '80s. Perhaps some collector has a 1978 newspaper press kit to promote the comic, so we will consider those first. Even items that date back to 1978 are hardly antiques, as an antiques store would define them. To be exact, an antique is defined as at least 100 years old. An antique store would simply consider them "collectibles".

Use this as a warning and don't buy something just because the seller tosses around emotion-causing words like, "vintage", "rare", "limited edition" or "hard to find". Do your homework before buying something that is hyped-up.

Tip #16: Don't Believe the Date

Copyright 1978 so the item must be old! – No, Garfield was first born in 1978, so most items will show "copyright 1978", but were manufactured much later. As Robert has already mentioned in this book and in his video, "How to sell your Garfield Collection", you can carbon-date Garfield items by looking at the eyes. The number one, biggest clue to know around when the item was produced is in the eyes.

Tip #17: Bid Against Yourself, Not the Seller

I absolutely hate reserve price auctions. If you are the seller, just set the price for the amount you are willing to accept. I also can't stand the best offer option either. As a buyer, I'm usually going to low ball my offer expecting the seller to counter my offer. Nothing drives me crazier than getting his automatic message that he refused my offer. Why bother putting that option if you are not going to counter the offer? Go up a couple bucks from my offer and you'll probably sell me the item.

Tip #18: Do Your Homework

Do your homework. If you see an item and are not sure of the details, check Google. You'll see people list the "Dear Diary" plates as a complete set. But is it really? How many plates were in that set? I say it all the time - there are really 10 Christmas houses for a truly complete Garfield Christmas Village, but most people think that it's complete with 6 houses. I'd like to think that most sellers are not purposely trying to deceive you, but maybe they just don't know. We can politely educate them and may even get a better deal.

Tip #19: Contact Seller if Unhappy

Finally, if you are not happy with an item once you receive it, contact the seller and try to work it out with him before leaving negative feedback or opening a case with eBay or PayPal. Most sellers care about their standing with eBay and will do what they can to make you happy. Be sure to leave the appropriate feedback once all issues have been resolved.

Happy Bidding!

CRAIGSLIST.COM (THE WHERE AND HOW TO)

C raigslist.com can best be described as a website that has regional classified ads. Items are broken down by categories.

Regional Placement

The idea behind Craigslist is that buyers and sellers should get together, inspect the goods for sale, count the cash, and transact in person. It is discouraged to conduct business around Craigslist.com over the phone or by email since there are many scammers, stolen credit cards, and identity thefts related to remote transactions.

The Advantage of Craigslist.com

The advantage of Craigslist is the ability to find out about thrift sales, estate sales, and entire collections that are for sale close to where you live.

Cathy and I purchased a 700-piece collection from someone who only lived 25 minutes from us. We were able to inspect the items for sale, rent a trailer, and come back with cash to purchase the collection.

We also purchased a very rare giant Macy's 25th anniversary Garfield on Craigslist.com. Shipping would have been a fortune.

Another Craigslist.com purchase we made was a complete Christmas Village. As a ceramic item, shipping would have been a fortune and most of the items could break in shipping. I was able to preview the pieces and carefully transport them in the trunk and back seat of my car. Everything made it home safely.

How to Use Craigslist.com to Find Garfield Items

It is very simple. Craigslist has the ability to search its database. Before you do that, you need to make sure you are searching in the right area of the country. Simply find the country and region that you live in and click on the name of the region. It will bring you to the proper database. I chose United States / New York / Long Island.

As you can see, since Long Island is not actually a city or state, Craigslist is broken down into common market areas. Long Island is made up of Nassau County and Suffolk County, and everything is within a reasonable driving distance.

Searching Craigslist

To narrow down your search, you can first click on a category. In the Garfield example, it is best to choose "collectibles." "Collectibles" is in the middle section labeled "For Sale."

Towards the top of the page there is an area labeled "Search Collectibles." Simply type in "Garfield" and press the little magnifying glass icon to start the search.

Like on eBay, you will run into President Garfield and Andrew Garfield search results.

If the item you are looking to purchase is not too large, try to meet the person selling in a public place. If that's not possible, don't go alone, bring someone with you. Especially if you will be carrying a large amount of cash on you. If you absolutely must go alone to their house, make sure someone knows where you are going. Make sure you let that person know you made it home OK.

There are other options similar to Craigslist popping up on the internet. Letgo is a fairly new site and I'm sure there are others. Use Google to search other options, talk to family and friends to find out what sites they use. Join Facebook groups that share the same types of interests you do. Members share information all the time about new items they have found.

HOW TO SELL A GARFIELD COLLECTION (THE HOW TO)

Because of the popularity of our website, www.LovesGarfield.com , even before Cathy held the world record, we were already among the most visible Garfield collectors in the world. I am a website developer and do video production and the website I made of Cathy's collection dominated Google for anything related to Garfield collectibles.

Almost two times a week, we would get a phone call from someone who either inherited, owned, or was helping a friend who wanted to liquidate his collection. I would take the time and say the same thing over and over again and give him helpful hints on how to sell the collection.

Video

After a while, I realized that I should just make a video with the same information that I was telling everybody over the phone. I put a notice on the website suggesting that people should watch the video first, and if they had any questions, they could give me a call. This cut down on hundreds of calls and standardized the quality of my answers. As of the writing of this chapter, the video had over 15,000 views.

Here is the interesting part: the average amount of time that people watched it was four minutes, or about 45% of the video. So hopefully, the people who called me watched the entire video before calling. The video is still available, so if you did not want to read this chapter, the information is pretty close.

The Parts are More Valuable than the Whole

We get calls about two times per week from people looking to sell their entire collection all at once. When I say "their collection", I mean a collection they inherited or one they need to liquidate for a family member or friend due to the fact that they are moving into a smaller space or perhaps a nursing home.

The phone calls almost always sound the same. They want to box it all up and sell it to one person.

People Want us to Buy the Collection

Personally, we have already purchased two entire collections on separate occasions. When we did, the circumstances were right. One collection was only a half-hour drive from our house on Long Island. It was an extraordinary collection and his asking price was extremely reasonable. We could walk around his house and see everything he had. His collection was so good that we offered him just $100 less than the asking price because we did not want to insult his intelligence, but knew we had to rent a trailer to get everything home in one trip.

The second collection was not as impressive, but it had some high-value pieces that justified the purchase price. They were also in New York, but much further away. We were also able to see the collection before we purchased it. We made two offers, one if we had to drive up again to pick up the collection and a second higher offer if they were willing to drive down and deliver the collection. We were glad to pay the higher price since they wound up driving to us and delivering the collection to our doorstep.

Why We Would Likely Not Purchase Your Entire Collection

The reality is that most of the time the circumstances are not right for Cathy to purchase collections from people for many reasons.

- We need to see the collection
- Many collections are out of state and may be difficult to look at
- We already have 12,000 pieces, so it's likely that there would be many duplicates
- We are not willing to pay top dollar for a collection and many people want to get full price
- We are out of space

We still might purchase more collections if . . .

- The price is realistic
- It is close to us
- It is a good value
- There are few duplicates

This chapter is not about us buying your entire collection. It is overall about selling your collection. Now that Cathy and I are eliminated as potential buyers, the following information should help you sell your collection.

The Sum of the Individual Pieces is More Valuable than the Sum of the Whole

Selling an entire collection all at once will likely not get you the best price. It might be quicker or more convenient, but it is unlikely you can make more money compared to selling it a little at a time.

Duplicates

Buyers will not want to pay top dollar for something they already have. Of course, there are exceptions. Someone may want to keep one safe and in the box, put another out on display, or dare I say, use the item for its intended purpose.

What You Paid Could be the Most Each Item is Worth

If you paid retail value for an item and you later tried to recover the value, in a way, the item is now used. Some items may go up in value, but as an entire collection, it is unlikely that every item in the collection will go up in value.

One Person May Not Have as Much Money as Hundreds of People Collectively

One person buying it all will probably not be prepared to pay $1,000 or $10,000 or $20,000. However, if you find 300 people to buy a 600-piece collection, on average they are only purchasing a couple of items and would probably be in the position to pay considerably more.

The Best Place to Sell Items

eBay

eBay is the largest auction website in the world. The buyers are looking in from all over the planet, not just from your hometown like a garage sale. People can search for exactly what they want and bidding can become competitive. Some people try to win just for the sake of winning.

eBay Tips:

Do Not Set a Reserve Price

A reserve price is a secret number that only you and eBay know that you will not sell the item until you reach the number. It is a guessing game. Someone might bid and not reach the reserve, and then bid again and still not reach the reserve. They get frustrated and stop bidding. It would be a better strategy to use a minimum bid instead of a reserve price. This way the bidder knows where to start the bidding.

Always Set a Minimum Bid or the Item May Sell for Too Little

On eBay, if an item does not have a minimum bid, you can end up selling a $300 Garfield cookie jar for $20. By setting the minimum bid to $150, you know you will either not sell it or get at least $150, which was the minimum you were willing to take.

Photograph Everything

It all starts with digital photographs. So many items look alike. They are all orange and they are all Garfield. The pictures will show exactly what the item looks like, what condition it is in, and any visible damage.

Disclose Damage

Your reputation is everything. List everything with integrity and disclose any damage.

Establish Positive Feedback

New sellers without a reputation are much more suspect than existing sellers. Open an account early, buy several items, and receive good feedback as a buyer and as a seller.

Smoking or Non-Smoking

Several times my wife has purchased something on eBay that smelled like an ashtray from the '70s. The odor of smoke was soaked into the item and hit our noses like a ton of bricks. It is likely she could have given negative feedback for lack of disclosure and the disappointment of the condition the item was in.

On the flip side, if the item comes from a smoke-free house, you should brag about that fact. Volunteer the fact that it is smoke-free so the buyer has one less thing to be concerned about.

Pack it Safely

This should be obvious but you should make sure the item is shipped with proper protection. Use padding. Wrap fragile items. Use a strong enough box. The shipping system does not care if it is a rare piece, it is just as vulnerable as any other package sent through the system.

Do not rely on the fact that you get insurance. When the buyer opens the box and sees that you tossed in a single paper towel leaving too much space for it to bounce around in, he will likely disclose this fact in the feedback section. It might read:

"Item came broken. Terrible packing job. I was looking forward to this item and now it is in five pieces. DO NOT DO BUSINESS WITH THIS SELLER. HE DOES NOT SEEM TO CARE."

Insurance

Insurance is often a very good idea. It is up to you to bundle it into the price or to offer it to the buyer on a voluntary basis. Even having insurance is not as convenient as it sounds when an item comes broken.

The post office once broke an item that Cathy had purchased. Although we bought the insurance on it, they insisted on keeping the broken item during the insurance claim processing. They ended up losing the item. The person who originally helped us lied on the claim. Then she retired. A supervisor took over and wasted six more months before finally disclosing that she had the authority to negotiate up to $99 and could process it herself if we settled for taking a loss of around $50. Could you imagine if we did not have insurance?

Group Items in a "Lot"

If you have 600 items to sell, you do not have to run 600 auctions. A "Lot" is a grouping of multiple items being sold together. You might bundle 5 to 10 items together as a single auction. You can combine cheaper items with

sought after items to enhance the sale and unload multiple items at once.

This also gives you the best shipping value. It does not make a lot of sense to pay $2 shipping for a single Garfield pencil. If you combine six pencils with an Enesco mug and two plushes, they can go together in one box to the buyer.

Other Places You Can Sell a Garfield Collection or Garfield Items

Besides eBay, there are other places you may be successful selling your items. Some items may be too large to ship, or perhaps too fragile.

If you are looking to sell the entire collection at once, eBay may not be the best place due to the number of boxes that need to be shipped and the fact that a buyer will probably rather view the collection in person than look at photos.

www.Craigslist.com

We found one of the collections that we purchased on Craigslist.com. Cathy saw a picture with a rare Garfield crystal and we called about the ad. The seller was also on Long Island and we were invited to see it in person.

Several advantages of Craigslist.com is the fact that the listing is free, you can leave the ad up until you sell the item, and people are more trusting about in-person transactions. Craigslist sales are usually completed in person. You pay the person when you are picking up the item(s).

Garfield Gathering (Garfield Convention) Swap Meet and Sale

If you are fortunate enough to be close to the Garfield Gathering, the last day always features a "sale and swap" meet. The tables are very reasonable to rent to display your items and the attendees are typically avid Garfield collectors.

Talk about needing the moon to align with the stars for this sales strategy. You need to be near the convention. You need to be willing to sell the collection in June only, since the event corresponds with Garfield's birthday. To add another wrinkle to the plan, we recently voted to have the Gathering every two years. Go to www.garfieldgathering.com to find out exactly when and where the next one will be.

Garfield Gathering Room Hopping

The Garfield Gathering swap meet was mentioned in the previous section. Assuming you can attend a Garfield Gathering, you can also sell items at what we call "room hopping." Attendees who want to have other attendees come around to their hotel room will add their room number to the room hopping list. During free time, people may visit your room and purchase items that you are selling.

Garfield Gathering Facebook Page

Use this one sparingly. Since the convention is a community, it is not uncommon to give other collectors a heads-up about collections for sale. The intended purpose of the Garfield Gathering Facebook page is to promote the Garfield Gathering, but if you are not annoying about it, other collectors may be happy to meet up and see what you are selling.

The Worst Place to Sell Garfield Items

Garage sales

What are the odds of living within a few blocks of an elite Garfield collector who just happens to be going to garage sales on a regular basis? Garage sales are typically marked down to pennies on the dollar.

Where to Establish a By-the-Book Price (we will cover the how later)

eBay

eBay is probably one of the best ways to establish a selling price. If you monitor an item that is being sold, the selling price will be revealed once the auction is over.

Books

As we mentioned earlier, there are a few books featuring Garfield collectibles. Keep in mind that when these books were published the internet was still in its infancy. There was not a lot of information available regarding Garfield items. Fast forward almost twenty years and there's now a wealth of information available on the internet about any topic.

You need to have patience and do some digging, but you can get a range of the value of an item by checking past sales. Be sure you are comparing apples to apples when it comes to the condition of an item. You can find an item that sold for $500 because it was mint in box and you can find the same item sold for $100 because it was removed from its box and played with.

- *Garfield Collectibles* (A Schiffer Book for Collectors) Paperback - June 1, 1998
- *Collecting Garfield: An Unauthorized Handbook and Price Guide* (A Schiffer Book for Collectors) Paperback - January 1, 2000
- *The Unauthorized Collector's Guide to Garfield and the Gang* (The Unauthorized Collection Guide) Paperback – April 2000 by Robert Gipson (Bob Gipson is one of the early organizers of the Garfield Gathering.)

I do not intend for this handbook to be a book review for these other books. Cathy and I do own them.

Garfield celebrated his 20th birthday in 1998. It's hard to say if the prices they listed for the items when these books went to print are still relevant.

Garfield Conventions

We already discussed the "Garfield Gathering" also known as "Garfest" earlier in the book. As it relates to this section there is an auction and "room hopping", where collectors can buy and sell items going from room-to-room of fellow collectors. Many of the collectors are aware of the true value of Garfield items. The live-auction is based on only a handful of collectors, who may or may not be caught up in the moment. Because something sold for hundreds of dollars at the auction could simply mean that the buyer did not want someone else in the room to win the item.

Swap Meet at the Garfield Convention

As I say in my video on YouTube, "How to Sell a Garfield Collection," the Garfield Gathering is one of the best ways to sell a lot of items if it is close enough to you and the timing is good.

During the event, there are a few hours set out for the swap meet. Even if you are not attending the entire event, you can still purchase a table at the swap meet for a few dollars and sell your collection. You are now in front of some of the biggest Garfield collectors in the country.

The biggest problem with this strategy is that the event only meets once every two years and it moves around the country. As it pertains to the next event, this assumes you are willing to transport your items for sale to Hershey, Pennsylvania in June 2019.

On the other hand, if you are near Hershey, Pennsylvania and have a collection to sell around June 2019, then for a few dollars you will do very well to be in front of this group.

Social Networking / Other Collectors

There are several Facebook (and other social networking website) pages where someone can ask about value and get opinions from other collectors. The Garfield Gathering website has often taken questions regarding the value of an item. Social networking websites and pages do not write themselves. It is other Garfield collectors and fans who help contribute to these pages.

More Details on How to Establish the Value of a Garfield Item

As we mentioned earlier, there really is not a set value for Garfield collectibles. At best, there might be a price range that they usually sell for. This is because Garfield collectors are all individuals. They all have different tastes. They also all have different reasons for wanting an item

Since we already established that people collect what they want for their own reasons, it is common for someone to overpay for something that he really wants. If nobody is paying attention on the auction websites, people can also underpay for an item. This is how my wife Cathy purchased most of her 12,000 items. Unlike stamps, coins, and paintings, where the market is firmly established, Garfield items do not necessarily have a set price.

Guidelines to Establish Prices

First Google it

Google, or your favorite search engine, is the fastest way to see how many types of markets the item may be available in. If the item is relatively new, it may still be for sale in retail stores and the price is the price. If the item is older, it might be for sale on www.Amazon.com, www.eBay.com, and other websites.

The results may also list websites about the item or even videos featuring the item. In the websites and videos, people may be telling their story about where they purchased it and what they paid. The information might be out-of-date, but every clue is useful in establishing a value.

It May Depend on What Someone Paid in the First Place

It is unlikely that someone will sell a Garfield gold ring that he purchased for $300 for much less that what he paid for it in the first place. It is safe to use the original price as a decent starting point to establish a value.

A Garfield phone could be around $30 to $50. A Garfield stuffed animal could be $5 to $20.

Shown below is "Bedtime for Garfield". When you add up the installments plus shipping, the original cost is $152.50. Depending on the market it may hold its value, drop in value or increase in value. Using the original cost gives a good starting point to predict the selling price.

The exception to this rule is when somebody is selling his collection in bulk. When selling off an entire collection, it is common to discount it just for the convenience of having one seller.

It May Depend on What They Frequently Sell for Online

If a Garfield cookie jar consistently sells for between $200 and $300, it is sending a message to the market that this is the logical range to buy or sell a Garfield cookie jar. Someone who really wants to win it might bid $350. A buyer might get lucky and snag it for $150 if the timing is good and nobody else is paying attention.

Seasonality of Garfield Items

If you have time and are not under pressure to sell your items quickly, you may do better if you can sell certain items at certain times of the year. For example, Halloween pieces will sell for higher prices close to Halloween. Easter-themed pieces will sell faster and for more money around Easter time. Christmas items can sell year-round, but again, you may get top dollar closer to Christmas. Family members of Garfield collectors may buy an item knowing that their relative has always wanted a certain piece or just know if they get anything Garfield, they will "be heroes." But they don't necessarily know the market, so they may pay a higher price to make their family member or friend happy.

Use eBay and Other Auction Sites and Pre-check What it Sells For

Using the Garfield fish aquarium as an example, since there was only one type ever made, you may be able to search auction sites for "Garfield Fish Tank/Aquarium." If you find one and you are not in a hurry to sell yours, add it to your "watching" list and see what it sells for. If there are several for sale, watch them all.

When I checked eBay a moment ago, there were six for sale. They were all in used condition ranging between $49 to $79. Several were "buy it now" status which meant the first person willing to pay that asking price was automatically the winner.

Unless you are selling a brand-new, unused Garfield fish aquarium that is still in the original box, it is likely the item is worth around $60. The first one will sell out at $47 and the rest will cost a little more money.

If you have the time, put each Garfield fish aquarium in your watch list and see if they even sell in the first place. Because there are already six of them for sale, this may signal to the market that they are common, abundant, and there is no rush to make a bid.

If there is only one for sale and it very seldom becomes available, there is more of a chance that the auction may have multiple bidders trying to win it.

Use Collectors' Sites and Ask Questions

I know we just mentioned this a few paragraphs above, but that was the "where" and this is the "how", so please forgive us. There are several Facebook groups, forums, and blogs that are specifically about collecting Garfield. Often, you can post a question to the group to ask what they think an item is worth. Many experienced collectors like Cathy are aware of the market and can give an accurate estimate. Other people may have just purchased one elsewhere and are happy to share what they paid.

As we said above, the Garfield Gathering group still has an audience of Garfield collectors even when an event is not actively being promoted. We are happy to help. I know this because I was the one who set up the group.

There is also the Garfield Collectors group and they are always available to offer their opinions on Garfield items. Currently, there are over 7,800 members so you are bound to get some feedback from them. Please be sure to follow their rules for posting.

Do Not Sell to Your Appraisal Source

It would be foolish to take someone's word for what something is worth and then sell it to him. It is a common truth that people lie. People might low-ball the estimate just because they know that they want to offer you money for it. There are dishonest people in every category of life, so it should come as no surprise that Garfield collecting should also include these crooks.

Cathy and I are often contacted by people who want to know the value of something. It would be easy to low-ball what it is worth if they seem like they are looking to sell it. In the name of honesty and integrity, I will first tell the person if Cathy has one, is looking for one, or wants one. I will also tell them not to sell to the person who values it for you. Finally, I will answer their questions with a range based on experience. I also point out that Garfield collectors are individuals and the item is ultimately worth what they are willing to sell it for and what the buyer is willing to pay.

21
FUN LITTLE STORIES NOT WORTHY OF A CHAPTER (THE WHO, WHAT, AND WHEN)

College - Thefts

Years ago, there was a strange period in time when people were smashing car windows and stealing Garfield Stuck-on-You plushes. These were Garfield stuffed animals that had suction cups on their feet. They would be stuck to the inside of car windows.

Nobody knows for sure how the thefts started. Nobody knows why they continued. Was it a copy-cat crime or were people rebelling over the popularity of the items?

When Cathy was in college, she fell victim to this Garfield theft and her plush Garfield Stuck on You was stolen from her car. Thankfully, they didn't break her car window, but they did destroy her door lock. She had to drive home with an extension cord tied from the driver's door handle to the passenger's door handle to keep her door from flying open on the Long Island Expressway.

Another time, her car was broken into and her Garfield ice

scraper was stolen. This fact alone does not necessarily qualify her to write a Garfield collectors book, but just like with the Woodstock concert, there are two types of people. People who went to the Woodstock concert and the  people who claimed they went to the Woodstock concert. Her car was actually broken into.

With the thefts of Cathy's plush and ice scraper, she was dragged into an episode in Garfield's history that was not so pleasant. It also cost her a car door lock, since the vandal destroyed it.

You are the Garfield People

One time, Cathy and I were eating out at a T.G.I. Friday's restaurant and the waitress saw Cathy's Garfield shirt and said, "Omigod! You are the Garfield people." At first, we assumed she served us before at Friday's, so we did not think much of it.

It turns out that she actually remembered us from seven years prior when she worked at the Fashion Bug clothing store. Cathy found out that Fashion Bug had many Garfield items on sale, including several types of Garfield waste paper baskets, a Garfield hamper, and other items.

The waitress remembers us rolling around the floor trying to separate the waste paper baskets that were packed together too tightly. I wrapped my legs around the can and pulled as hard as I could. Apparently, to her, it was very memorable.

Book Signing at the World-Famous Book Revue – June 17, 2003

It was just supposed to be a regular book signing. Jim Davis was invited, no lured, to the world-famous Book Revue bookstore in Huntington, New York. The Book Revue is a small privately-owned bookstore known for hosting book signings. They probably have at least a dozen signings per month with some very famous authors.

The interesting spin on the story is that Jim Davis and company were told the bookstore was only an hour from New York City. The truth was it was at least two hours away, factoring in rush hour. Rush hour out of New York City around 5:00 PM is among the worst in the world.

The event started a little late, but Jim gave a great talk, similar to the chalk talk he gave on the 25th Birthday cruise. It's always amazing to watch him draw Garfield in person. He starts with a blank page and within minutes, there's Garfield on the page and you can tell his attitude with the little subtleties Jim gives him.

This book signing was only a month after the Garfield cruise. Cathy and I wore our cruise t-shirts to the signing. Jim noticed them and commented how great the cruise was when he was autographing Cathy's items. She brought the photo album she put together with the cruise photos. Since she already had her 25th Birthday book signed on the cruise, she was able to get other items signed by Jim. He even saw the Garfield jacket she had with her and offered to sign that, too. Jim's wife, Jill, was with him and she was thrilled that we asked her to sign a professional photo we purchased of us on the cruise. Jim stayed until every book was signed.

Winning Two Giant Macy's 25th Anniversary Christmas Plushes

In 2003, for Garfield's 25th anniversary, the Macy's Christmas special promotion was a small Garfield wearing a Santa hat holding an Odie with reindeer antlers and a book titled "Garfield's Night Before Christmas". Embroidered on Garfield's left foot is Limited Edition 25 years. They were available for $16.95 with any purchase.

As part of the promotion, each store was to raffle off one 5-foot-tall, 50-pound giant Garfield plush. We were ready to do everything in our power to try and win one.

First, we went around to every Macy's nearby and loaded the

ballot box with entries. According to the rules, there was to be only one entry per person per store. We got out our phone book and wrote down the names and phone numbers of the 43 most reliable friends, family members, and co-workers.

We remember driving to one Macy's in the middle of a blizzard. There was two feet of snow on the ground and, to make matters worse, the Macy's parking garage was on a steep, ice-covered incline.

After we exhausted the Macy's stores on Long Island, New York, we moved on to New Jersey, Pennsylvania, Massachusetts, and New Hampshire. In total, we submitted around 43 names in each of 13 Macy's in 5 states.

In the end, we won two giant Garfields. One winning name was mine at a Long Island store and the second winning name was her boss, at a different Long Island store, right around the corner from our house. It was so funny watching Cathy's petite boss carrying out a 5-foot-tall, 50-pound Garfield out of the mall. It was bigger than she was! We actually had another friend win at another store on Long Island, but somehow that wound up being a 5 foot tall Kermit the Frog doll. It was 3 feet of legs and a 2 foot torso. The store claimed that it was their second prize.

We later purchased a third giant Macy's Garfield on Craigslist.com. For a brief moment, we owned three of these huge items, but we immediately sold the third to a friend of ours who also collects Garfield. We charged her exactly what we paid for it. It wasn't in the best condition, there was some stains on it and some of the threads were loose.

To the best of our knowledge, there are only 300 of these giant Garfields in the world and we are lucky to own two of them. The bad news is that I can no longer move in my office.

Oh… Those Old Things

When I was in Port Jefferson, New York, a quaint and charming touristy town on the north shore of Long Island with a college friend, my "Gardar" went off while walking past a gift store. "Gardar" is like Radar for Garfield items. It is why Cathy keeps me around.

On the front counter of the store was a large pile of Garfield Enesco Christmas ornaments marked down half off an already silly price. I am not a poker player, but I am smart enough not to scream, "Holy cow! Do you have any idea what these things are worth?".

I said very calmly, "My wife likes Garfield a little, (WOW, THAT'S THE LIE OF THE CENTURY!), do you have any more of these?" The person said, "Oh ... Those old things." She had a whole boxful that she came across downstairs and she was getting rid of them. I said, "My wife might think they are cute; I will take them all." I was trying very hard not to smirk or show my excitement.

Lake Compounce RV Trip – September 2006

Years ago. Cathy and I picked up an old 1976 Dodge RV off Craigslist. We decided it would be a trial RV. If we liked it, we would get a good one. It was old, and it was not much of a looker. Our motto was, "We thought we had a piece of junk RV until we learned that we were preservationists". This was because apparently the old beast qualified to be a classic.

In September 2006 we took the RV to Lake Compounce Amusement Park in Bristol, Connecticut with good friends. It was the same amusement park featured in the Garfield Gathering in 2005. We did not know about the Gathering in 2005, so Cathy and I did not attend.

At the time, Lake Compounce licensed the Garfield character for its theming. Rides, games, and shows were all centered around Garfield. It was heaven.

These days, Lake Compounce

no longer has the license to use Garfield items, so it was a good thing that the Garfield Gathering and our friends went there before it no longer featured Garfield.

Shampoo bottle acquisition

In 1998, Cathy was working the trade show booth for the cosmetic division of the company she works for at the Javits Center in Manhattan. She was walking up and down the trade show aisles and out of the corner of her eye, she saw Garfield shampoo bottles on a display shelf of a bottling company. They were tall, plastic, orange bottles in the shape of Garfield.

She went over to one of the people in the booth and asked about the Garfield bottles. They had produced them for a company that had a line of bath products - shampoo, conditioner and bubble bath. They like to show them off at the trade shows because they are a great representation of what their company can manufacture. Cathy explained that she was a huge Garfield collector and asked if she could have them. The person said no, they could not give them away.

Now this was the last day of the trade show and most of the items that Cathy's company was displaying were going to be thrown out instead of being brought back to the office. So, Cathy figured she had nothing to lose, so, she gathered up as many containers, packaged applicators and brushes she could and went back to the bottle booth. They were packing up their booth as well and Cathy went over to the person she had spoken with earlier and offered her all the items in exchange for the three Garfield bottles.

The person was so thrilled with the items Cathy brought over, she said that even though they had just packed them up, she would go find them and give them to Cathy. She was thrilled to get them. Cathy said she learned valuable lessons that day. One, always have your Gardar (Garfield radar) turned on because you just never know when you will spot an item. Two, persistence can pay off. If she hadn't gone back to the booth, she would not have gotten the bottles. Three, sweeten the pot, if possible. Cathy figured the items were only going to be thrown out, so it couldn't hurt to take the containers and only the bagged applicators and brushes. She wasn't going to offer the person a handful of cotton balls.

Cathy told her father the story, since he was retired from the cosmetic industry, and might know the bottle company. Turns out that he didn't, but a friend of his did, and a couple of days later another couple of bottles showed up in our mail.

These are real cute bottles because they are orange with a figural shape of Garfield. The labels reveal a different sea creature when they get wet.

The Checkers Value Meals

One year, Checkers restaurants offered Garfield game cards with its Value Meal. There were several different types of card games to choose from. The cards also came in a paper bag with Garfield graphics on it. For collectors, this is the bonus plan.

The promotion lasted four weeks. Within the four-week period, Cathy and I collected over 80 sets of cards. Some days, we purchased the meal deals for both lunch and dinner. We even served the sandwiches to our dogs to help us eat the food. It was probably our dogs' happiest weeks of their lives eating fast food day and night.

Knoebels Amusement Park, Elysburg, Pennsylvania – 2014

Since the conventions switched to every other year starting in 2013, there wouldn't be another formal convention until 2015. Knowing that many collectors are from the Northeast region of the United States, we decided to have an unofficial meeting in 2014.

We asked Nancy to help us get the word out to other collectors.

She suggested that we have it at Knoebels Amusement Park. Knoebels is an old-fashioned amusement park. You don't pay to park and there's no admission charge. On the weekdays, you can purchase a "pay one price" wristband and have unlimited rides on all of the attractions, but they don't offer the "pay one price" option on the weekends.

Cathy and I wanted to be able to take advantage of all the rides, so we went a day early. It's a good thing we did because the amusement park is situated in a valley so cell phone reception was horrible at best. One of the rides is a 14-minute chairlift ride that takes you up and back down the mountain. On Friday, we rode the chairlift about 10 times making phone calls, checking e-mail and sending texts to coordinate with everyone.

On Saturday, every ride up the chairlift cost about $4 for the 2 of us, so we kept track of everyone we needed to contact and limited our rides to about 2. It also helped that other collectors were there and had better cell phone service than we did. It was funny that we ran into another collector who was there for a family reunion! She had her dog with her. Knoebels is pet-friendly.

Auctioneer Trying to Fool Us

Have you ever been on a cruise that made a big deal about the art auctions held onboard? They tell you about the latest up-and-coming artists who are going to increase in value. The art auction department has a sense of confidence in them as if everything they say is the law.

Cathy and I are not art experts, but when it comes to Garfield collectibles, there are very few people who know more. This little story might come off as arrogance or our ego talking, but we share this story because we are trying to help others not get taken advantage of on a cruise.

Just about every time we go on a cruise, we might pop in the auction room to see if they have any Garfield items for sale. We give them a few minutes to pretend to be art experts and tell us how rare, limited, and valuable the items are. Most of the time, we just leave knowing we will not be playing their game. Other times, we might show our hand and find out the real price for the items. Eventually, when they find out Cathy has the world record, they might lose the act and start being realistic about the prices.

A few times, we were able to purchase a complete set of lithographs for less than the display price of one. Think about this for a moment, we purchased six for around the price of one.

Ironically, when the cruise ends and you return home, you often see the same cruise ship cels being sold online for a third of what people pay on the ship. As we said to the person in the cruise ship art department, "We may not know fine art, but we know Garfield."

Another Cruise Art Story That Proves Our Point

When we were younger and naïve, we went to the art auction on a ship. The rules were, if you identified an item you were interested in, you were guaranteeing the ship that you will buy it at the opening bid.

On one cruise, we were interested in a Garfield cel and the opening bid was not too unreasonable. We put our name down that we wanted it up on the block for bidding. When the item came up for bid, there was another couple also bidding on the item and driving the price up. Knowing we did not need another Garfield item that badly, we eventually dropped out and let the other couple win.

At that moment, the auctioneer said, "Good news. We have more than one of these in the warehouse and both bidders will win it at the price where we dropped out." They just doubled their money for a print that is heavily stocked.

Custom Acrylic – (The program probably went away because of us)

One year, Paws Inc., the parent company of Garfield, came out with a custom acrylic painting program. It was a chance for collectors to have a picture of Garfield playing their favorite sport or doing their favorite hobby. Looking back, the samples that they showed for the program were all pictures that were already produced for a specialty book, calendar or coloring book.

When we contracted with American Royal Arts, a sales entity for the program, the sales rep asked us what Cathy's favorite hobby was. Expecting to hear an activity such as soccer, ice-skating, or golf, they could have gone easily to the coloring book and found a sample of Garfield doing that activity.

Instead, we answered, "Collecting Garfield." Seeing how perplexed he was, we had to elaborate on our answer. I even went so far as to create a mock-up using a computer graphics tool. After all, I am a website developer and I am no stranger to computer graphics. They modeled a one-of-a-kind painting after my computer-generated mock-up, but we said it wasn't busy enough. It didn't reflect Cathy's out-of-control collection.

I told the sales rep we did not want to see any white space (referring to the wall in the painting). When it was ready, they added a few more Garfields and painted the wall blue. They showed us . . . no white space.

Jim Davis signed the piece of art as a final step and they also included a behind-the-scenes photo book of them making it. We love it. The caption reads, "What this place needs is more . . . more me!" It is a fantastic piece and one of our favorites.

We suspect that because we were so high-maintenance, the program was quickly discontinued. I guess if Cathy liked ice-skating, soccer, or golf, the program might still be around today.

Not Taboo Enough for TV Show - "My Crazy Obsession"

Sometime in 2013, we were contacted by a producer of a TV show called "My Crazy Obsession." We filmed a demo DVD for them. This was easy for me since I own professional video cameras for my business and do video production. The producer told us we were on the short list for being filmed, but she kept asking us, "Do we do anything out of the ordinary such as dress up like Garfield when we leave the house?" At the time, I did not realize that this is what the show was about. It was to shock viewers.

The best we could come up with was that we sometimes dust the collection with a shop compressor. We also ate about 80 fast food Value Meals, with the help of our dogs, during a Garfield promotion at Checkers just to get 80 Garfield decks of cards and the Garfield-themed bags that they came in.

We later found out that the program began as a series about collecting and notable collections. Over time, it transformed into a show featuring people who did some pretty scary, disgusting, and taboo things. In essence, the series evolved into a freak show.

Fortunately, Cathy and I did not qualify for the show since we were just normal people who have a lot of Garfield items in our house.

In the end, we were not chosen. We take this as a compliment since other people who were featured were filmed doing some pretty creepy and sick things. Every guest of the show had bizarre, freakish habits that would make your skin crawl. You might think I am making this up, but one of the shows that they filmed was about a woman who drinks her own urine.

"Shipping Wars" Loves Garfield

One day, Cathy received an email that had the subject line, "Shipping Wars Loves Garfield." The body of the email introduced one of the producers of the show and mentioned that the program likes popular culture.

The television show "Shipping Wars" contacted us to see if we had any unusual items that needed to be shipped. This was not long after we had already paid to have the kiddie amusement ride crated and shipped to our house. The shipping cost almost as much as the ride itself. But, we were actually looking at a Garfield Tabletop Slot Machine. I suggested to the producer to look into the legality of moving slot machines across state lines.

When they got back to us, their research also indicated that it was probably not a great idea flaunting to the authorities an item that was regulated in several states as a gambling machine.

In time, we may be in the position to contact them again to transport a large, yet legal, Garfield item.

College Student Film School Graduate Project

One time, we were contacted by a graduate student who found our collection on the internet. She went to Stony Brook University and was a film student. She filmed and interviewed us for a project. As a video producer, as part of my business, it was interesting to be on the other side of the camera.

She got an A.

Subject of a Report in South Africa

It is not a major part of our credibility and history, but in 2015, we were contacted by someone in South Africa. His son was doing a report and he loved Garfield. The kids had to pick a world record and research it deeper. The man wanted to know more insights about Cathy's world record for his son's report.

Insurance Company Garfield / New World Record

In October 2014, right after the newspaper article came out from the book signing with Jim Davis, Cathy got a package in the mail from Ritchie Insurance, Inc., a broker of Indiana Farmers Insurance Company. It seems that Indiana Farmers Insurance Company had licensed Garfield for advertising purposes and they made up a plush of a Garfield wearing their company shirt.

The Garfield plush came with a nice note congratulating Cathy on her world record. The note said, "Here is another Garfield to add to your collection."

What they did not know was that we already captured some memorabilia from their company, Ritchie Insurance, Inc. when we pulled off the road to photograph a Billboard with Garfield advertising their company.

It just goes to show that when you are a Garfield collector you cannot turn it off. Spoiler alert, this item will be one of the items used when we re-submit and break Cathy's own world record. It has been a few years, and we have accumulated many more items not originally counted.

Contacted about Hong Kong Mall Tour

In March 2016, we received an email from a company planning a three-month mall tour of Garfield. They wanted to know if we could provide 200 to 300 of our best collectibles for the exhibit.

As a skeptical New Yorker, the whole proposal sounded like a really bad idea. Even if the organization was real and legitimate, just the logistics involved would make our heads spin. Being without our best pieces, we would be at the mercy of international law to enforce whether or not we would get our items back.

Even if they did ship our items back, it would almost be a guarantee that a percentage of the items would be broken or perhaps stolen.

We were flattered that once again another group found us due to the visibility of www.lovesgarfield.com, but it would have been a disaster if we actually took the proposition seriously.

Probably Will Appear on New History Channel Collectors Show in the Near Future

In 2017, we were contacted by a producer of a new TV show for the History Channel. The show will be all about collectors. The host is a collector and also a known TV personality. It will be aired in segments, both in studio and on location.

Since they film out of New York City, it would be a no-brainer to feature Cathy in our home. The latest news is that the production has been delayed, but we are definitely on the short list.

The only stipulation we gave them was that we required at least three weeks' notice to organize our collection, or else they will be filming an episode of "Hoarders."

The Vanity Shelf

I saved this for last because it sums up our silly book about a silly subject with a silly story. I have a desk in the dining room. The dining room used to be my office before it was taken over by Garfield items. On the top of the desk is a shelf where I put all of my trophies for business recognition, achievements, certificates of appreciation, and plaques.

On this shelf is salt and peppered some Garfield items that would ordinarily be considered a dime-a-dozen, lackluster, or just plain cheap. These not-so-collectible items each hold a special meaning in my heart for the simple fact that they remind me of things that I enjoy doing.

There is a wind-up SCUBA diving Garfield, and I am a certified SCUBA diver, Master Scuba Diver, Rescue Certified, and completed the level of Assistant Instructor in SCUBA Diving. This silly little wind up Garfield reminds me of my accomplishments and the sport that I enjoy.

There is a small Garfield keychain with Garfield holding a microphone. I love this trinket because I love public speaking. I was the first person in my High School to be exempt from the final exam speech in public speaking class. Ironically, not being able to talk one more time is more like a punishment when you like to talk as much as I do. In my professional life I never shy away from giving a seminar or running a monthly networking meeting. Once again, this cheap little keychain holds a lot of power, reminding me of what I enjoy.

There is an Odie ceramic that says, "I Like My Computer" and a Garfield statue holding a chainsaw over a computer that says, "Compute This". I have a Minor in computer science and I am a website developer as one of my businesses, so you can probably connect the dots.

I have a Garfield clock with Garfield wearing a necktie. As a businessperson I own many neckties.

My point is that you don't have to have slot machines, pachinko machines, and amusement rides in your living room to collect items that speak to you where it counts. I said it earlier: some people collect what they can relate to, such as golf, soccer, or even firefighting!

In a way, even though Cathy is the Garfield collector and I am just the cataloger, these seven to ten items are my collection that qualifies me to be part of a fun-loving community.

If you have a "Garfield World's Greatest Dad" mug and it makes you happy, then you are a collector, too.

In a world where we take things too seriously it is nice to know that there is something out there just for pure amusement.

Behold, a picture of my vanity shelf:

THE FUTURE OF GARFIELD COLLECTIBLES AND COLLECTING (THE WHO, WHAT, WHEN, WHERE AND WHY)

Only Jim Davis and the people at Paws, Inc. know the future of the cat. Jim has said many times that his only goal was to go ten years so Garfield would get syndicated. Much to his surprise, the syndication happened sooner, and Garfield is at the 40-year mark as of June 19, 2018.

The company owns a private jumbo jet and holds the world record for the most syndicated cartoon in the world. Jim Davis has won prestigious awards such as Emmys and lifetime achievement awards.

Garfield started as a comic strip, and merchandising soon followed. After retail, several fast-food companies piled on and made meal toys for kids. Amusement parks licensed them for character experiences and entertainment.

Videotape cartoons, TV specials, and major motion pictures followed.

In the past few years, there was a Garfield play that was not a "skip and wave" kiddie show. The play was scheduled to appear in several theaters.

What's a Comic Strip?

Weekly cartoons on cable TV now define Garfield to a younger generation. Their parents knew him as a comic strip, but since TV and movies have replaced the daily newspaper, younger people know Garfield as a TV show or other multimedia concept.

International Boom

The United States is keeping Garfield alive on a reactive level. What we mean is that manufacturers approach Paws Inc. for licenses when they come up with ideas.

Overseas, Garfield is exploding on a proactive level. In Asia, Garfield is incredibly popular. There are even current projects in China.

Wild Guesses

Will Jim Davis retire? Will the creative team not need Jim? Will they sell the rights to a bigger company such as Disney? Nobody but Jim Davis knows. It is possible that the talent pool will live on for years and years. Perhaps Jim's children or grandchildren will carry on the company. As an outsider, your guess is as good as ours.

"If We Take Care of the Cat, the Cat Will Take Care of Us"

There is a sign at Paws, Inc. that says, "If we take care of the cat, the cat will take care of us." Even as just the husband of the world record holder, the motto rings true.

Cathy and I have seen some amazing cities, just blindly following the path of where the next Collectors Convention will be. Pigeon Forge, Tennessee was never on our radar for a vacation, but Dollywood and the surrounding entertainment "strip" in Gatlinburg, Tennessee were two of the most fun cities we have ever visited.

We walked the sacred halls of the Alamo fort in San Antonio, Texas and rode the boat ride of the River Walk.

Just driving to the conventions and to Muncie, Indiana, we stopped at some of the greatest amusement parks and rode the country's most amazing roller coasters. King's Dominion Amusement Park was one thrill after another. Its roller coasters were tall and fast. Cedar Point Amusement Park was a half-way stop when visiting Muncie. We were blown away by some of the longest and fastest roller coasters on the planet.

We cruised the Caribbean for Garfield's 25th birthday with 400 of the craziest people that we have ever met and actually felt sane (or at least normal) for a week at sea.

The People

The greatest win was meeting all of the wonderful people who collect Garfield and share the love of collecting. The bonds that we have made have carried into our everyday life. Since some of our friends from the convention only live in the next county or next state over, we don't have to wait a year or two to get together. We meet all the time.

It's not just other collectors who have made this journey so enjoyable, but also the people of Paws, Inc. Jim Davis and his staff have given us moments of great joy and memories. We have been welcomed into their world several times to film Jim for the conventions, to interview staff for bonus video, and Cathy has even been interviewed with Jim Davis for the local media.

It is great to have a company like Paws run by such a kind and approachable person as Jim Davis. The irony is not lost on him that so many people are making such a big deal over a cartoonist who created a character that people can relate to. When you meet Jim Davis you realize that he is the first person who expects to wake up some morning as if this all was a dream.

Behind everything that Garfield stands for, there is a line that Jim and Paws never will cross. In an edgy world where doing shocking things gets the most media attention, Jim Davis has stated that he always wants Garfield to be a safe space for parents and families. After all, how much trouble can you get into making fun of eating, sleeping, and occasionally squashing a spider?

The Best of Both Worlds

Part of Cathy's life is being a somebody without being anybody. Cathy is a regular everyday person who works in medical purchasing. Because she has the biggest documented collection of Garfield collectibles, she has garnered some attention.

No paparazzi, no invasion of privacy, no bodyguards, just a hobby that takes up a lot of space with minimal downside. Cathy and I stand out a bit in our own sub-culture without the negatives involved with public life.

As one of the segments to kill time at a Garfield Gathering, Nancy and I came up with the funny idea of crowning Cathy the Queen. I wanted to use a toilet plunger as her scepter and a Burger King hat as her crown to downplay the ceremony. Nancy found a foam crown and a foam wand. Anything nicer would wreck the joke.

The truth is that it really does not matter if anyone else has a bigger collection than Cathy. The convention is not a place to divide. The convention is a place to celebrate our common hobby and enjoy each other's company.

Even without the world record, we would still be who we are. We would be answering everyone's questions online because they found www.lovesGarfield.com and we would be helping with audio-visuals and games at the convention because we like to help. I would probably be the auctioneer at the Garfield Gathering because it was my loud mouth that put me on the short list and the fact that I hosted games in the past.

Even before the world record, we were invited to Paws, Inc. to film and everyone was already nice to us and accommodating.

I say this to anyone out there, "If you find something that you enjoy, it is likely that other people out there enjoy it, too." If you are a social person, join a group around it. If you are an introvert, quietly enjoy it yourself.

This book could have easily been as universal to "President Garfield" collectors who are always running into that darn cartoon cat when they are on eBay. The point is that to some, collecting Garfield is a community. This community communicates, buys, sells, and sometimes gets together. I hope everyone feels as comfortable as we do when they are with their own ragtag group of nuts who share the same crazy obsession. It is more fun laughing in groups than laughing alone.

ACKNOWLEDGMENTS

Acknowledgment

There are always people to thank, so we should start with Jim and Jill Davis, Doc Davis, Kim Campbell, Sherri and Neil Greer, and the people at Paws, Inc. As they say... If we take care of the cat, the cat will take care of us.

To North Shore Animal League America, who give us meaning and purpose and a legacy to deserving animals, even though we are donating some proceeds to you, in a way, you are really enriching us. To any people who adopt from any shelter, anywhere, you are the people who make shelters work.

The Garfield Gathering is one of the groups that give our lives as collectors texture, many fun stories, and good friends. Without them, Cathy would simply be a lady with way too many Garfields in the house. Nancy and Manny Vega have been the catalysts who have kept the group together since we began to attend. Gary Skinner is the godfather of the group. Jo Hermann and Gary Wagner were our first friends in the group when we were just a married couple experiencing the convention for the first time. Tricia and Tina Lazrovitch are our newest Garfield friends that prove that when you click, you click.

Thank you to our fellow Garfield Gathering hosts, who handed the torch from person to person, city to city, year after year.

Bret and Liz Savit edited the book for the first round, from the goodness of their heart and the strength of our deep friendship.

Stephanie Larkin, Owner of Red Penguin Books saw the potential in this exciting project and was onboard from the moment she met us. You have been a wonderful partner.

To Cathy's brothers, Joe and Paul and my sister Margaret, who contributed to the insanity of Cathy's collection, buying her presents. My parents, Dan and Elaine for always finding or making Cathy Garfield items, I blame you all.

Credit must go to Cathy parents, Jack and Doris, AKA "Garfield Collection South" who should probably charge us rent for all the Garfield and Christmas items we leave in Florida to make us feel at home during the Christmas holidays. We love you all.

Finally, to our friends, co-workers, and family who have ever given Cathy something Garfield, did they ever think that their appreciated gifts would actually contribute to a world record?

Thank you all.

www.ingramcontent.com/pod-product-compliance
Lightning Source LLC
Chambersburg PA
CBHW071258110526
44591CB00010B/709